how loathsome
ted naifeh   tristan crane

www.howloathsome.com
www.nbmpub.com
www.tristancrane.com
www.tednaifeh.com

ISBN 1-56163-386-0, cloth
ISBN 1-56163-387-9, pb.
© 2004 Ted Naifeh & Tristan Crane
Printed in Singapore

5   4   3   2   1

Library of Congress Cataloging-in-Publication Data

Crane, Tristan.
  How loathsome/Tristan Crane, Ted Naifeh.
     p. cm.
   ISBN 1-56163-386-0 (cloth) -- ISBN 1-56163-387-9 (pbk.)
    I. Naifeh, Ted. II. Title.

 PN6727.C69H68 2004
 741.5'973--dc22

                                                      2004040210

how loathsome

created and written by
tristan crane & **ted naifeh**

illustrated by
ted naifeh

lettered by
tristan crane

introduction by
danielle willis

introduction
by danielle willis

My first reaction to 'How Loathsome' was total freakout.

I was lying on a couch in Cleveland waiting for my drug dealer
to fucking show up, when my lover tossed a manila envelope onto
my lap. It was from my friend Sherilyn in San Francisco and
contained what I was fairly certain was a comic book version
of my life, written and illustrated by people I'd never met.
Either that or I'd gone totally delusional and was indulging
in the sort of bitter old drag queen 'Madonna wrote that song
about me' bullshit I've always found incredibly tiresome in
bitter old drag queens.

To make a long story short, I went back to San Francisco in
July of '03 and met Tristan Crane and Ted Naifeh, who confirmed
my suspicion that the Catherine Gore character was in fact
based loosely on me; turns out Ted saw my one-woman show
'Breakfast in the Flesh District' back in '94 and now I get to
write the introduction to the 'How Loathsome' collection. Quite
an honor, not to mention a massive ego stroke.

Too many stories set in the San Francisco 'underground' read
like the kind of Nash Bridges episode where Don Johnson has to
go undercover as a meth-addled uniform freak to investigate a
series of suspicious deaths at a sinister new bondage club.
Did I say Nash Bridges?

Maybe I meant 'Basic Instinct'. Oh well, same thing.

Then there's those 'stark and unflinching' pseudo-journalistic
gazes into the abyss featuring 15 year-old runaways shooting
up in the pay toilets at 16th and Valencia, and other similar
affronts to civic pride. The subject of heroin (and drug use
in general) is yet another potentially literary minefield that
How Loathsome manages to navigate unscathed by cliché́s,
hyperbole, or dead babies crawling upside down across kick-room
ceilings. Drugs can be a daily routine, something too many
writers forget while rushing their characters through a series
of melodramatic overdoses and jailhouse detoxes on their way
to some inevitable hogarthian bottom. Cigarettes will kill you
too, but you don't see characters who smoke suddenly clutching
their throats and dropping to their knees as bloody foam spews
from their nostrils.

Finally there's stuff by folks who really live here, but can't
write. At best penning the alternative lifestyle versions of
'Letters to Penthouse Forum', or if they're setting their
aspirations a little higher, modern queer-core pastiches of
Armistead Maupin full of characters who are little more than a
few mannerisms and eccentricities cobbled together and given
names.

To say that Ted and Tristan manage to avoid these pitfalls is
an understatement. The San Francisco they create in How
Loathsome is one I not only recognize, but have lived in for
the last twenty years. Hell, I've been to that alien insect
bar Nick stumbles into in Issue 3. In fact I've had a guy who
could easily have been Nick living in my closet on Webster
street for six months. He used to shove speed crystals into
his pee hole and saw demons on a semi-regular basis. We all
sort of believed him.

Before 'Nick', that same closet was inhabited by a pair of
young hustlers against whose frail shoulders I've nodded out
countless times, like Catherine and Alex. With characters this
good it would really suck if the artist decided to use them as
an excuse to indulge in a bunch of uber-shiny, Matrix-meets-
the-Hunger fetish porno. To be sure there is plenty of bondage
gear in these pages, not to mention goth clubs and gender-queer
sex scenes, but Ted Naifeh renders these with a gaunt elegance
and economy of style that meshes beautifully with Tristan
Crane's understated prose.

It's a perfect translation, from the rocker-boy androgyny of
Catherine Gore and Chloe's brittle poise, to the surrealistic
ever-mutating streets of San Francisco itself. These are people
and places I know intimately. Even minor characters are sharply
delineated, in particular that trio of owlishly voyeuristic
Germans hanging out in Pacific Heights. Yes. They are cool.
This is a very cool comic series.

The creators of 'How Loathsome' have managed a labor of love.
In just four parts this book chronicles with elegance the lives
of this clique of denizens. Their own lives become the
mysteries to solve, and this is what makes How Loathsome stand
on its own, without gimmicks. The questions which arise are
just reasons for me to keep reading.

This book will help you understand. We are not definable.
We are not straight. We are not gay.

We are, however, Loathsome.

Danielle Willis
2003

chapter 1

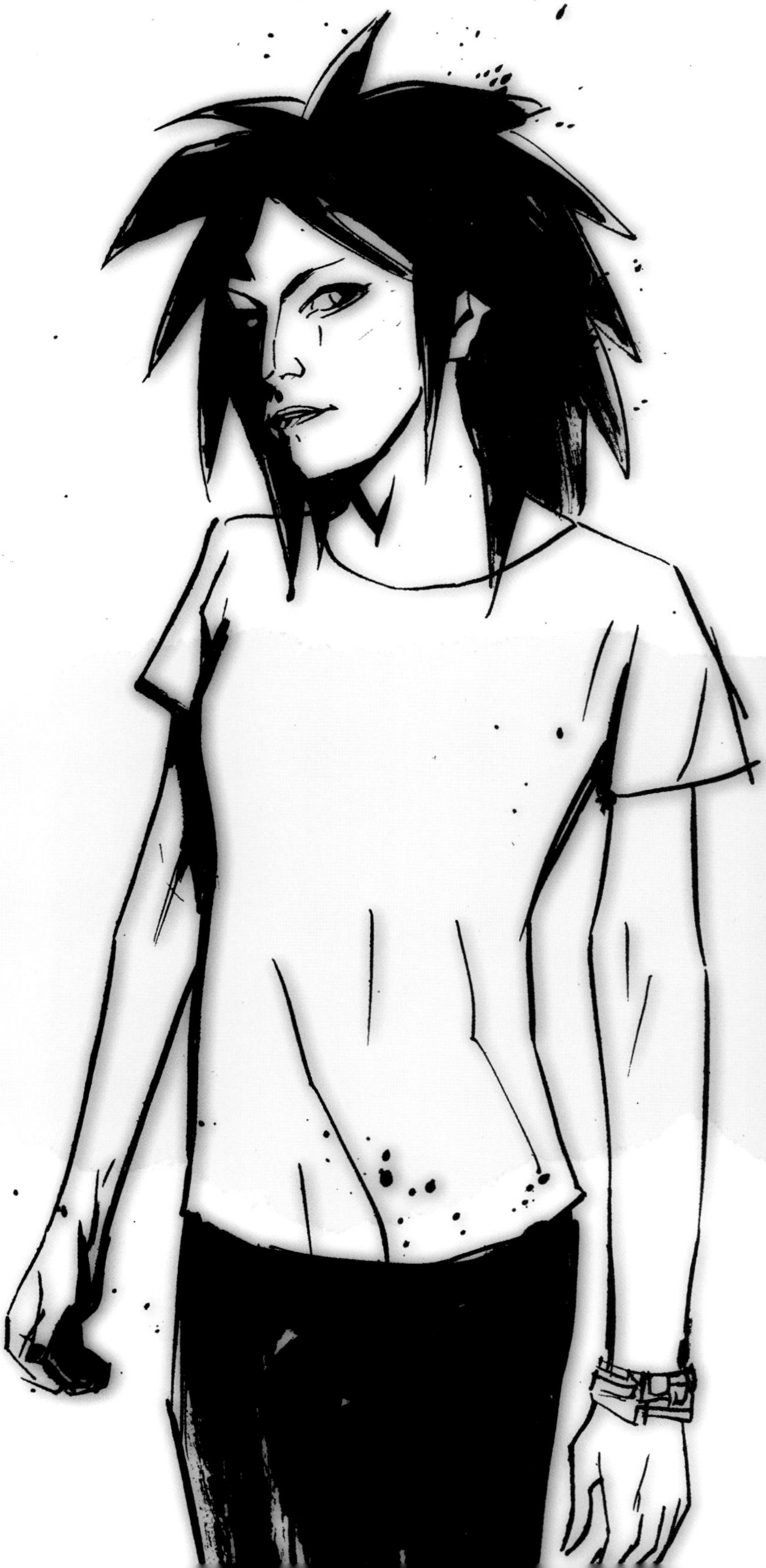

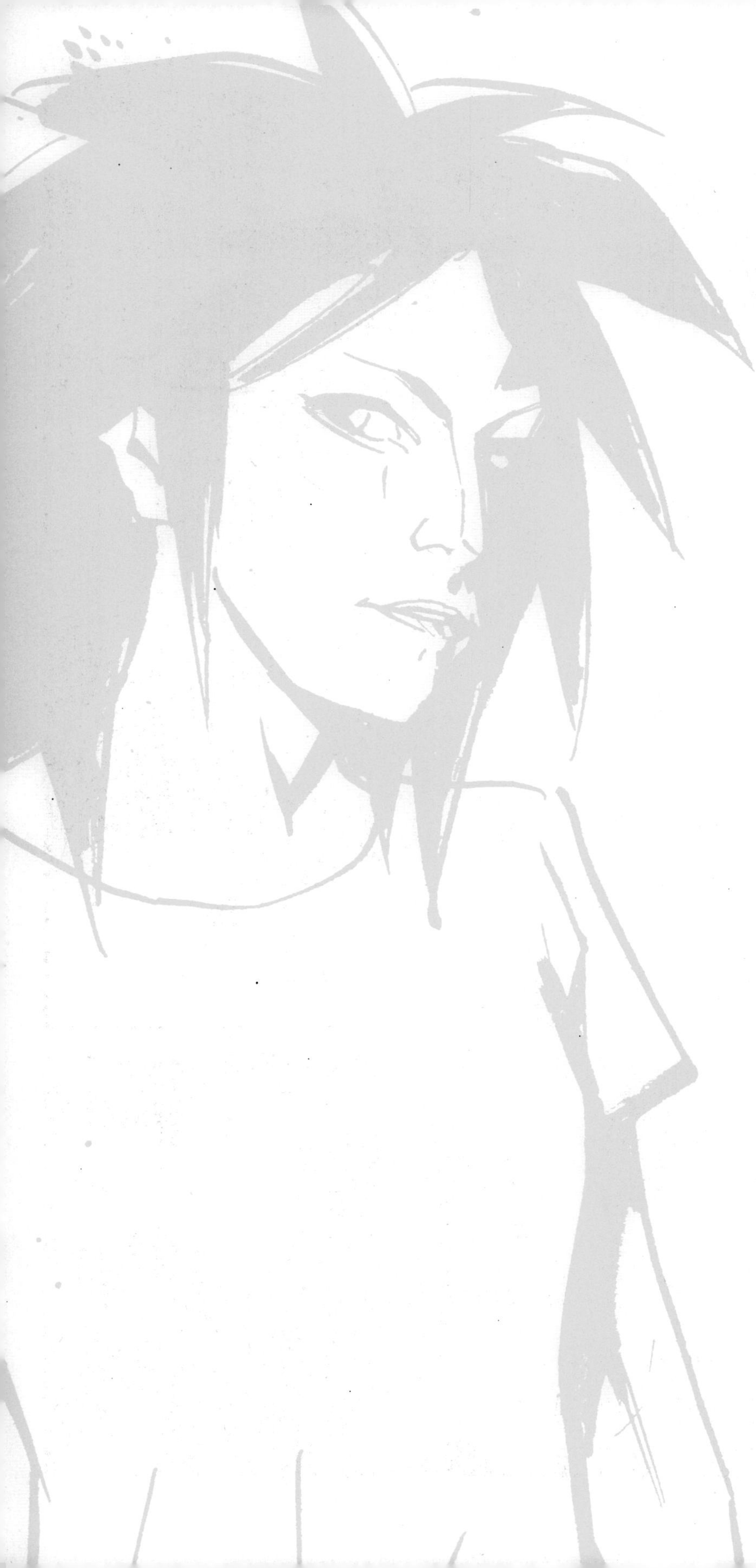

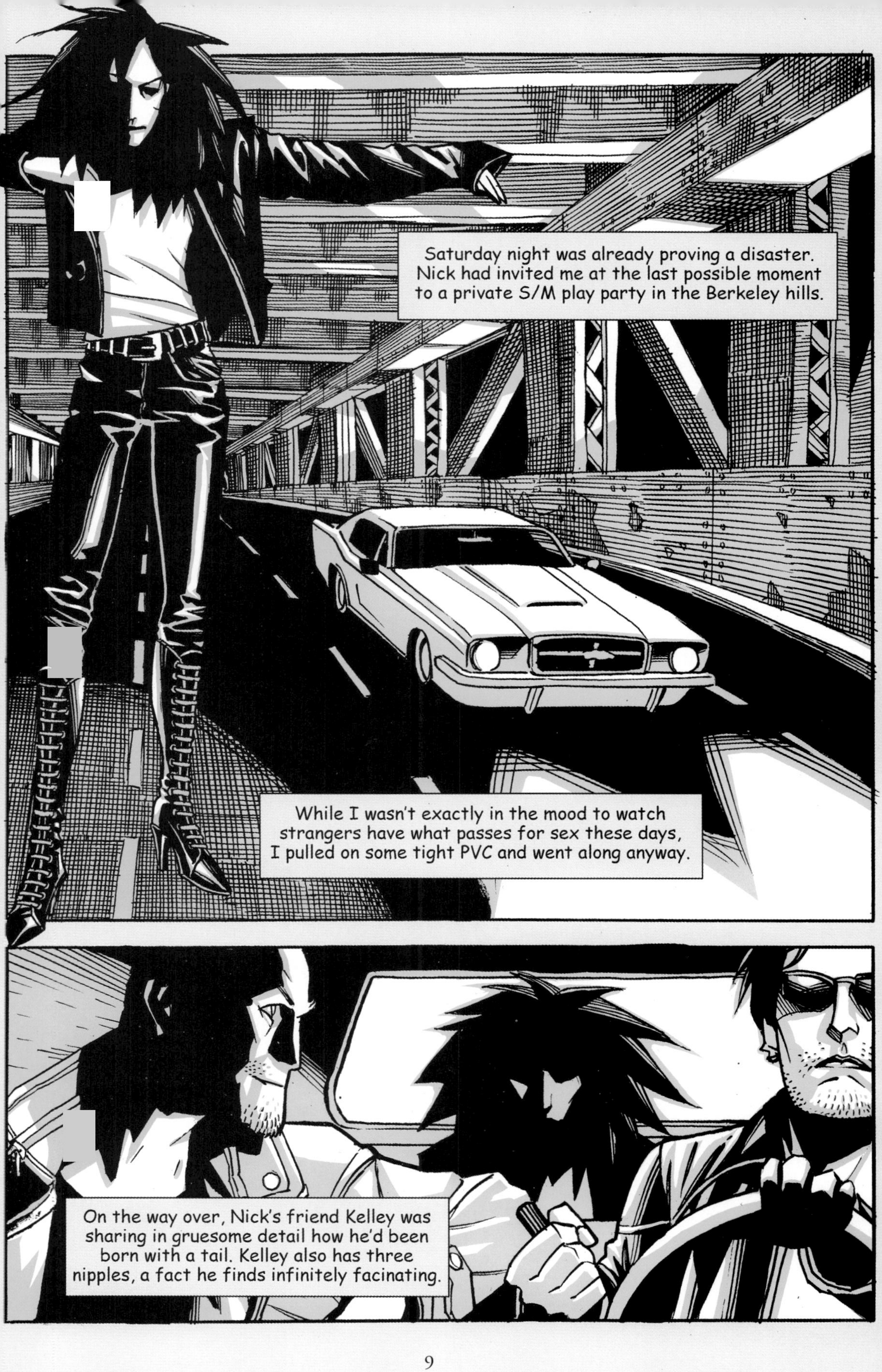
Saturday night was already proving a disaster. Nick had invited me at the last possible moment to a private S/M play party in the Berkeley hills.
While I wasn't exactly in the mood to watch strangers have what passes for sex these days, I pulled on some tight PVC and went along anyway.
On the way over, Nick's friend Kelley was sharing in gruesome detail how he'd been born with a tail. Kelley also has three nipples, a fact he finds infinitely facinating.

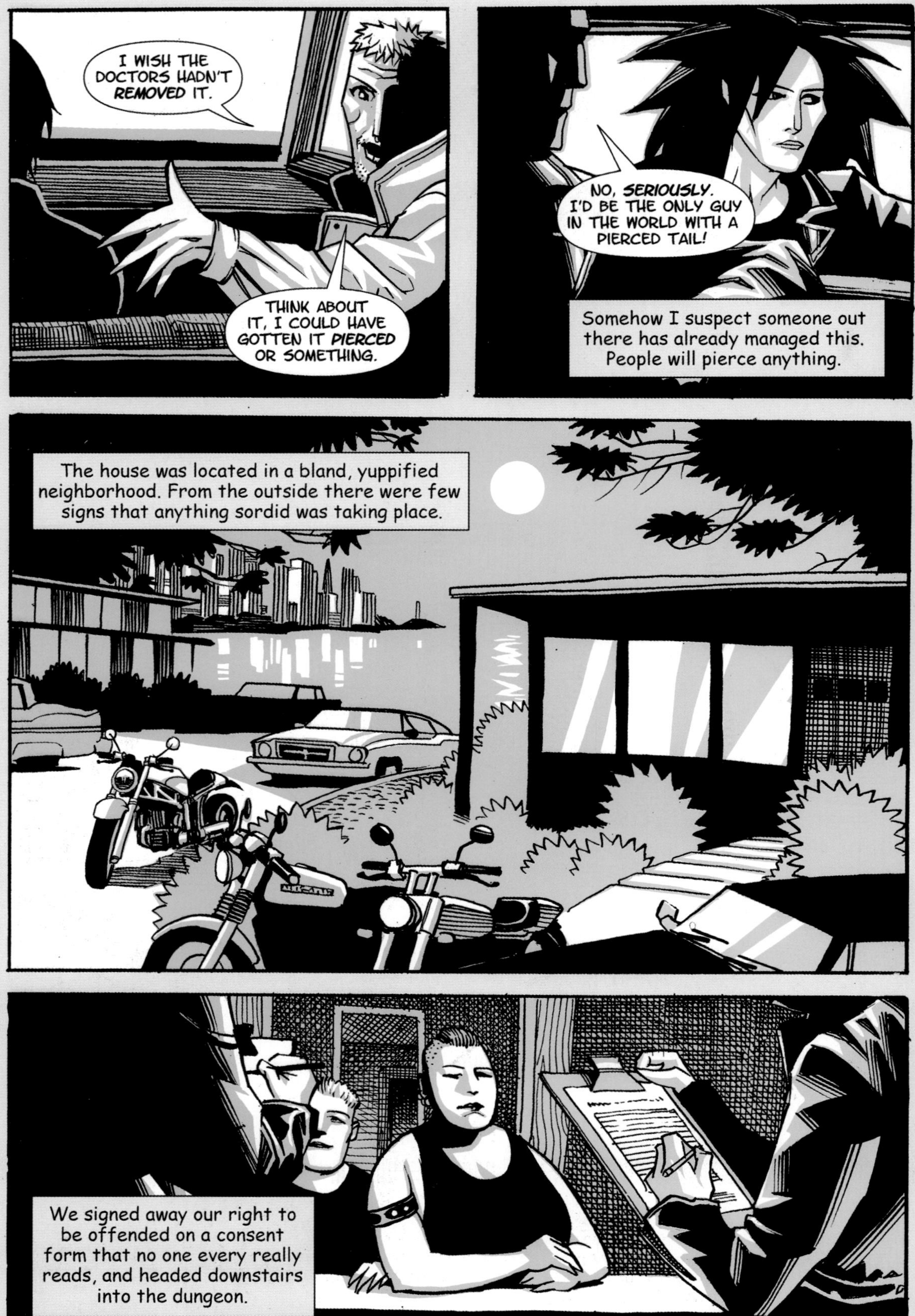
I WISH THE DOCTORS HADN'T *REMOVED* IT.
THINK ABOUT IT, I COULD HAVE GOTTEN IT *PIERCED* OR SOMETHING.
NO, *SERIOUSLY*. I'D BE THE ONLY GUY IN THE WORLD WITH A PIERCED TAIL!
Somehow I suspect someone out there has already managed this. People will pierce anything.
The house was located in a bland, yuppified neighborhood. From the outside there were few signs that anything sordid was taking place.
We signed away our right to be offended on a consent form that no one every really reads, and headed downstairs into the dungeon.

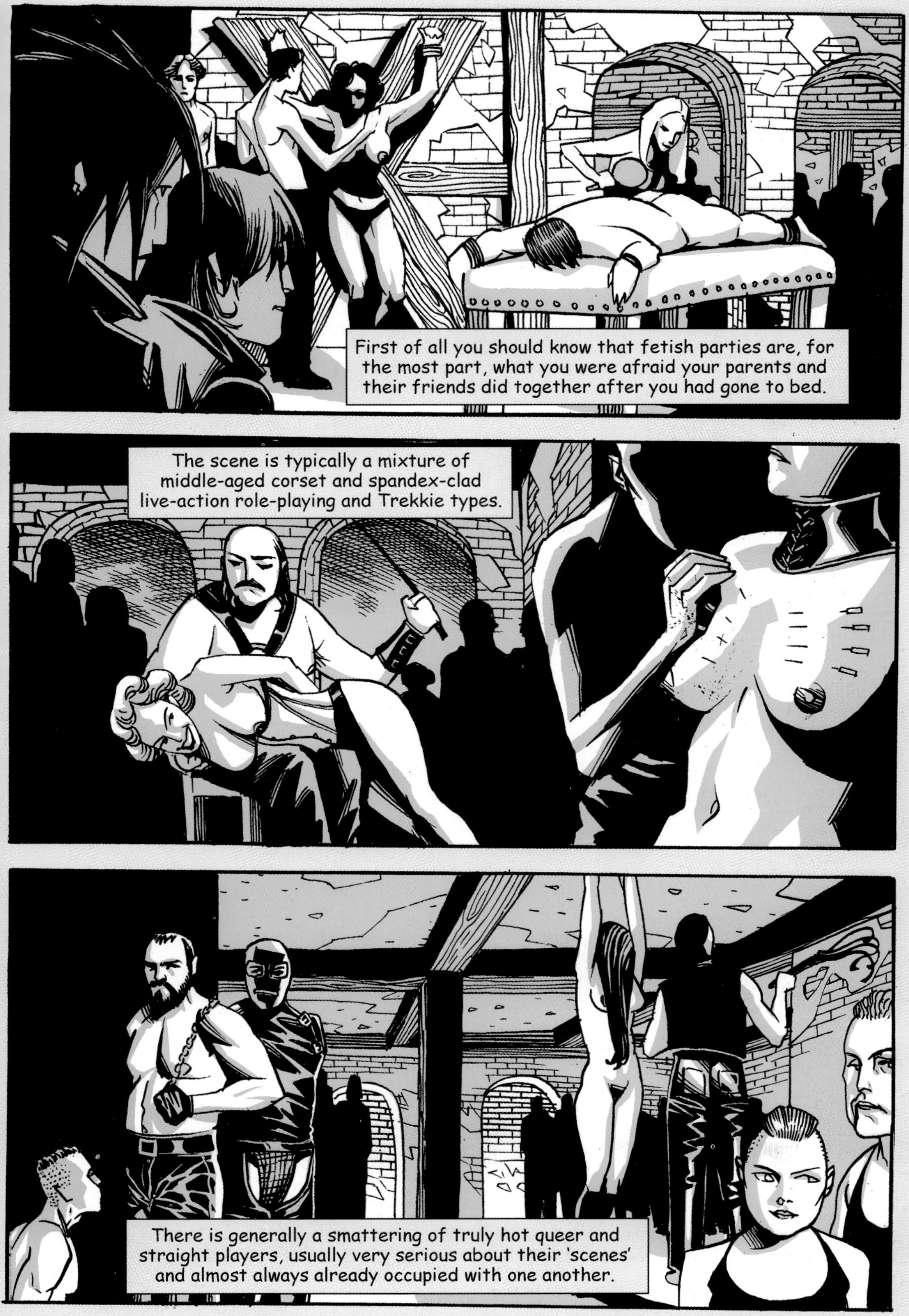
First of all you should know that fetish parties are, for the most part, what you were afraid your parents and their friends did together after you had gone to bed.
The scene is typically a mixture of middle-aged corset and spandex-clad live-action role-playing and Trekkie types.
There is generally a smattering of truly hot queer and straight players, usually very serious about their 'scenes' and almost always already occupied with one another.

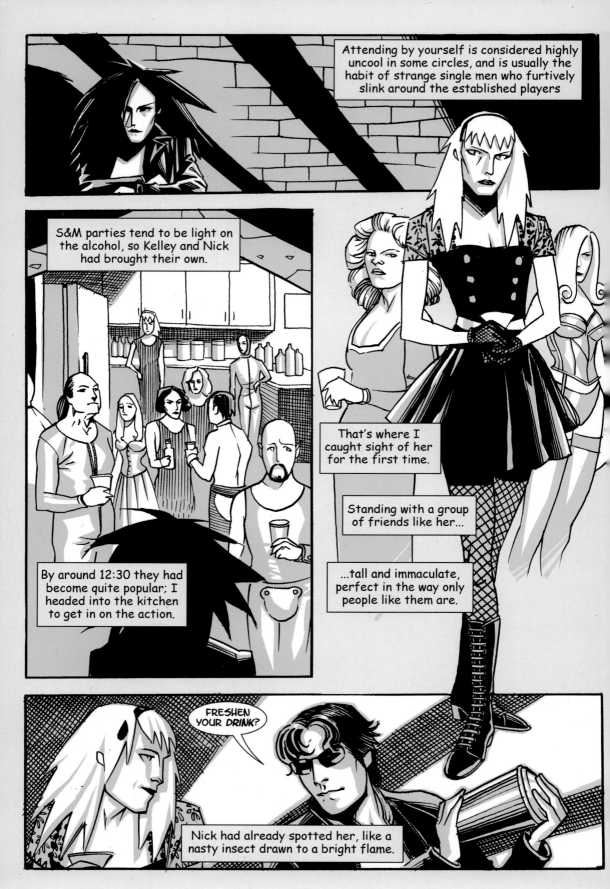

Attending by yourself is considered highly uncool in some circles, and is usually the habit of strange single men who furtively slink around the established players

S&M parties tend to be light on the alcohol, so Kelley and Nick had brought their own.

That's where I caught sight of her for the first time.

Standing with a group of friends like her...

By around 12:30 they had become quite popular; I headed into the kitchen to get in on the action.

...tall and immaculate, perfect in the way only people like them are.

FRESHEN YOUR DRINK?

Nick had already spotted her, like a nasty insect drawn to a bright flame.

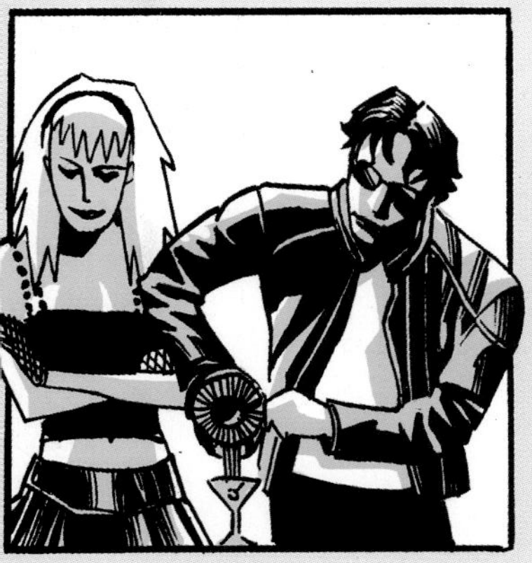

He seemed to be doing well, but I'm not sure he fully grasped the situation.

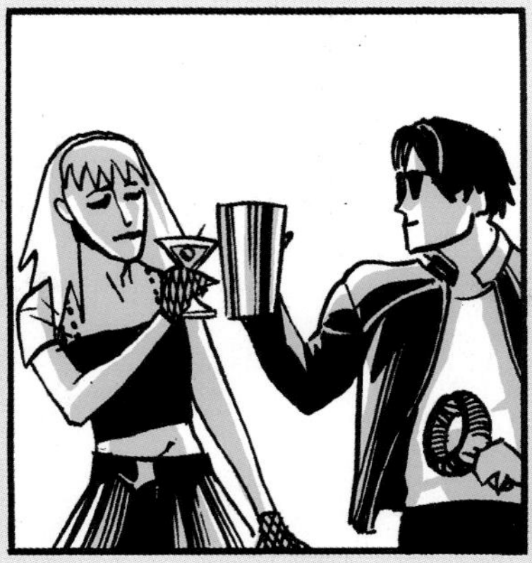

She was taken with him though, which isn't that suprising really.

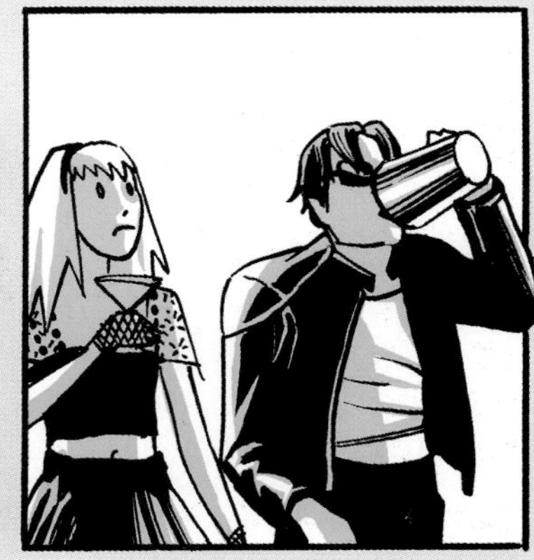

Nick, while not actually charming, is just repulsive enough to be great company.

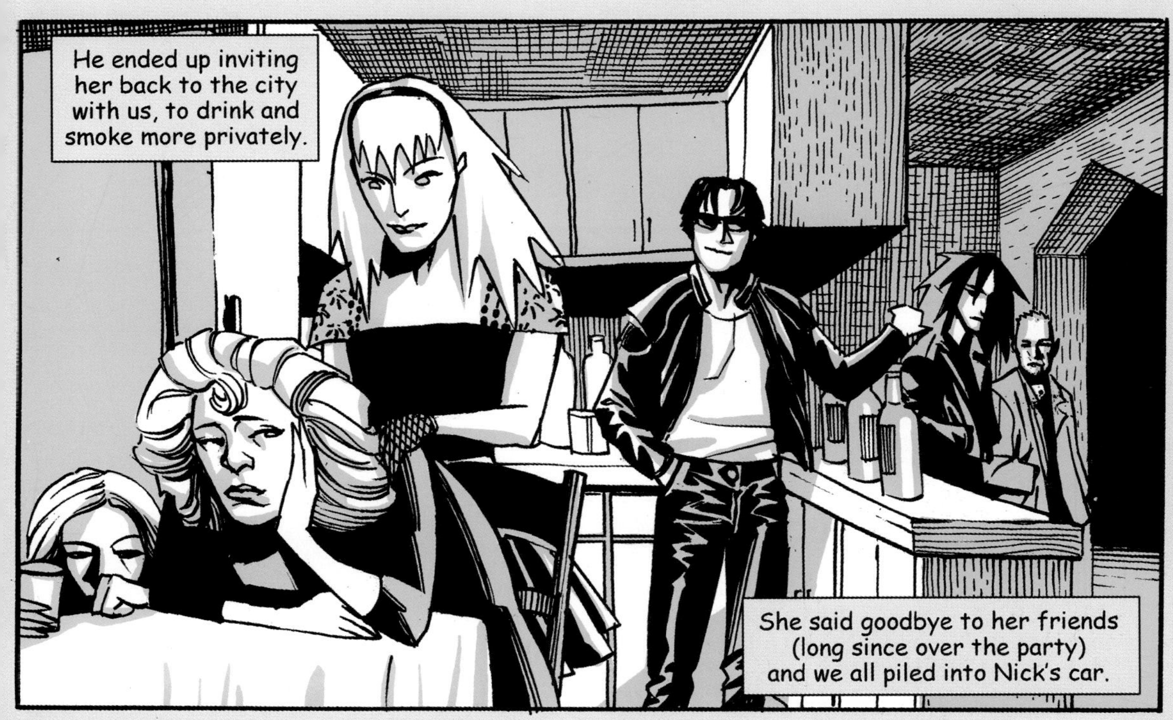
He ended up inviting her back to the city with us, to drink and smoke more privately.
She said goodbye to her friends (long since over the party) and we all piled into Nick's car.

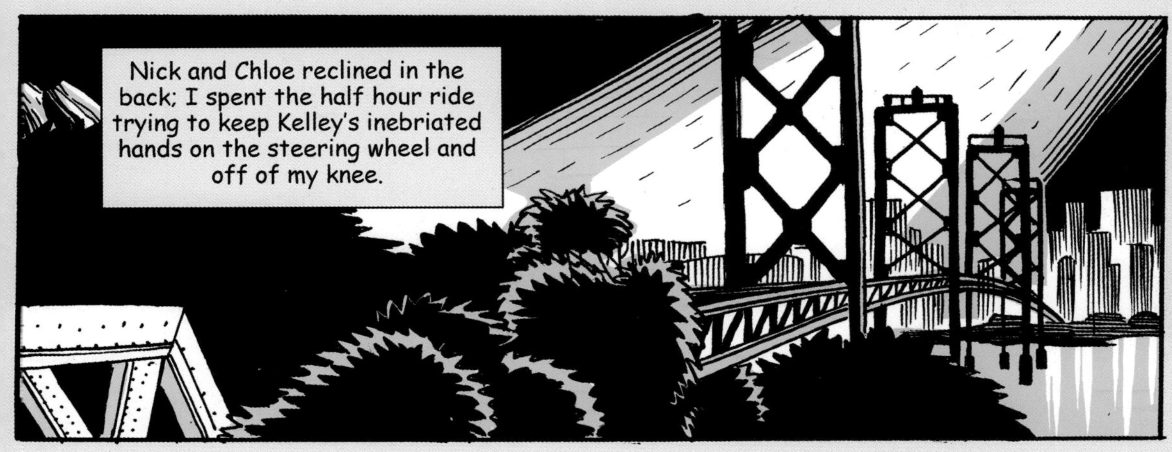
Nick and Chloe reclined in the back; I spent the half hour ride trying to keep Kelley's inebriated hands on the steering wheel and off of my knee.

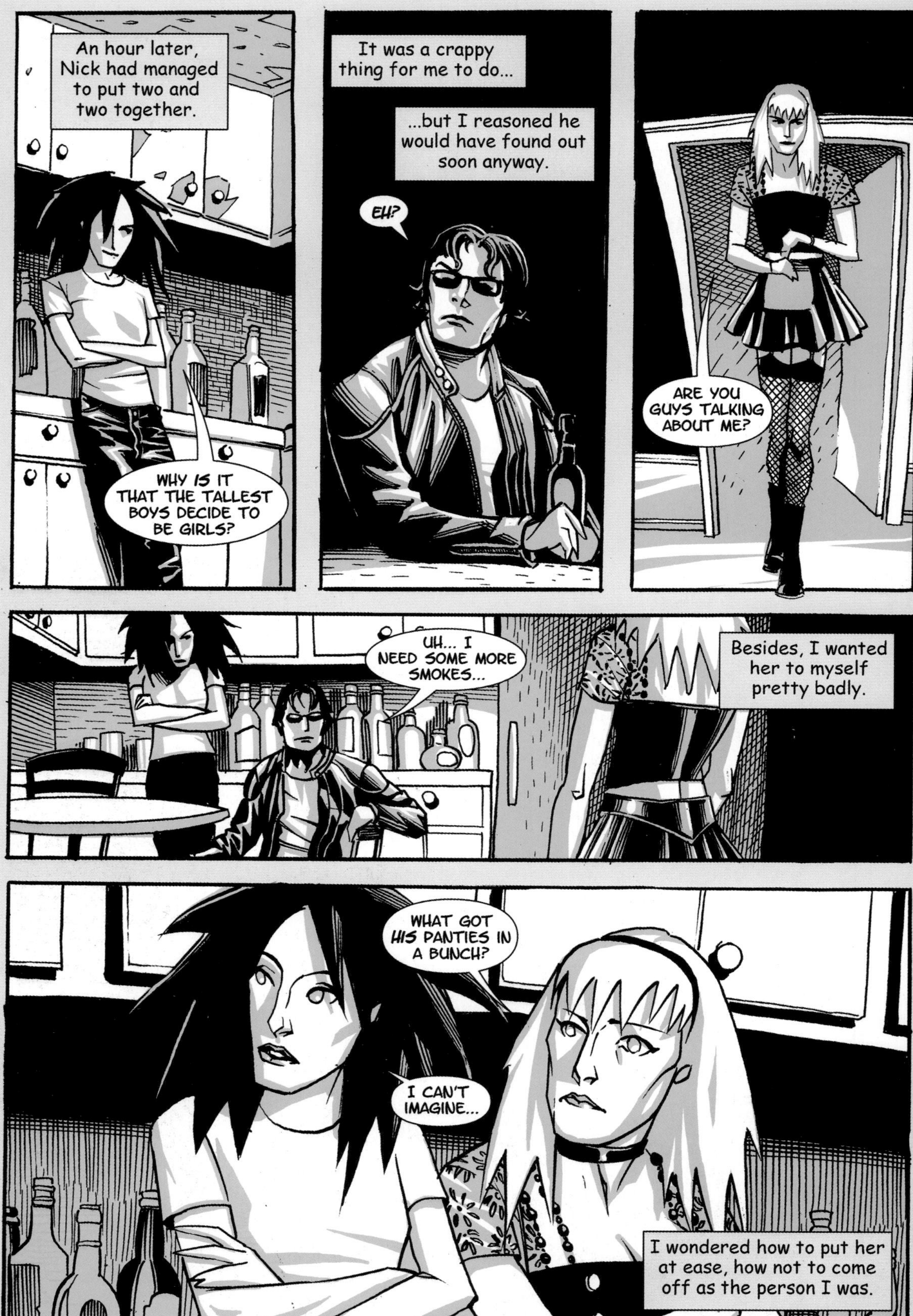

An hour later, Nick had managed to put two and two together.
WHY *IS* IT THAT THE TALLEST BOYS DECIDE TO BE GIRLS?
It was a crappy thing for me to do...
...but I reasoned he would have found out soon anyway.
EH?
ARE YOU GUYS TALKING ABOUT ME?
UH... I NEED SOME MORE SMOKES...
Besides, I wanted her to myself pretty badly.
WHAT GOT *HIS* PANTIES IN A BUNCH?
I CAN'T IMAGINE...
I wondered how to put her at ease, how not to come off as the person I was.

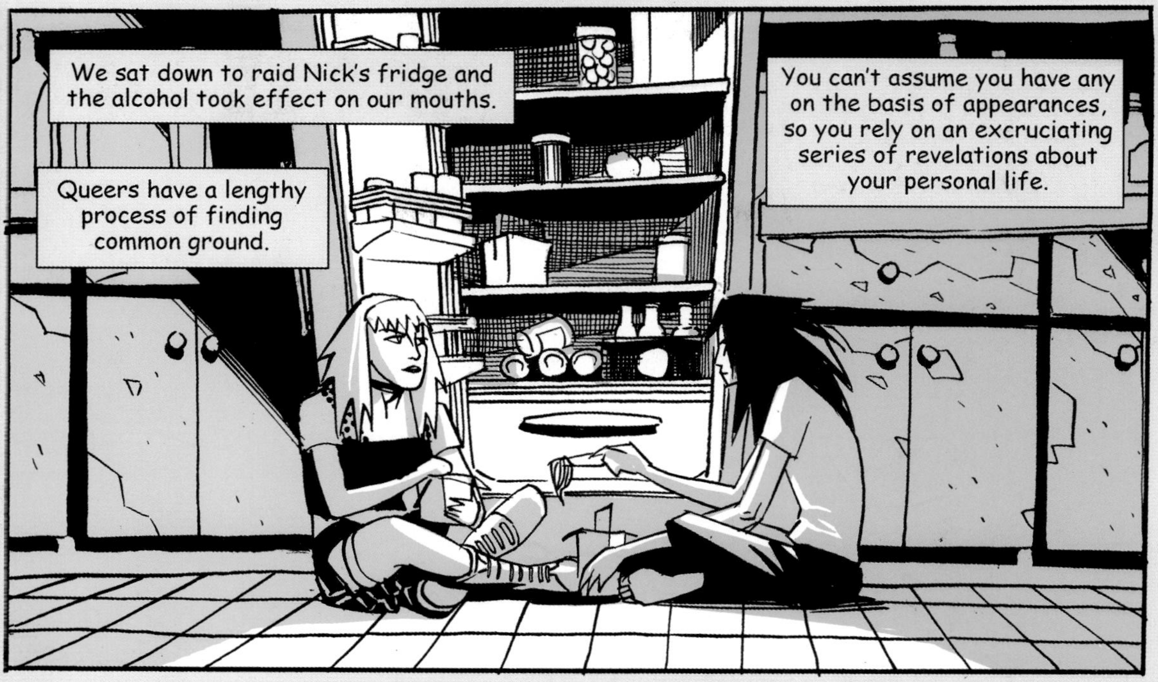
We sat down to raid Nick's fridge and the alcohol took effect on our mouths.
Queers have a lengthy process of finding common ground.
You can't assume you have any on the basis of appearances, so you rely on an excruciating series of revelations about your personal life.

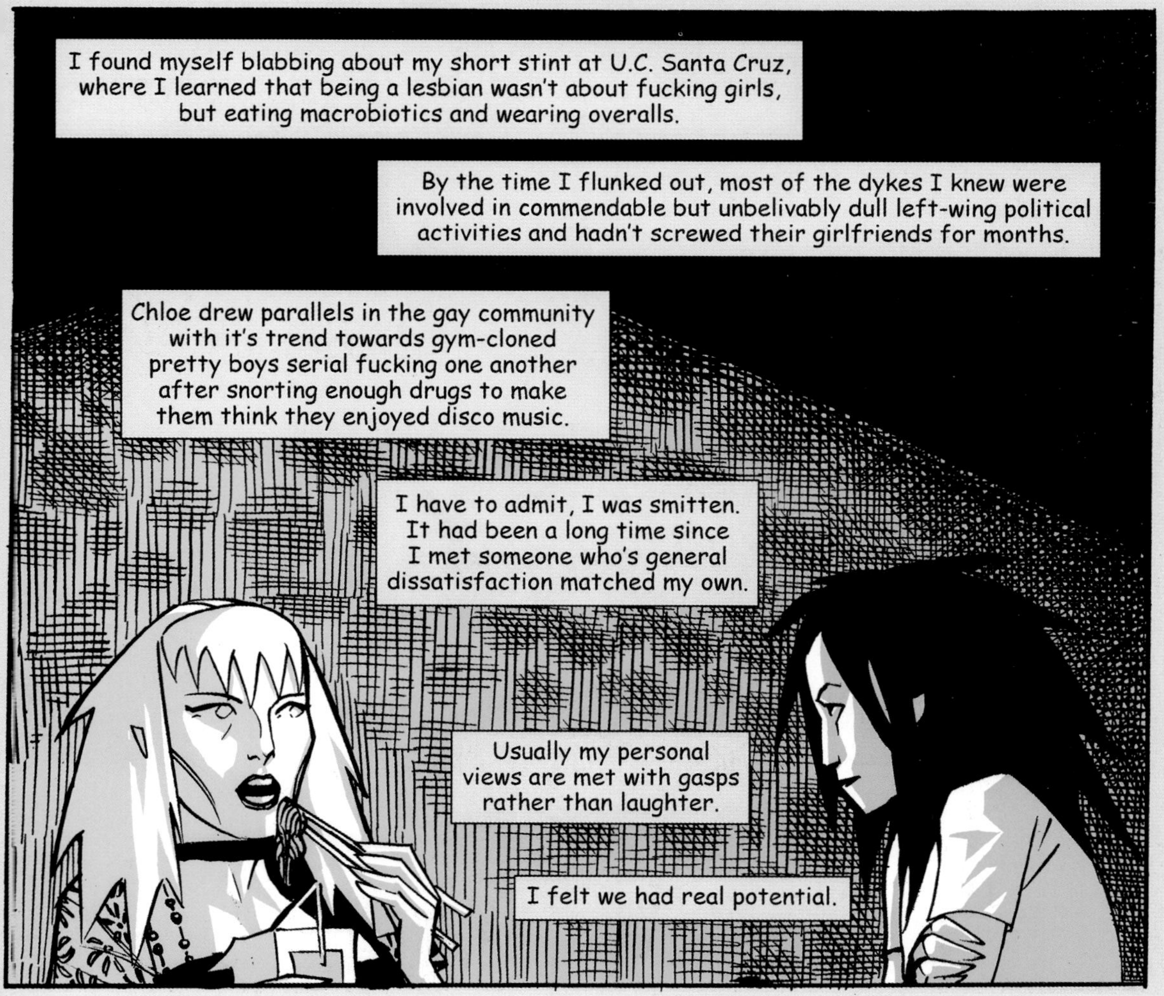
I found myself blabbing about my short stint at U.C. Santa Cruz, where I learned that being a lesbian wasn't about fucking girls, but eating macrobiotics and wearing overalls.
By the time I flunked out, most of the dykes I knew were involved in commendable but unbelivably dull left-wing political activities and hadn't screwed their girlfriends for months.
Chloe drew parallels in the gay community with it's trend towards gym-cloned pretty boys serial fucking one another after snorting enough drugs to make them think they enjoyed disco music.
I have to admit, I was smitten. It had been a long time since I met someone who's general dissatisfaction matched my own.
Usually my personal views are met with gasps rather than laughter.
I felt we had real potential.

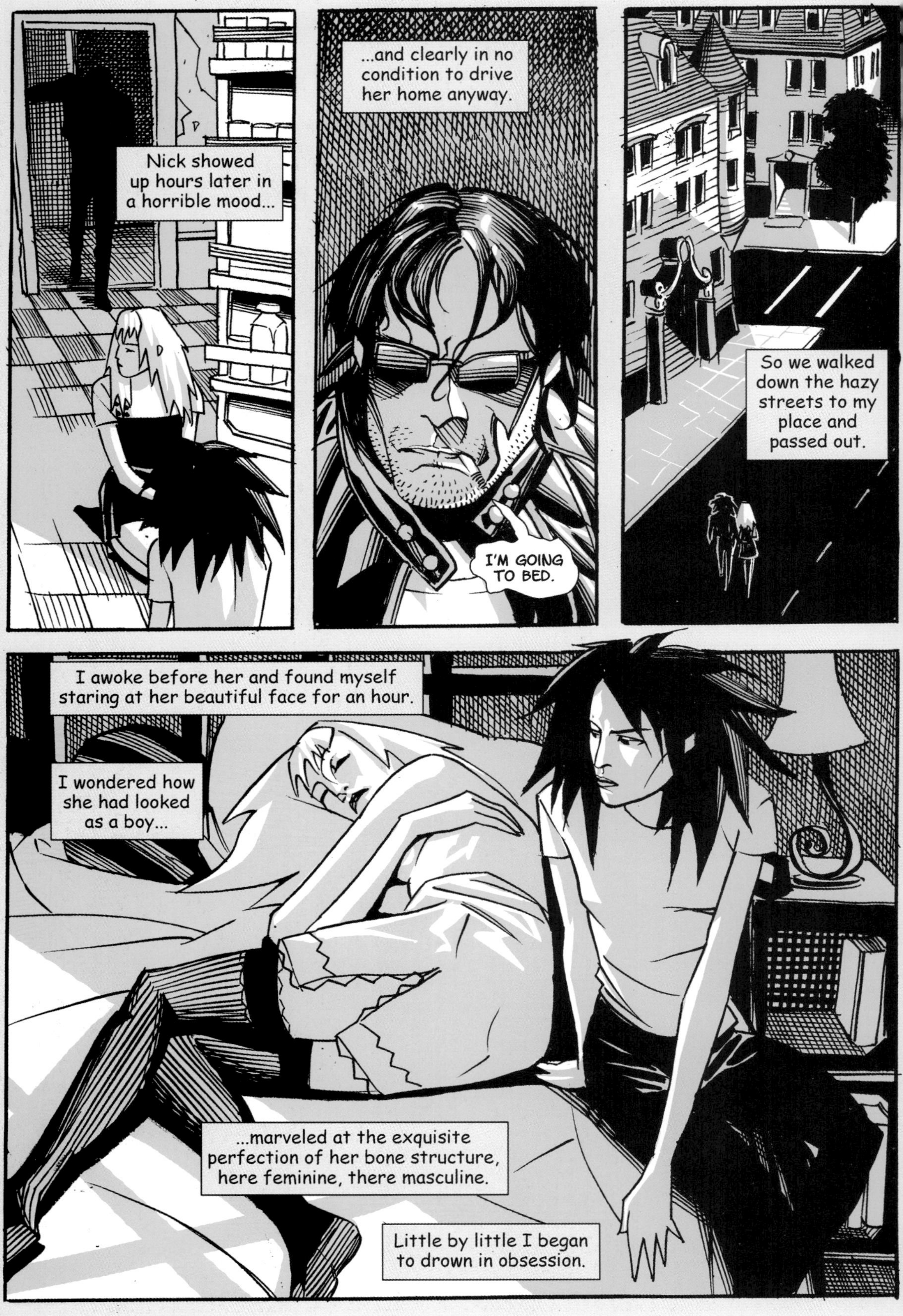
Nick showed up hours later in a horrible mood...
...and clearly in no condition to drive her home anyway.
I'M GOING TO BED.
So we walked down the hazy streets to my place and passed out.
I awoke before her and found myself staring at her beautiful face for an hour.
I wondered how she had looked as a boy...
...marveled at the exquisite perfection of her bone structure, here feminine, there masculine.
Little by little I began to drown in obsession.

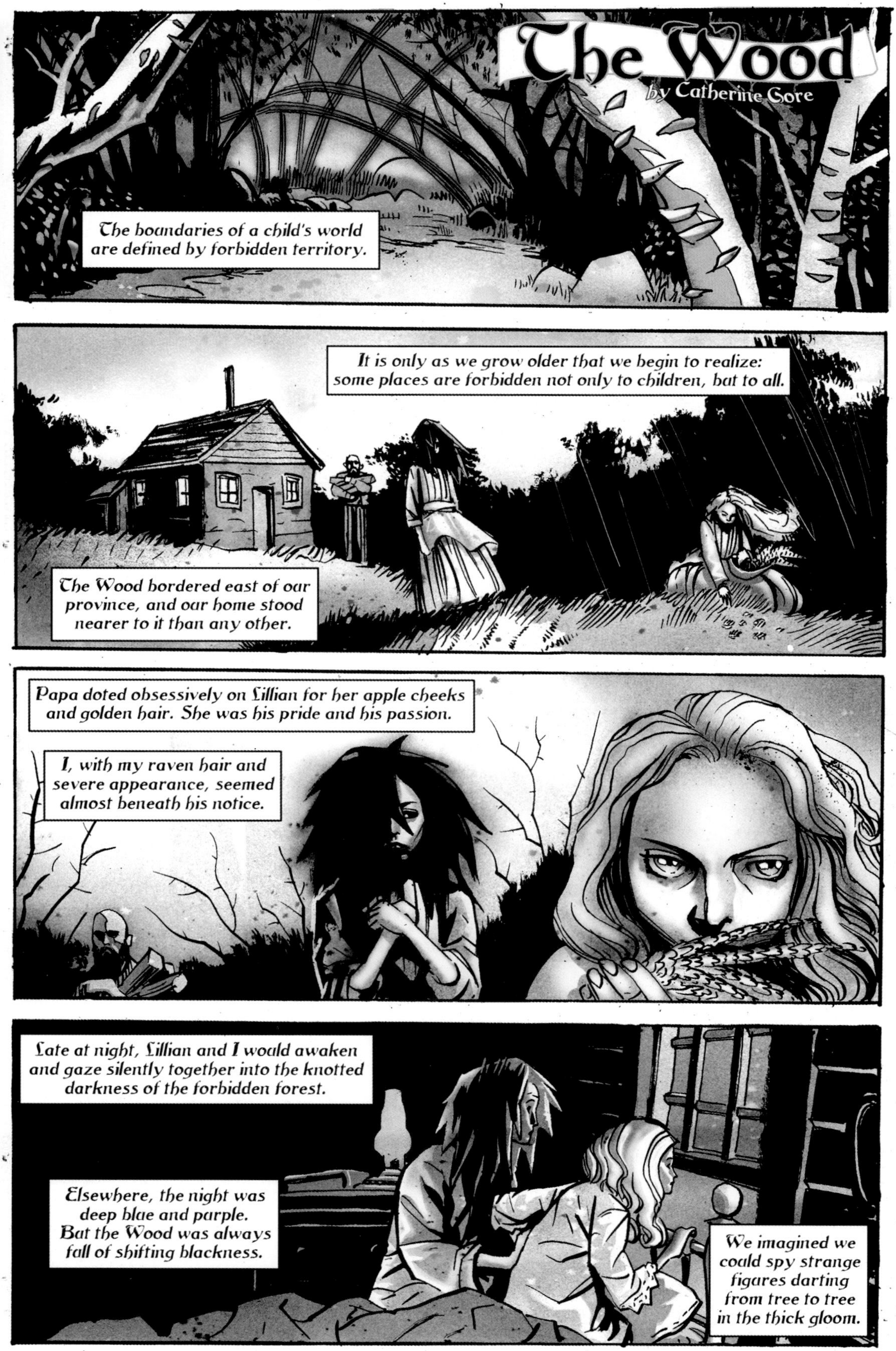
The Wood
by Catherine Gore
The boundaries of a child's world are defined by forbidden territory.
It is only as we grow older that we begin to realize: some places are forbidden not only to children, but to all.
The Wood bordered east of our province, and our home stood nearer to it than any other.
Papa doted obsessively on Lillian for her apple cheeks and golden hair. She was his pride and his passion.
I, with my raven hair and severe appearance, seemed almost beneath his notice.
Late at night, Lillian and I would awaken and gaze silently together into the knotted darkness of the forbidden forest.
Elsewhere, the night was deep blue and purple. But the Wood was always full of shifting blackness.
We imagined we could spy strange figures darting from tree to tree in the thick gloom.

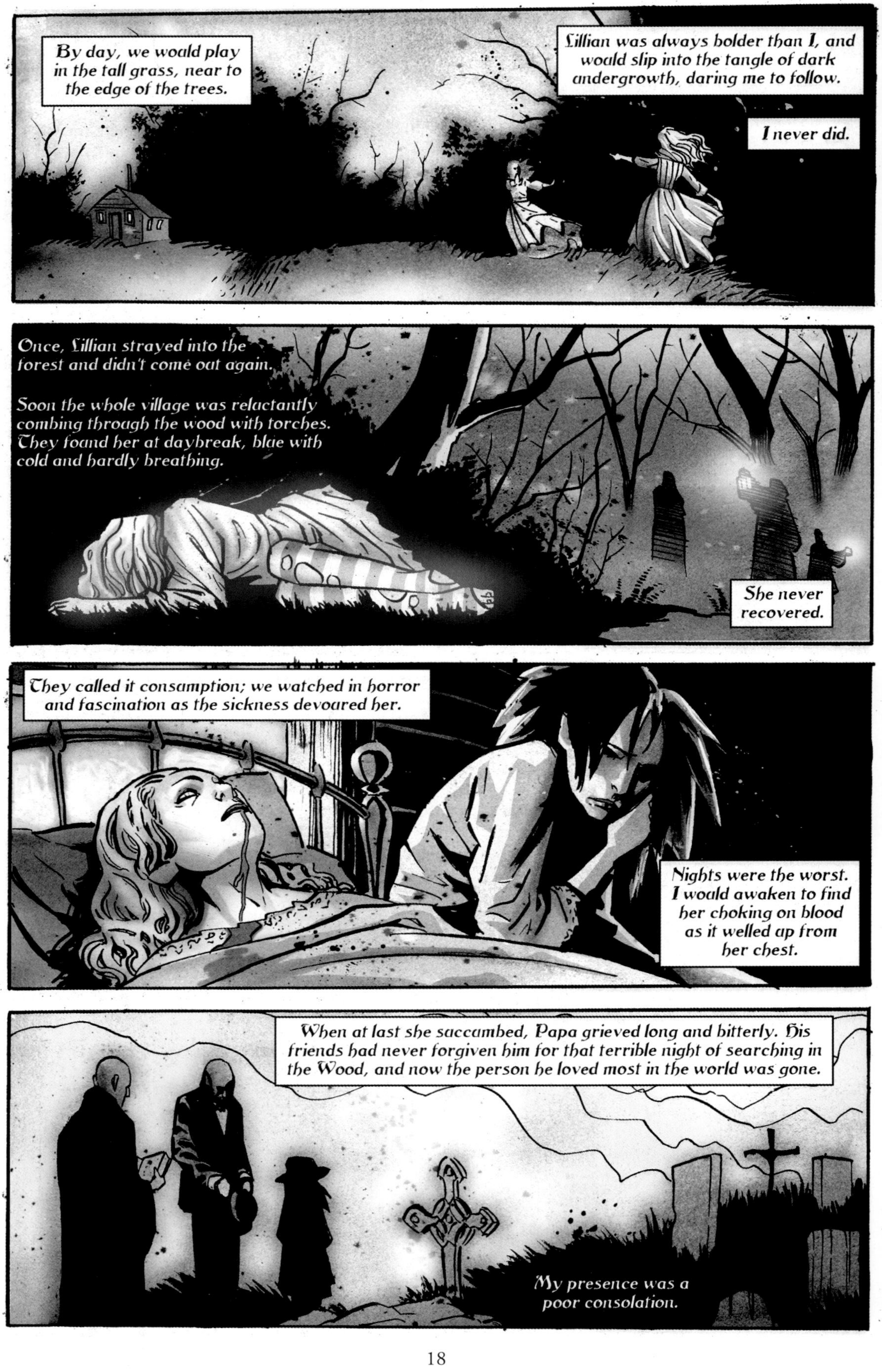
By day, we would play in the tall grass, near to the edge of the trees.
Lillian was always bolder than I, and would slip into the tangle of dark undergrowth, daring me to follow.
I never did.
Once, Lillian strayed into the forest and didn't come out again.
Soon the whole village was reluctantly combing through the wood with torches. They found her at daybreak, blue with cold and hardly breathing.
She never recovered.
They called it consumption; we watched in horror and fascination as the sickness devoured her.
Nights were the worst. I would awaken to find her choking on blood as it welled up from her chest.
When at last she succumbed, Papa grieved long and bitterly. His friends had never forgiven him for that terrible night of searching in the Wood, and now the person he loved most in the world was gone.
My presence was a poor consolation.

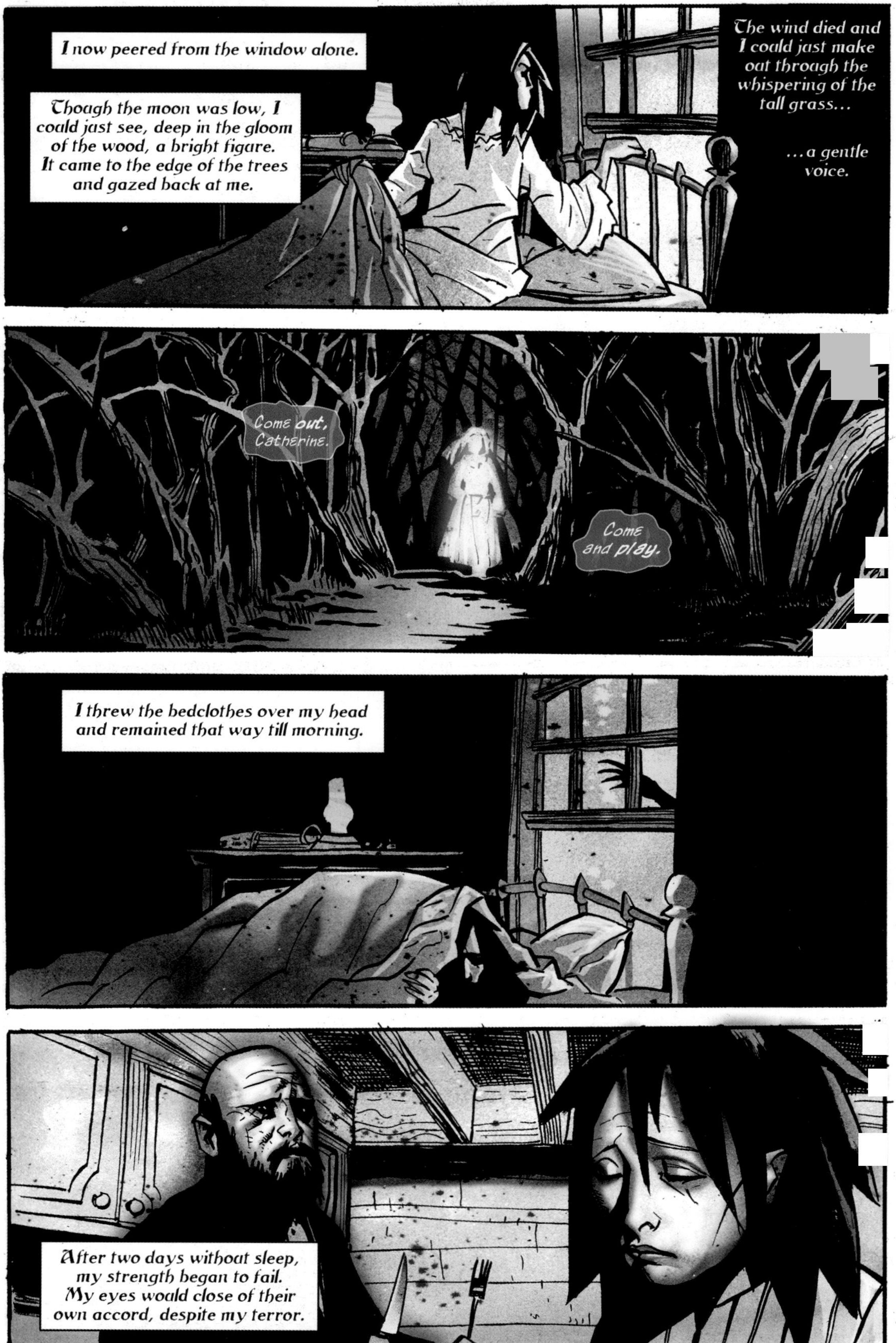
I now peered from the window alone.
Though the moon was low, I could just see, deep in the gloom of the wood, a bright figure. It came to the edge of the trees and gazed back at me.
The wind died and I could just make out through the whispering of the tall grass...
...a gentle voice.
Come out, Catherine.
Come and play.
I threw the bedclothes over my head and remained that way till morning.
After two days without sleep, my strength began to fail. My eyes would close of their own accord, despite my terror.

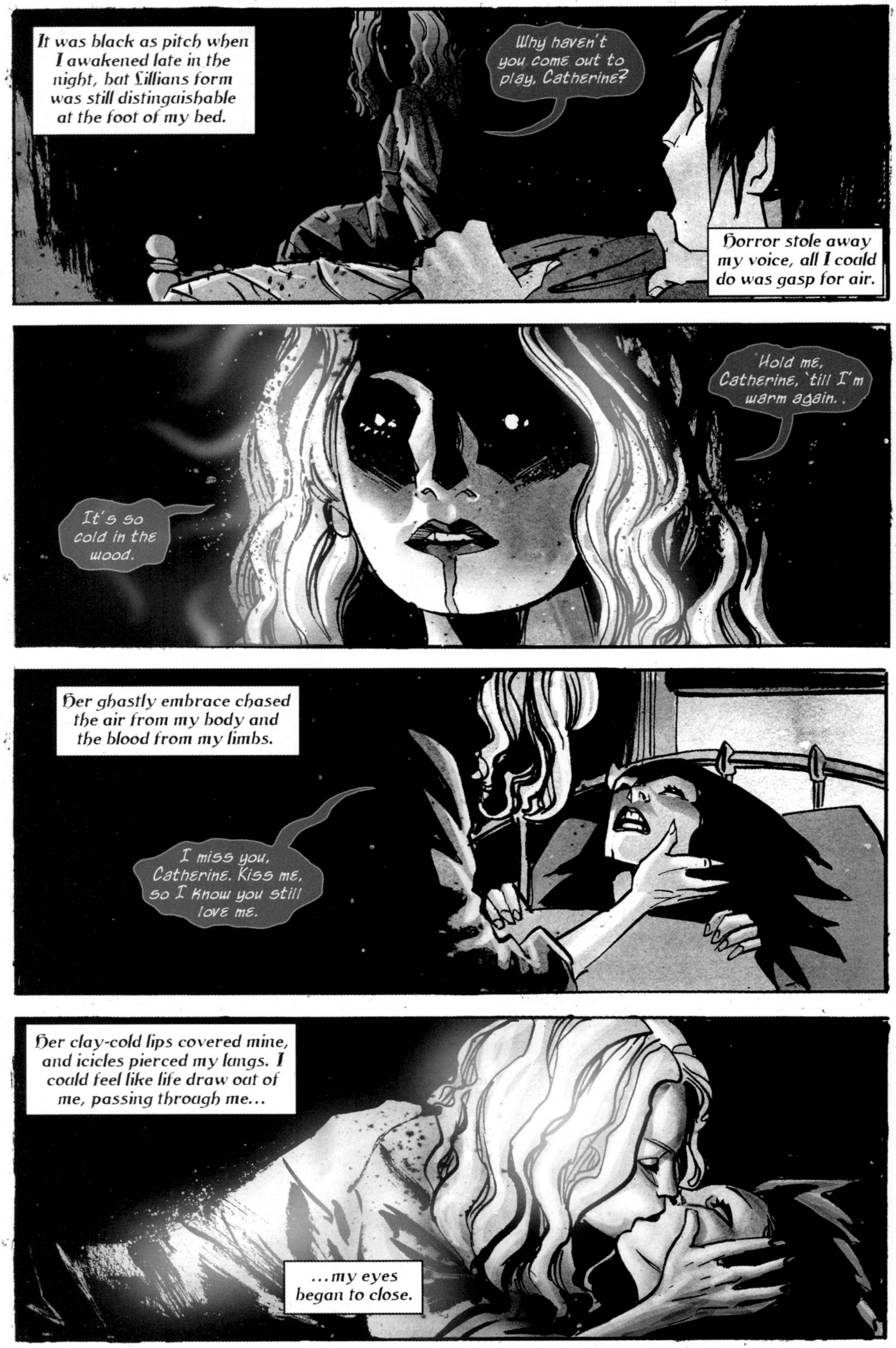
It was black as pitch when I awakened late in the night, but Lillians form was still distinguishable at the foot of my bed.
Why haven't you come out to play, Catherine?
Horror stole away my voice, all I could do was gasp for air.
Hold me, Catherine, 'till I'm warm again.
It's so cold in the wood.
Her ghastly embrace chased the air from my body and the blood from my limbs.
I miss you, Catherine. Kiss me, so I know you still love me.
Her clay-cold lips covered mine, and icicles pierced my lungs. I could feel life draw out of me, passing through me...
...my eyes began to close.

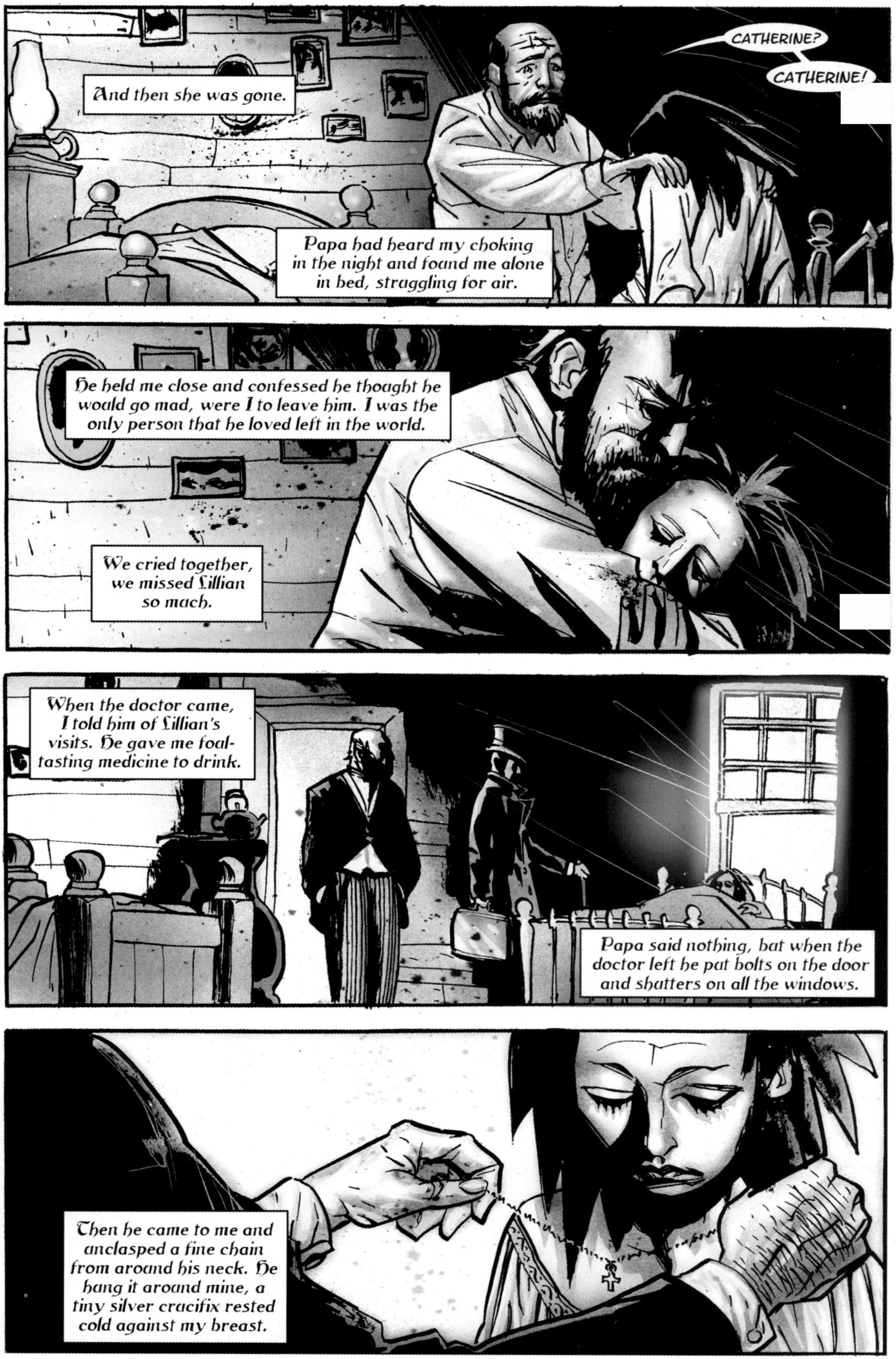
And then she was gone.
CATHERINE?
CATHERINE!
Papa had heard my choking in the night and found me alone in bed, struggling for air.
He held me close and confessed he thought he would go mad, were I to leave him. I was the only person that he loved left in the world.
We cried together, we missed Lillian so much.
When the doctor came, I told him of Lillian's visits. He gave me foul-tasting medicine to drink.
Papa said nothing, but when the doctor left he put bolts on the door and shutters on all the windows.
Then he came to me and unclasped a fine chain from around his neck. He hung it around mine, a tiny silver crucifix rested cold against my breast.

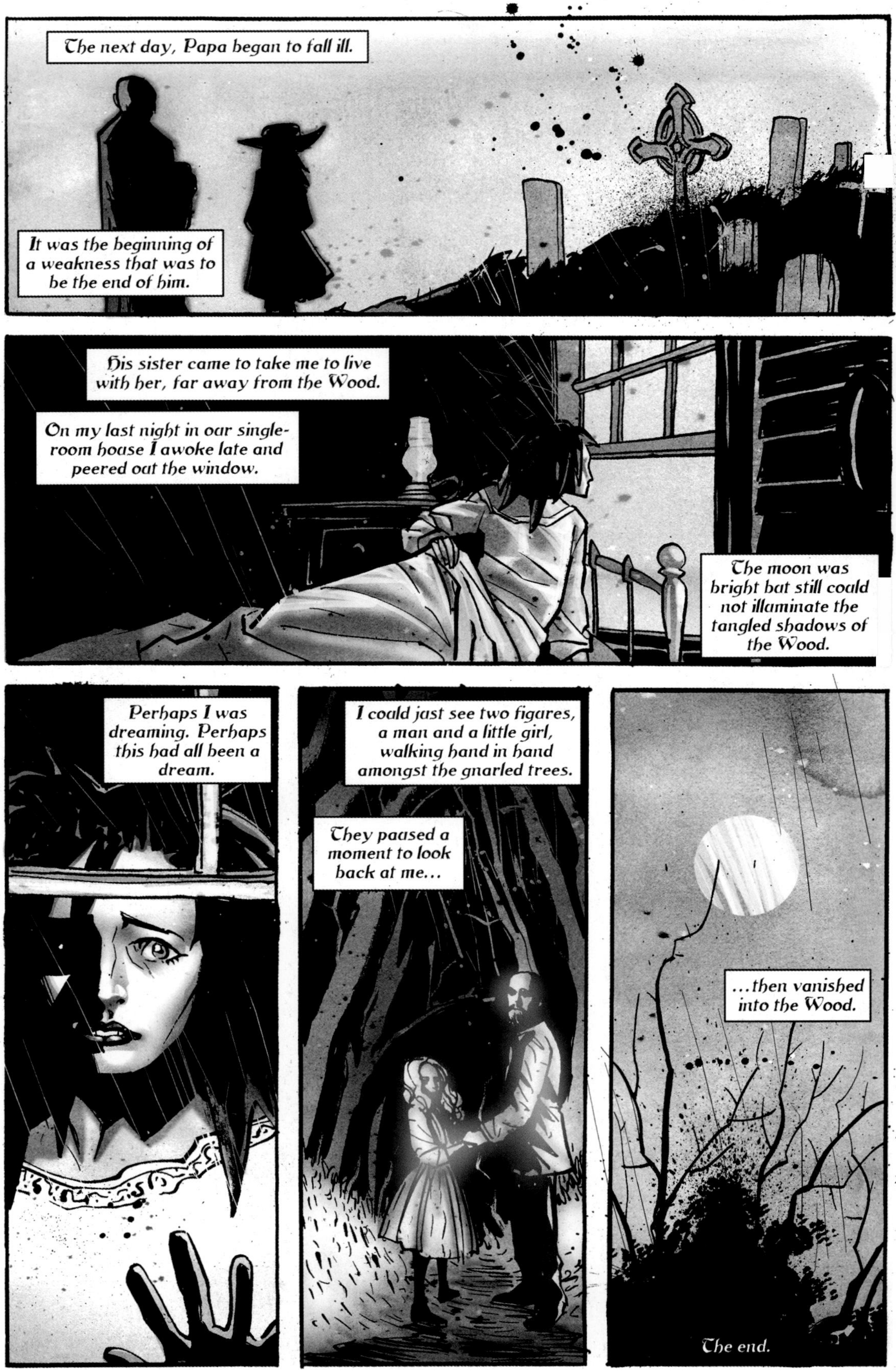
The next day, Papa began to fall ill.
It was the beginning of a weakness that was to be the end of him.
His sister came to take me to live with her, far away from the Wood.
On my last night in our single-room house I awoke late and peered out the window.
The moon was bright but still could not illuminate the tangled shadows of the Wood.
Perhaps I was dreaming. Perhaps this had all been a dream.
I could just see two figures, a man and a little girl, walking hand in hand amongst the gnarled trees.
They paused a moment to look back at me...
...then vanished into the Wood.
The end.

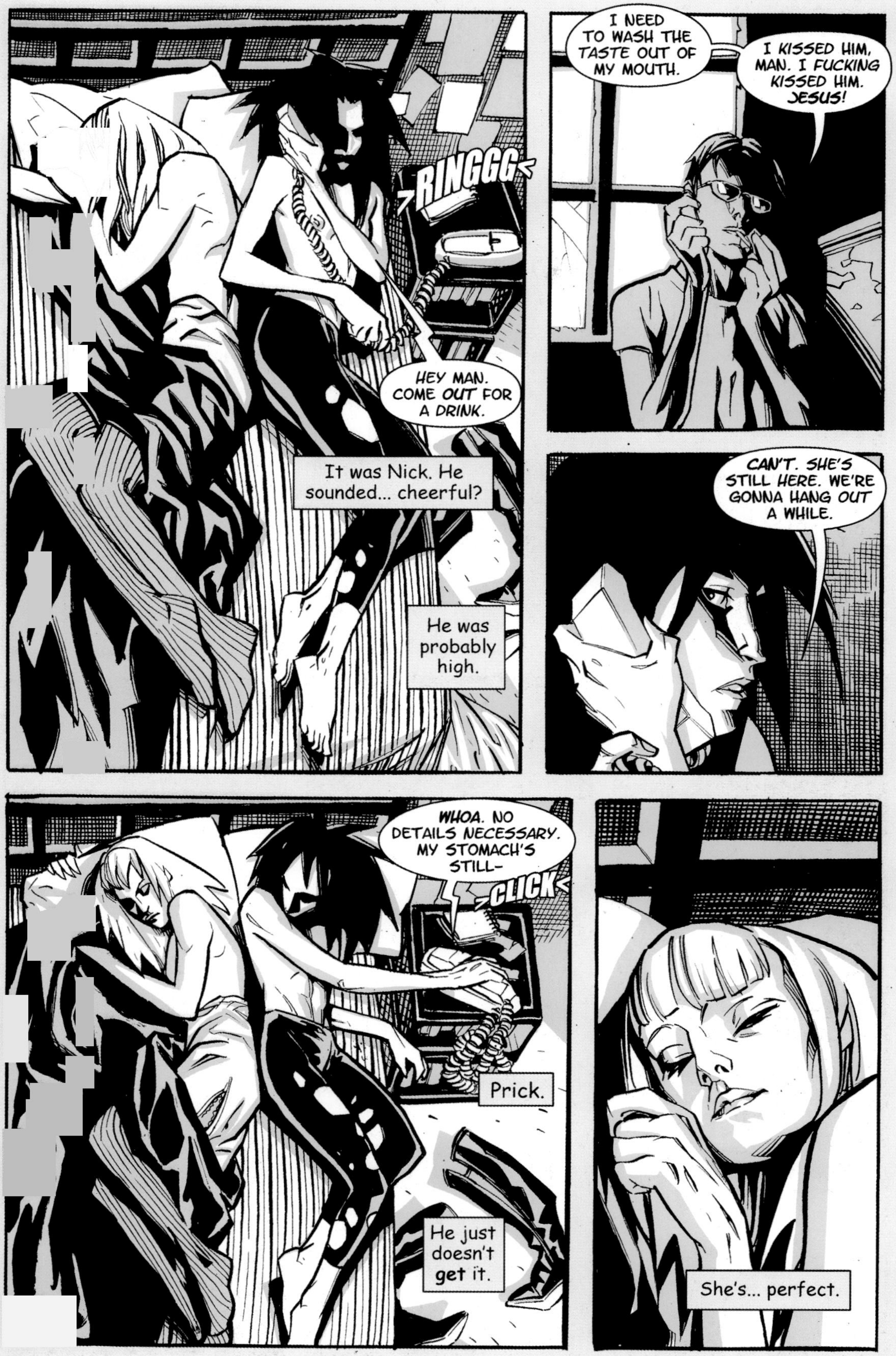
RINGGG
HEY MAN. COME OUT FOR A DRINK.
It was Nick. He sounded... cheerful?
He was probably high.
I NEED TO WASH THE TASTE OUT OF MY MOUTH.
I KISSED HIM, MAN. I FUCKING KISSED HIM. JESUS!
CAN'T. SHE'S STILL HERE. WE'RE GONNA HANG OUT A WHILE.
WHOA. NO DETAILS NECESSARY. MY STOMACH'S STILL-
CLICK
Prick.
He just doesn't get it.
She's... perfect.

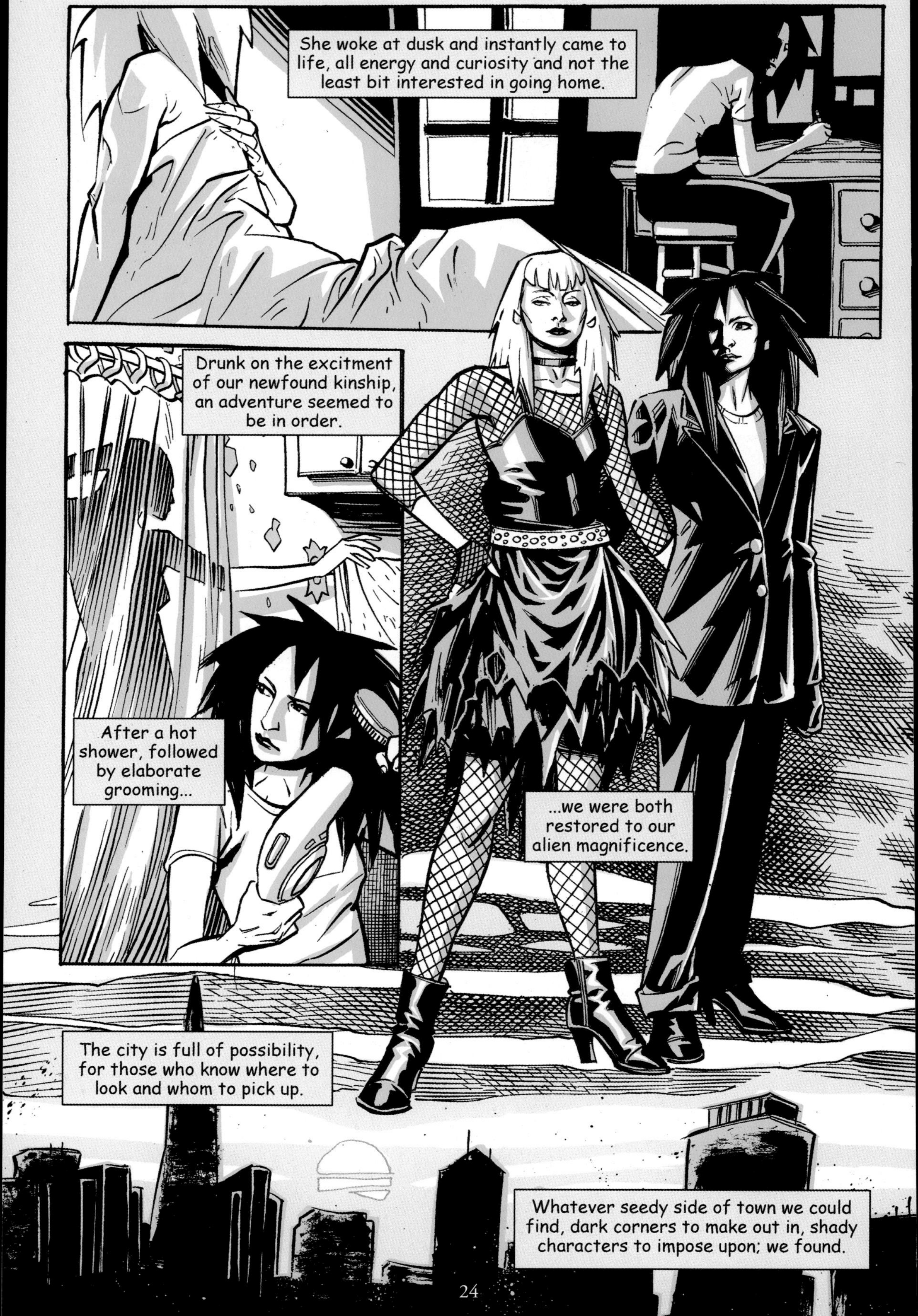
She woke at dusk and instantly came to life, all energy and curiosity and not the least bit interested in going home.
Drunk on the excitment of our newfound kinship, an adventure seemed to be in order.
After a hot shower, followed by elaborate grooming...
...we were both restored to our alien magnificence.
The city is full of possibility, for those who know where to look and whom to pick up.
Whatever seedy side of town we could find, dark corners to make out in, shady characters to impose upon; we found.

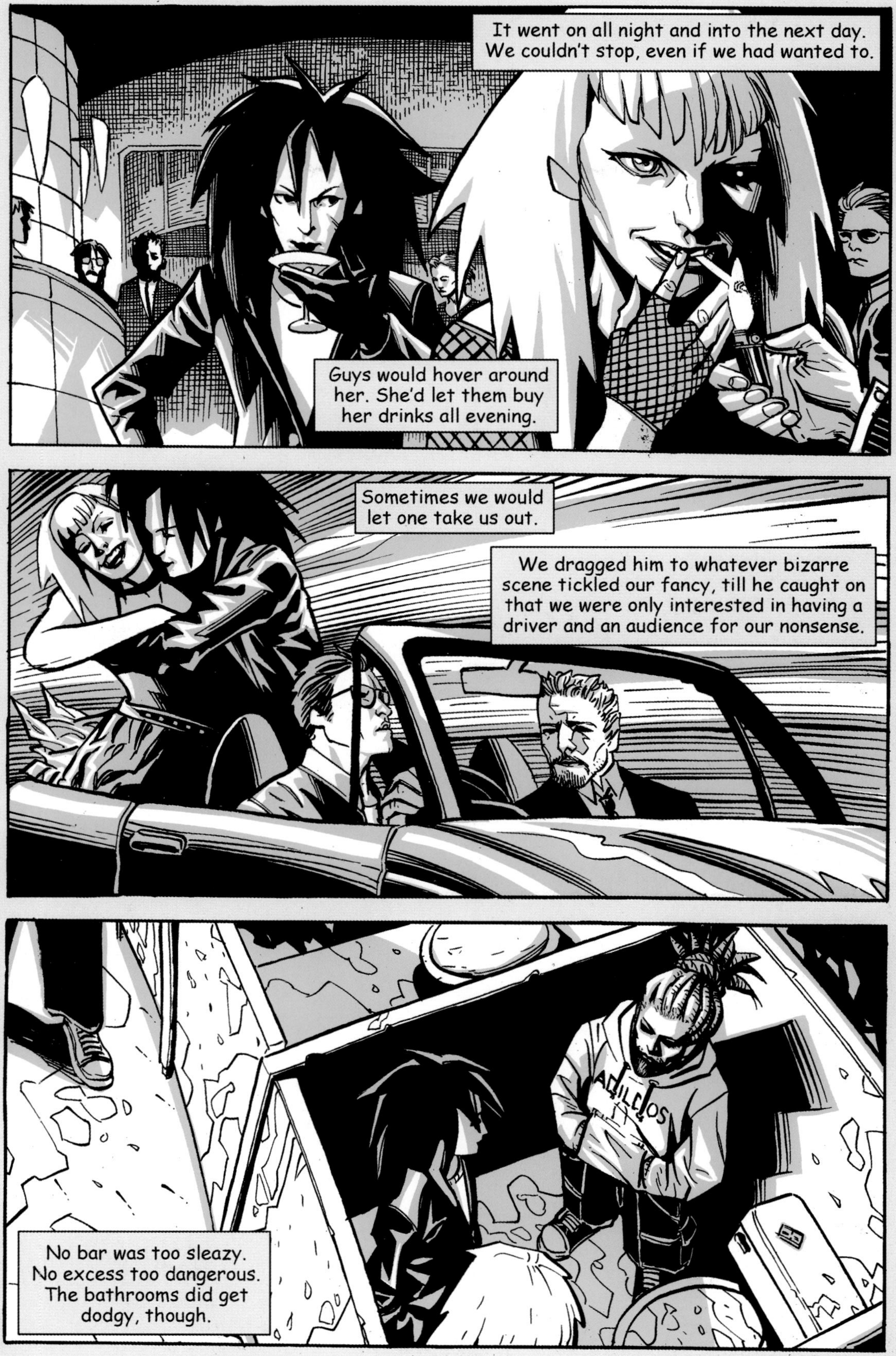
It went on all night and into the next day. We couldn't stop, even if we had wanted to.
Guys would hover around her. She'd let them buy her drinks all evening.
Sometimes we would let one take us out.
We dragged him to whatever bizarre scene tickled our fancy, till he caught on that we were only interested in having a driver and an audience for our nonsense.
No bar was too sleazy. No excess too dangerous. The bathrooms did get dodgy, though.

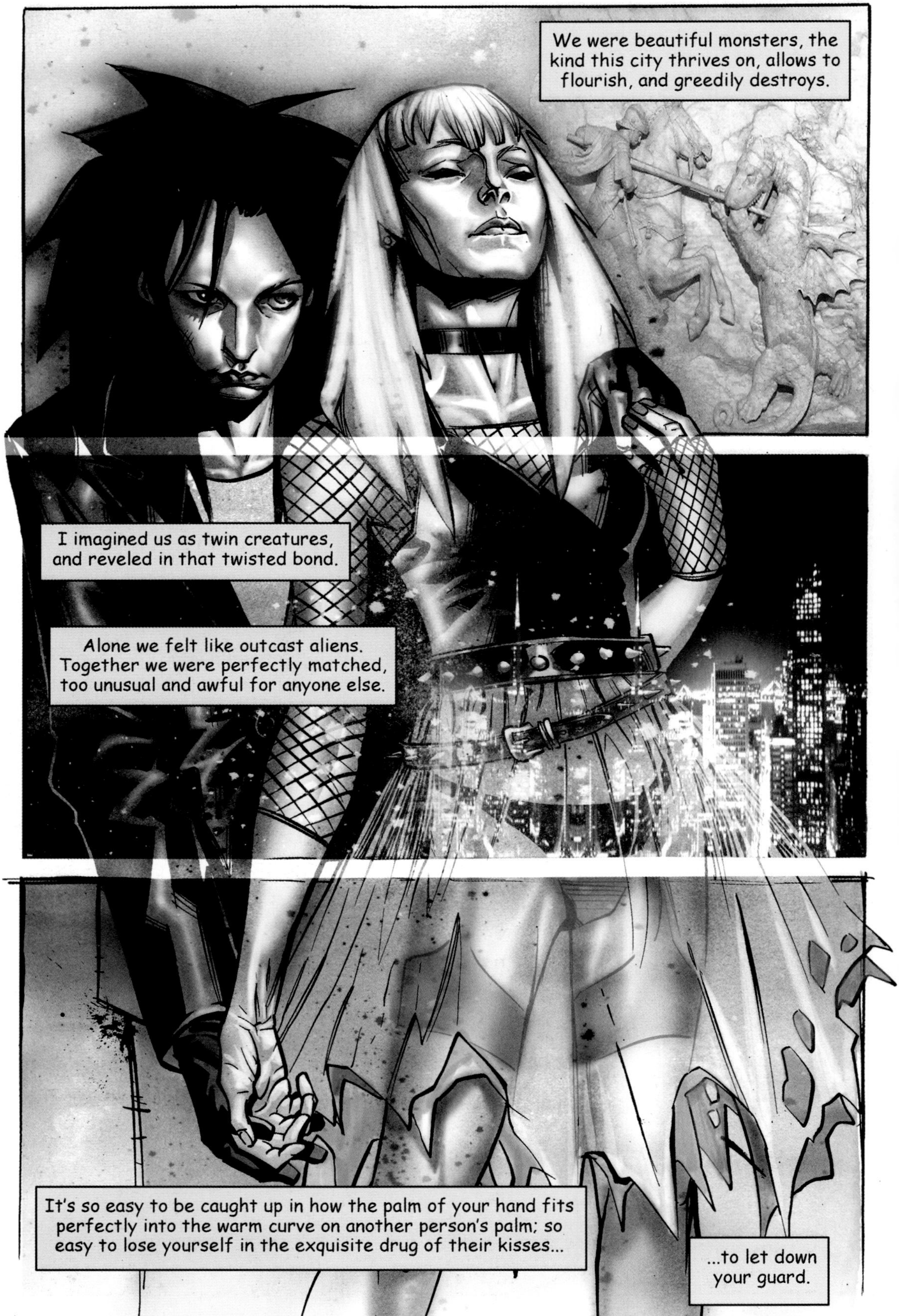
We were beautiful monsters, the kind this city thrives on, allows to flourish, and greedily destroys.
I imagined us as twin creatures, and reveled in that twisted bond.
Alone we felt like outcast aliens. Together we were perfectly matched, too unusual and awful for anyone else.
It's so easy to be caught up in how the palm of your hand fits perfectly into the warm curve on another person's palm; so easy to lose yourself in the exquisite drug of their kisses...
...to let down your guard.

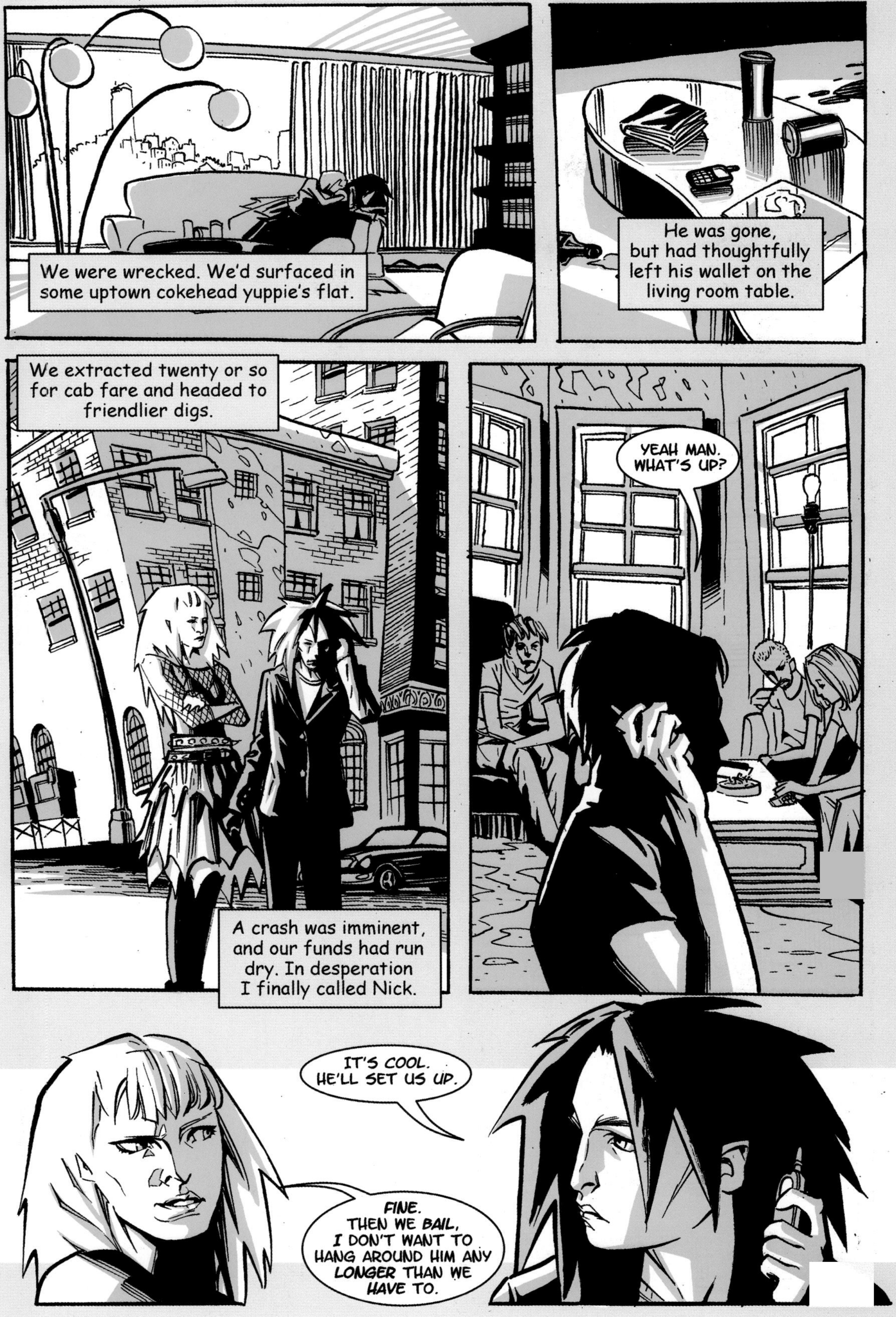
We were wrecked. We'd surfaced in some uptown cokehead yuppie's flat.
He was gone, but had thoughtfully left his wallet on the living room table.
We extracted twenty or so for cab fare and headed to friendlier digs.
A crash was imminent, and our funds had run dry. In desperation I finally called Nick.
YEAH MAN. WHAT'S UP?
IT'S COOL. HE'LL SET US UP.
FINE. THEN WE BAIL, I DON'T WANT TO HANG AROUND HIM ANY LONGER THAN WE HAVE TO.

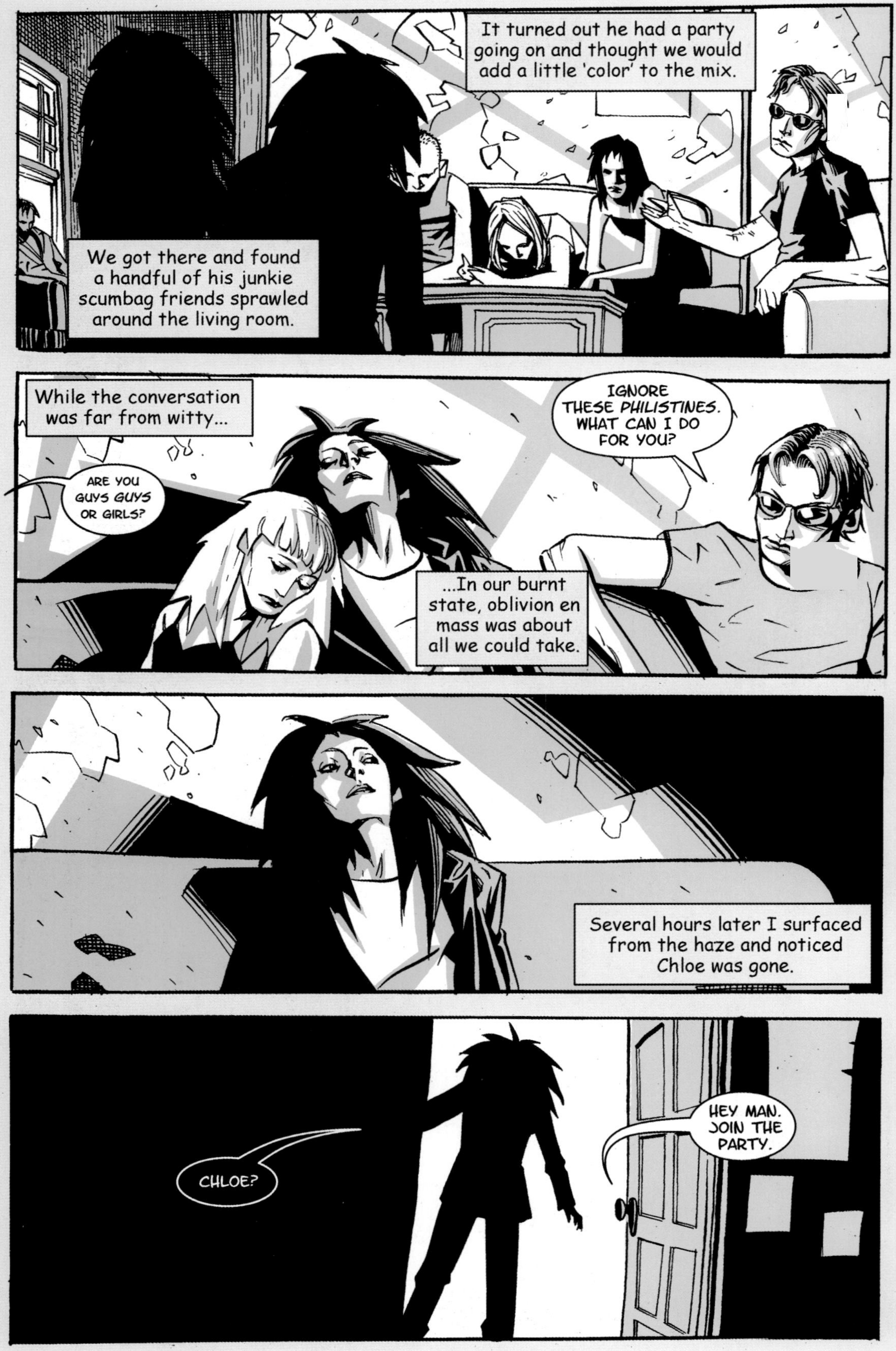
We got there and found a handful of his junkie scumbag friends sprawled around the living room.
It turned out he had a party going on and thought we would add a little 'color' to the mix.
While the conversation was far from witty...
ARE YOU GUYS GUYS OR GIRLS?
IGNORE THESE *PHILISTINES.* WHAT CAN I DO FOR YOU?
...In our burnt state, oblivion en mass was about all we could take.
Several hours later I surfaced from the haze and noticed Chloe was gone.
CHLOE?
HEY MAN. JOIN THE PARTY.

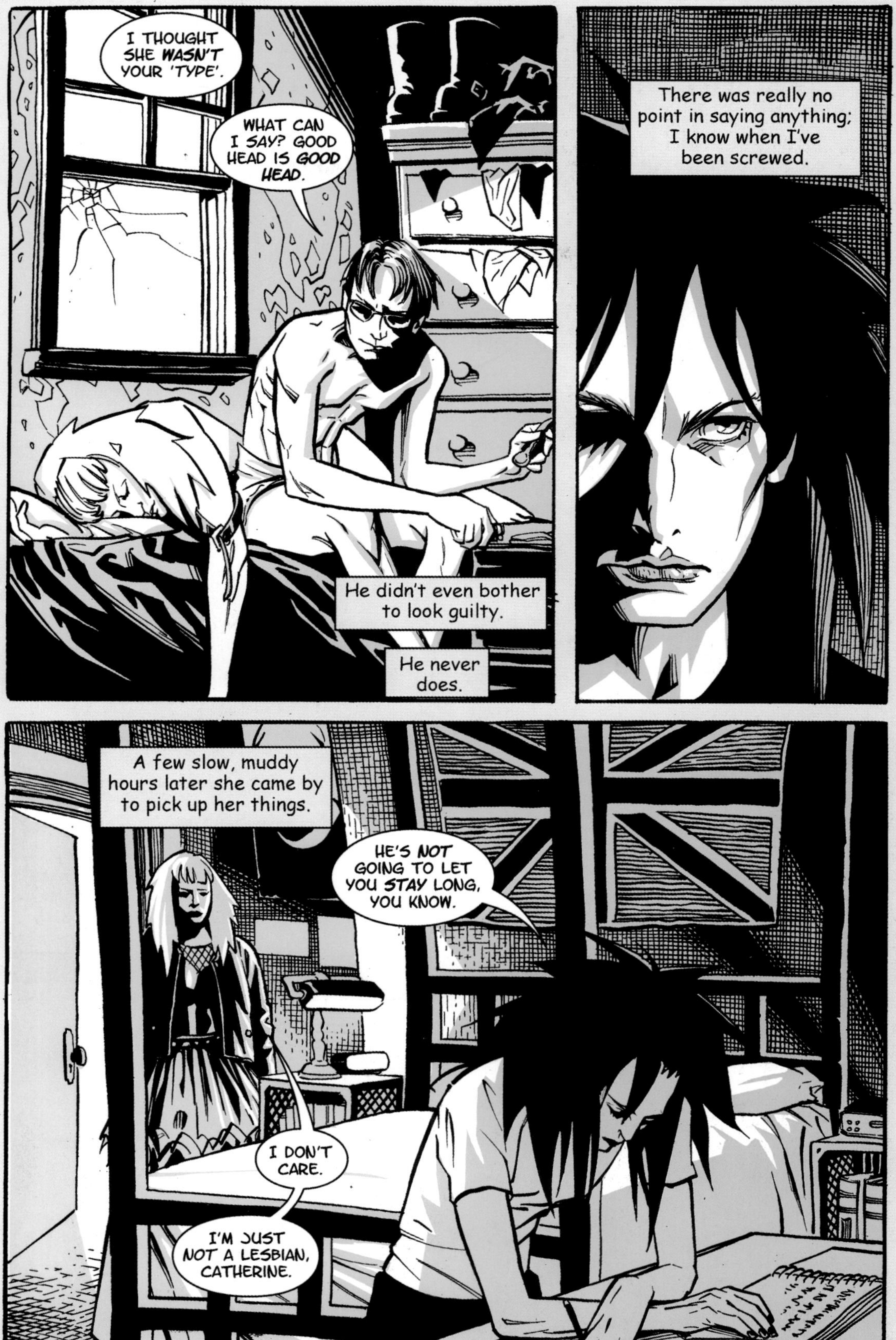

I THOUGHT SHE WASN'T YOUR 'TYPE'.
WHAT CAN I SAY? GOOD HEAD IS GOOD HEAD.
He didn't even bother to look guilty.
He never does.
There was really no point in saying anything; I know when I've been screwed.
A few slow, muddy hours later she came by to pick up her things.
HE'S NOT GOING TO LET YOU STAY LONG, YOU KNOW.
I DON'T CARE.
I'M JUST NOT A LESBIAN, CATHERINE.

I CAN'T PRETEND YOU'RE SOMETHING YOU'RE NOT.

BUT YOU EXPECT HIM TO 'PRETEND' WITH YOU.

FUCK YOU! I'M NOT LIKE YOU. I'M NOT PRETENDING.

YOU SPEND SO MUCH TIME TALKING ABOUT WHAT YOU'RE NOT, YOU HAVE NO IDEA ANYMORE WHAT YOU ARE.

That night I gazed at my empty bed sheets, willing her body to appear.

I marveled at the delicate sinews and exquisite lines, her fragile, developing breasts.

Her soft, sculpted lips.

The surreal and extraordinary presence of her penis.

Chloe once told me that I sometimes stared at her ravenously, as though I wanted to climb up inside her until I could see out through her eye sockets.

But to be honest...

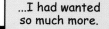

...I had wanted so much more.

chapter 2

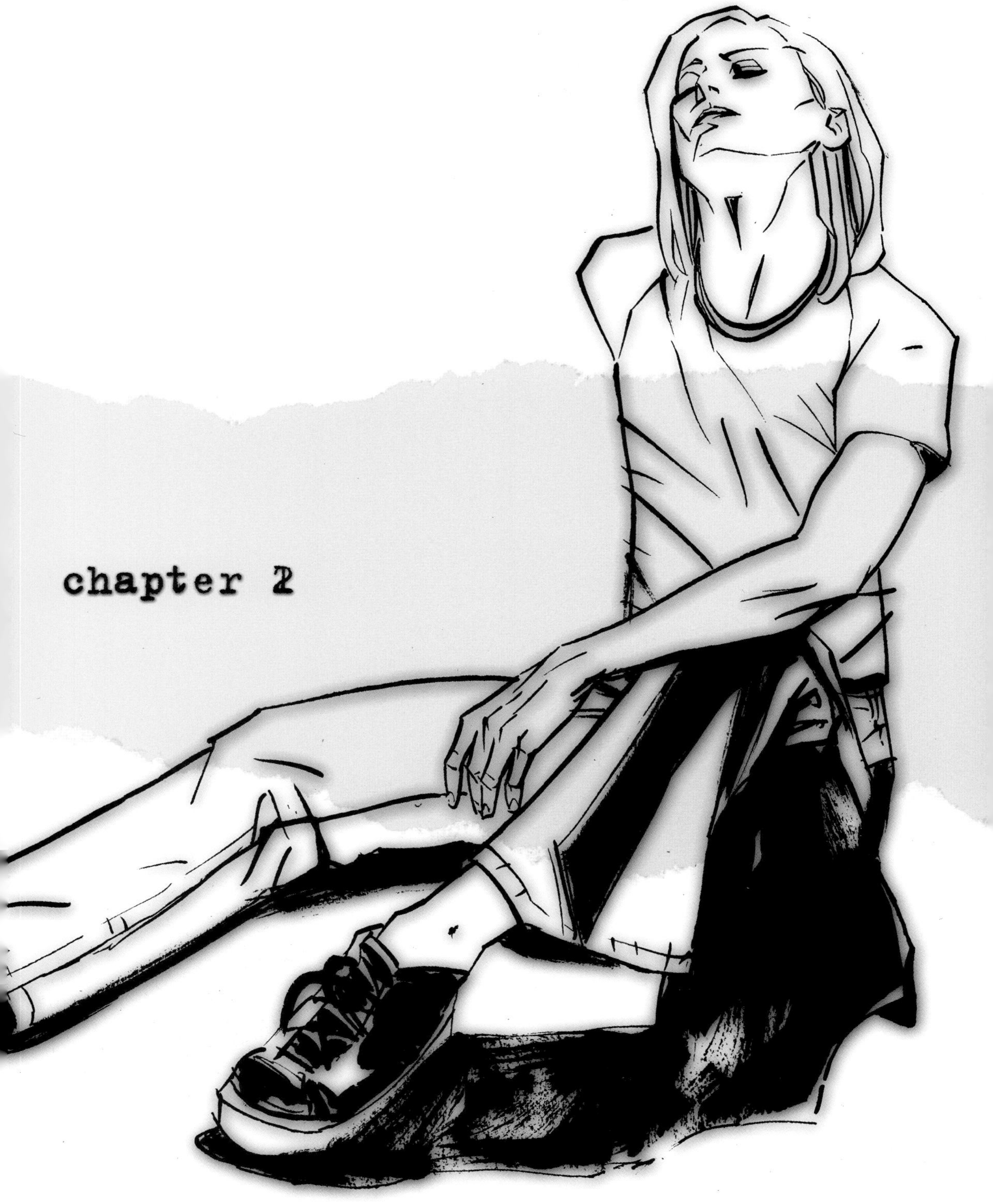

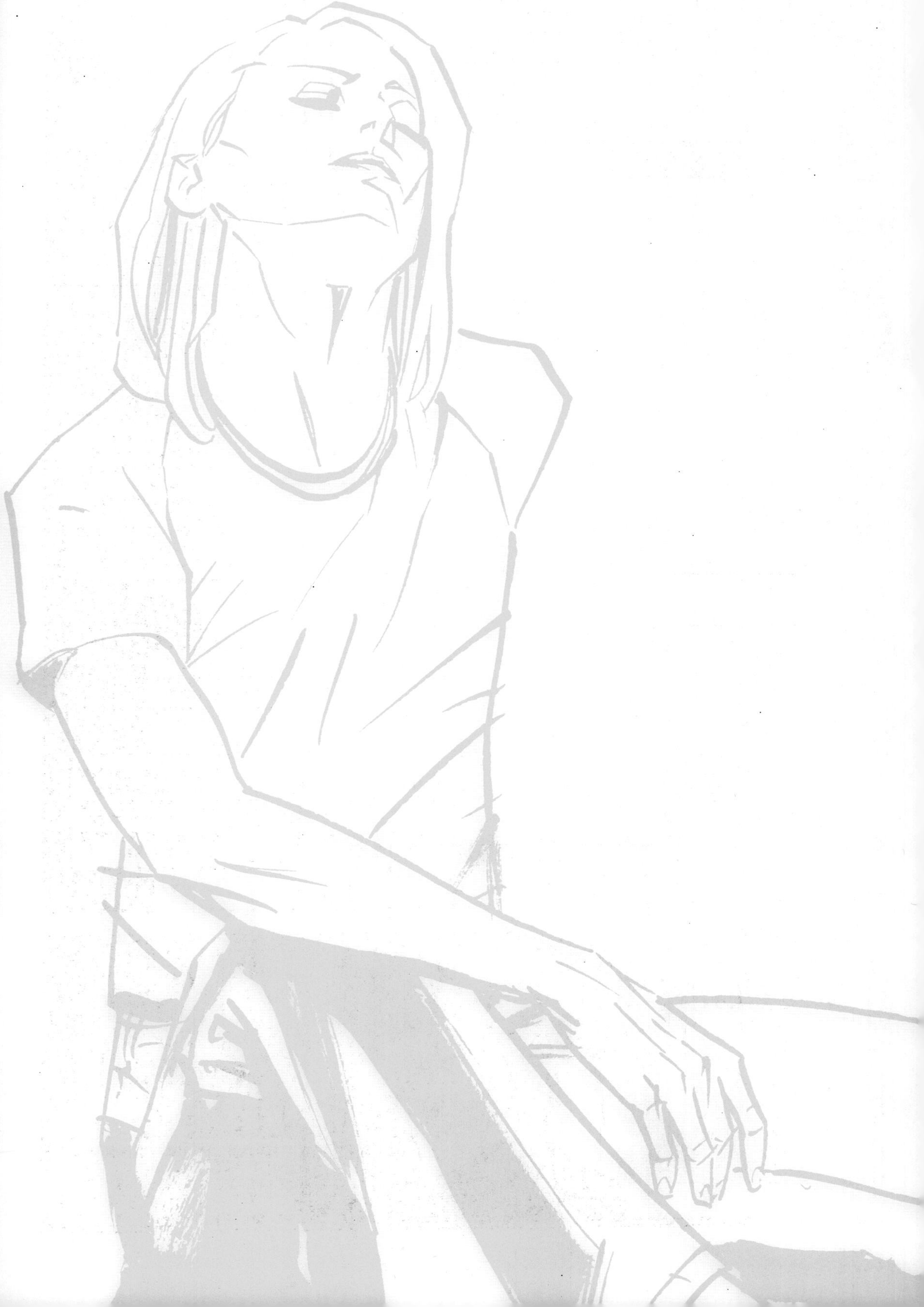

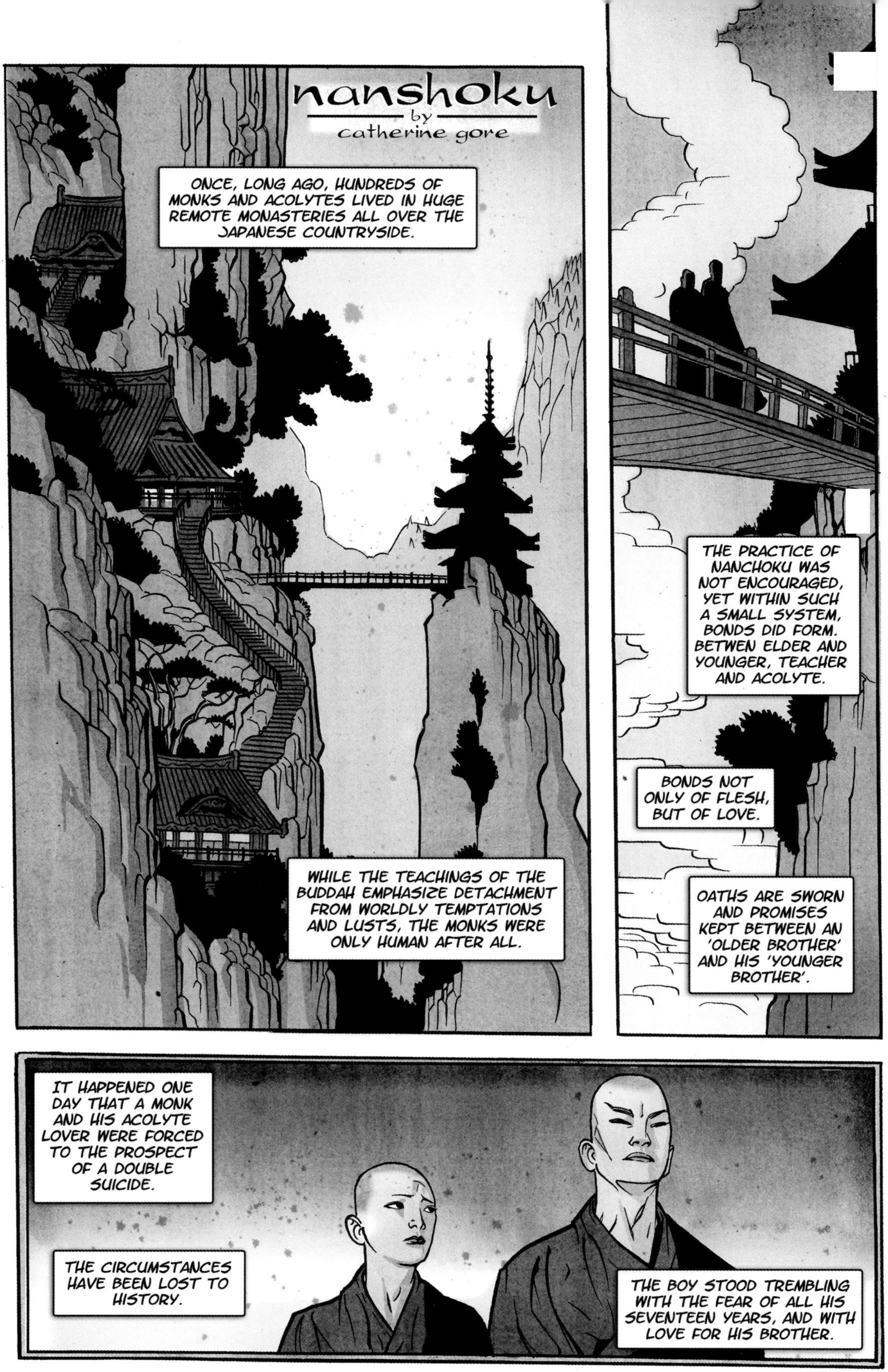
nanshoku
by
catherine gore
ONCE, LONG AGO, HUNDREDS OF MONKS AND ACOLYTES LIVED IN HUGE REMOTE MONASTERIES ALL OVER THE JAPANESE COUNTRYSIDE.
WHILE THE TEACHINGS OF THE BUDDAH EMPHASIZE DETACHMENT FROM WORLDLY TEMPTATIONS AND LUSTS, THE MONKS WERE ONLY HUMAN AFTER ALL.
THE PRACTICE OF NANCHOKU WAS NOT ENCOURAGED, YET WITHIN SUCH A SMALL SYSTEM, BONDS DID FORM. BETWEN ELDER AND YOUNGER, TEACHER AND ACOLYTE.
BONDS NOT ONLY OF FLESH, BUT OF LOVE.
OATHS ARE SWORN AND PROMISES KEPT BETWEEN AN 'OLDER BROTHER' AND HIS 'YOUNGER BROTHER'.
IT HAPPENED ONE DAY THAT A MONK AND HIS ACOLYTE LOVER WERE FORCED TO THE PROSPECT OF A DOUBLE SUICIDE.
THE CIRCUMSTANCES HAVE BEEN LOST TO HISTORY.
THE BOY STOOD TREMBLING WITH THE FEAR OF ALL HIS SEVENTEEN YEARS, AND WITH LOVE FOR HIS BROTHER.

THEY VOWED TO MEET TOGETHER IN THE AFTER-LIFE, IN PASSIONATE WORDS BEST LEFT TO THEIR EARS ALONE.

AFTER ONE FINAL KISS, THE BOY FLUNG HIMSELF FROM THE HEIGHT.

SOMETHING HELD THE ELDER BROTHER BACK.

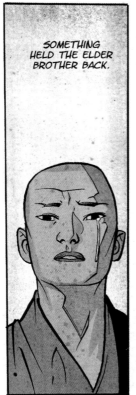

HE GAZED DOWN ONTO THE BLOODY ROCKS, AT THE RUIN OF HIS LOVER'S BODY.

HE RECALLED THE YEARS OF LOVE BETWEEN THEM, THE DAYS OF QUIET STUDY AND MEDITATION, NIGHTS OF EXQUISITE PLEASURE...

AT LAST THE MONK TURNED AWAY, AND LIKE A GHOST WALKED BACK INTO HIS TEMPLE.

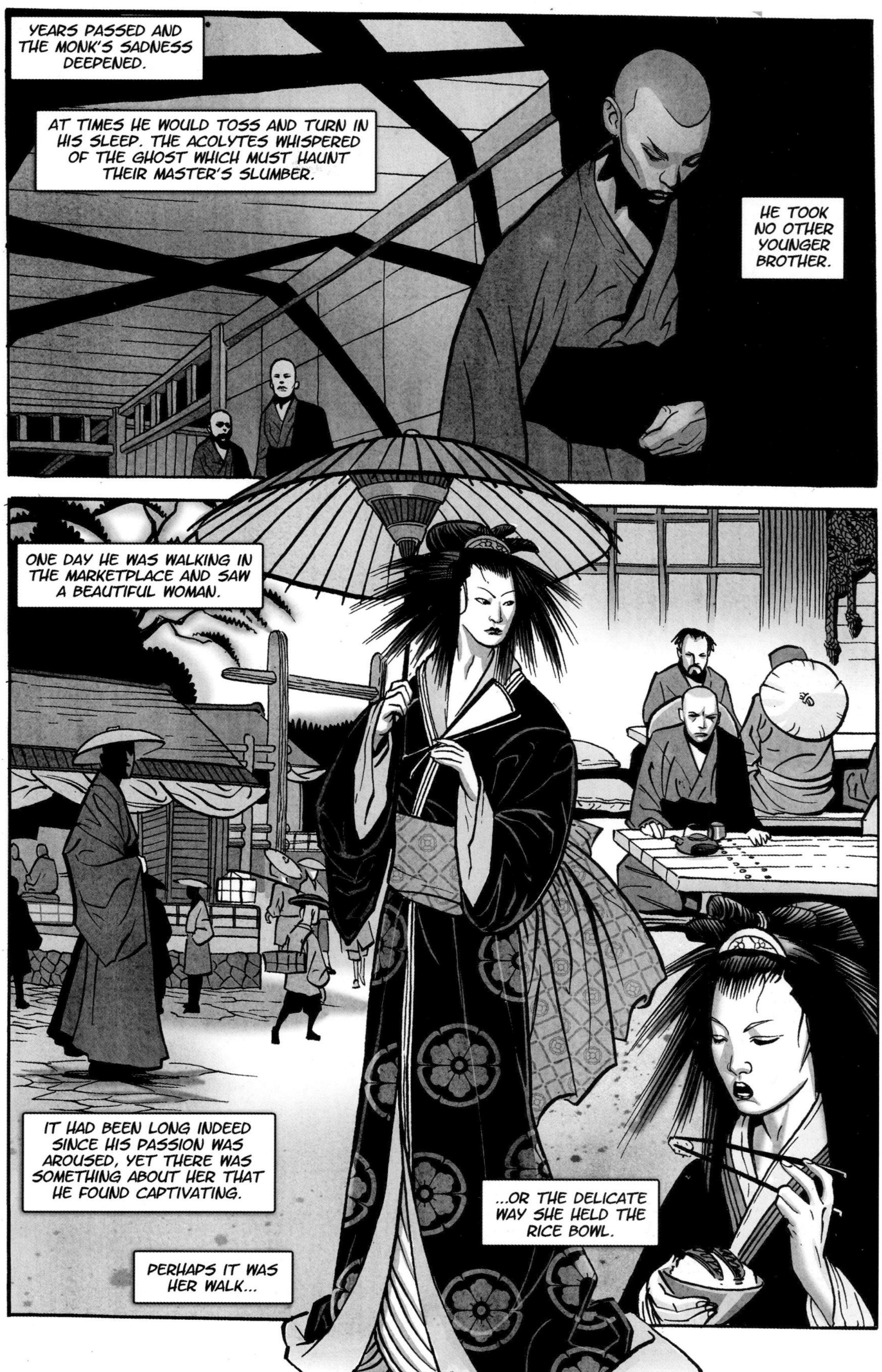
YEARS PASSED AND THE MONK'S SADNESS DEEPENED.
AT TIMES HE WOULD TOSS AND TURN IN HIS SLEEP. THE ACOLYTES WHISPERED OF THE GHOST WHICH MUST HAUNT THEIR MASTER'S SLUMBER.
HE TOOK NO OTHER YOUNGER BROTHER.
ONE DAY HE WAS WALKING IN THE MARKETPLACE AND SAW A BEAUTIFUL WOMAN.
IT HAD BEEN LONG INDEED SINCE HIS PASSION WAS AROUSED, YET THERE WAS SOMETHING ABOUT HER THAT HE FOUND CAPTIVATING.
PERHAPS IT WAS HER WALK...
...OR THE DELICATE WAY SHE HELD THE RICE BOWL.

HE LOST SIGHT OF HER AMONG THE CROWDED MARKET STALLS, AND ALTHOUGH HE SPENT THE REST OF THE AFTERNOON LOOKING FOR THE MYSTERIOUS WOMAN, SHE DID NOT APPEAR AGAIN.

THE PEACEFUL REST THE MONK CRAVED ELUDED HIM THAT NIGHT.

HE DREAMED AGAIN OF HIS YOUNGER BROTHER.

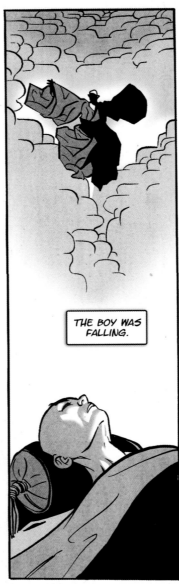

THE BOY WAS FALLING.

HE HIT THE ROCKS; HIS BEAUTIFUL BODY SHATTERED.

THEN HIS YOUNGER BROTHER LOOKED UP FROM WHERE HE LAY ON THE ROCKS, SOMEHOW STILL ALIVE, AND HE SPOKE...

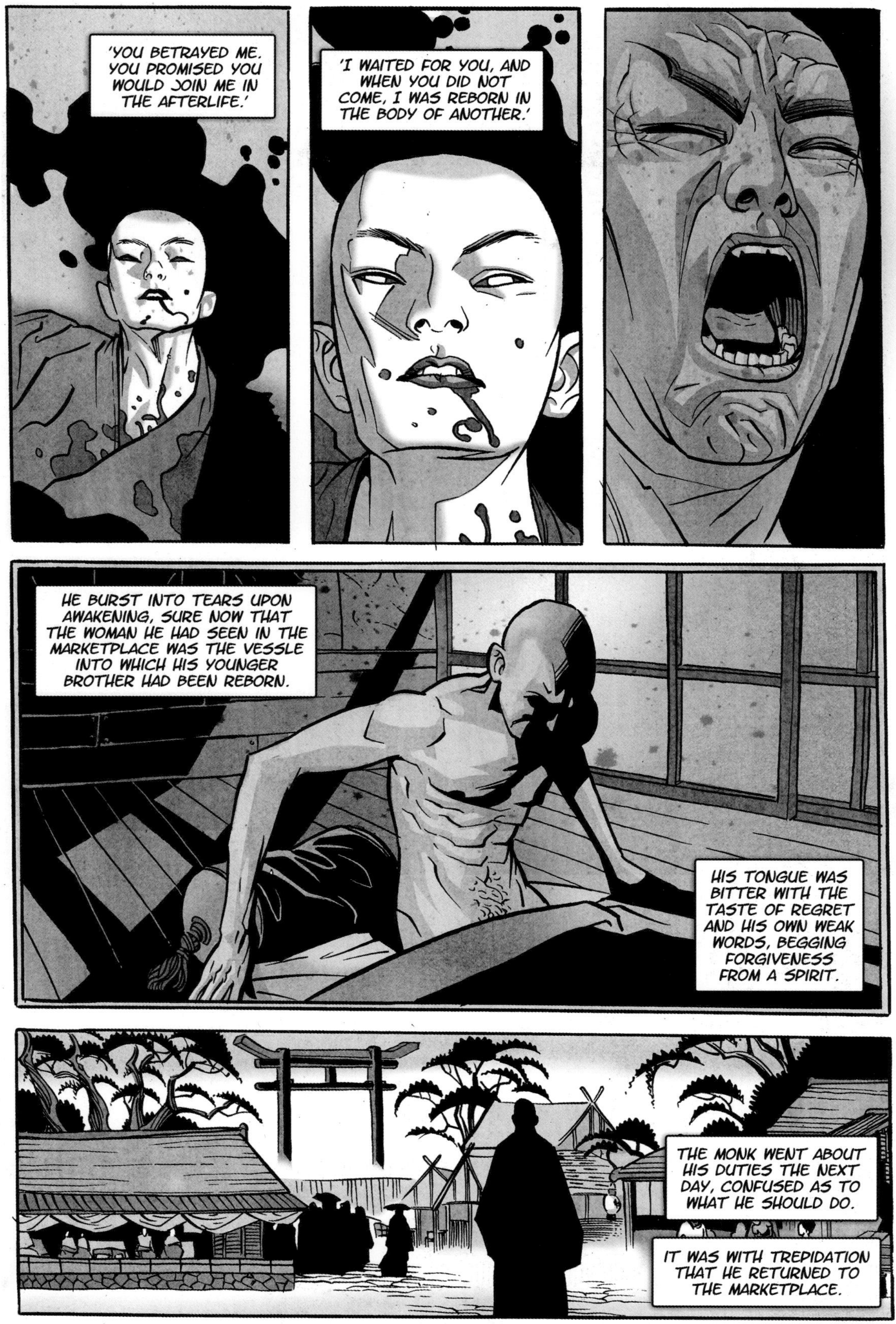
'YOU BETRAYED ME. YOU PROMISED YOU WOULD JOIN ME IN THE AFTERLIFE.'
'I WAITED FOR YOU, AND WHEN YOU DID NOT COME, I WAS REBORN IN THE BODY OF ANOTHER.'
HE BURST INTO TEARS UPON AWAKENING, SURE NOW THAT THE WOMAN HE HAD SEEN IN THE MARKETPLACE WAS THE VESSLE INTO WHICH HIS YOUNGER BROTHER HAD BEEN REBORN.
HIS TONGUE WAS BITTER WITH THE TASTE OF REGRET AND HIS OWN WEAK WORDS, BEGGING FORGIVENESS FROM A SPIRIT.
THE MONK WENT ABOUT HIS DUTIES THE NEXT DAY, CONFUSED AS TO WHAT HE SHOULD DO.
IT WAS WITH TREPIDATION THAT HE RETURNED TO THE MARKETPLACE.

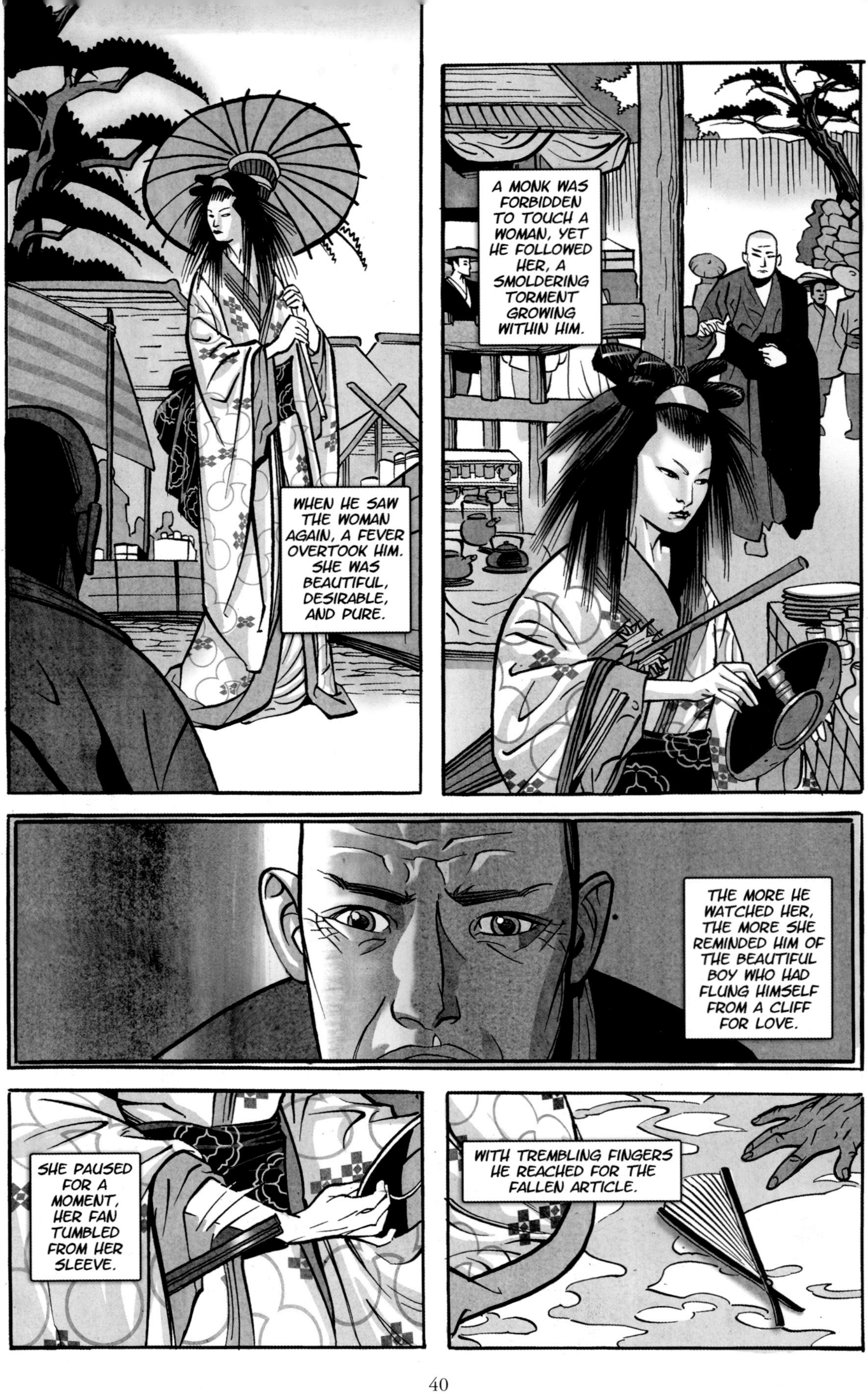
WHEN HE SAW THE WOMAN AGAIN, A FEVER OVERTOOK HIM. SHE WAS BEAUTIFUL, DESIRABLE, AND PURE.
A MONK WAS FORBIDDEN TO TOUCH A WOMAN, YET HE FOLLOWED HER, A SMOLDERING TORMENT GROWING WITHIN HIM.
THE MORE HE WATCHED HER, THE MORE SHE REMINDED HIM OF THE BEAUTIFUL BOY WHO HAD FLUNG HIMSELF FROM A CLIFF FOR LOVE.
SHE PAUSED FOR A MOMENT, HER FAN TUMBLED FROM HER SLEEVE.
WITH TREMBLING FINGERS HE REACHED FOR THE FALLEN ARTICLE.

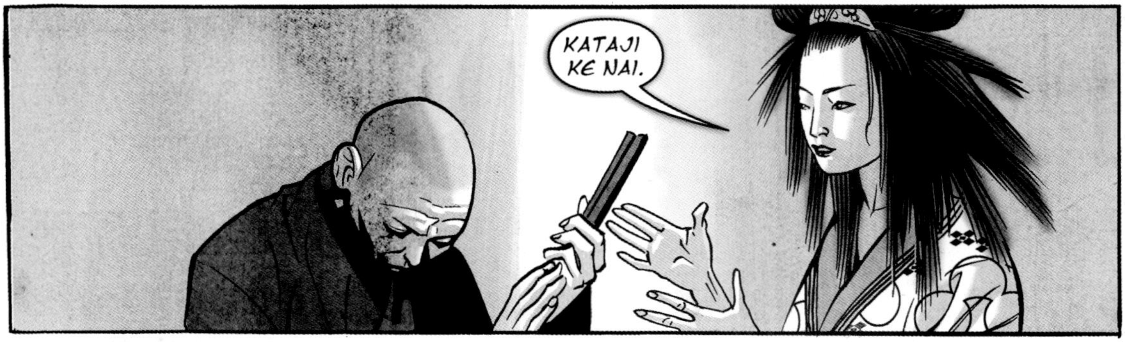
KATAJI KE NAI.

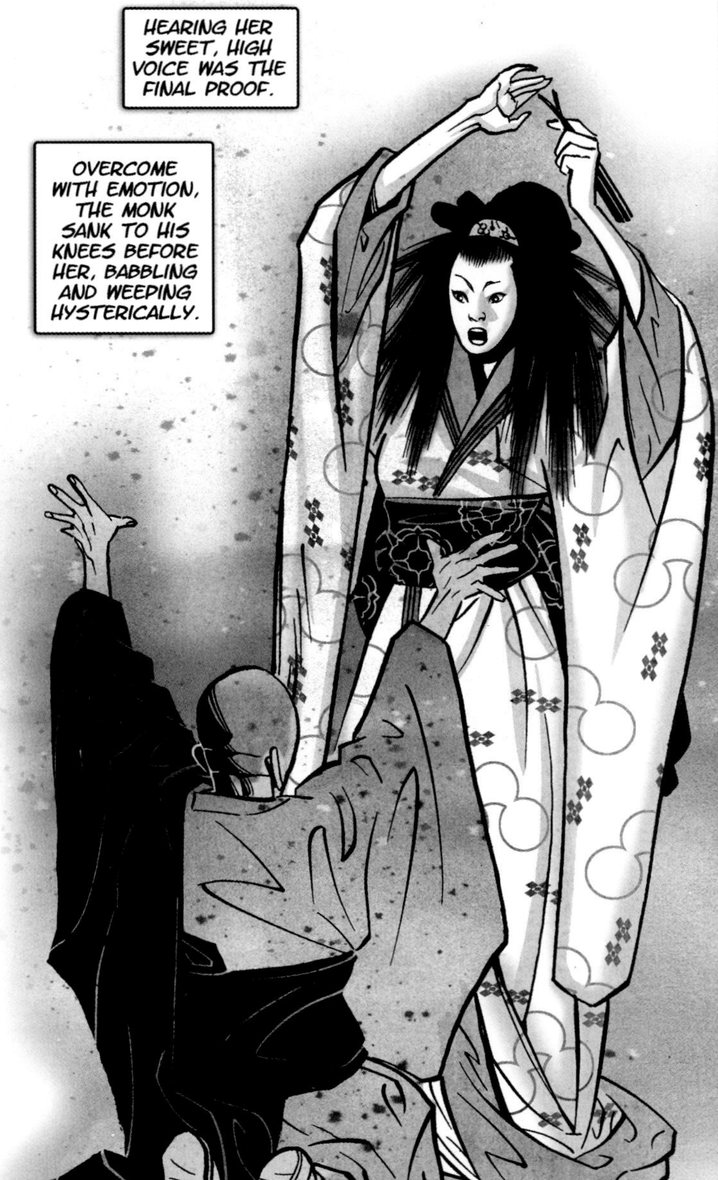
HEARING HER SWEET, HIGH VOICE WAS THE FINAL PROOF.
OVERCOME WITH EMOTION, THE MONK SANK TO HIS KNEES BEFORE HER, BABBLING AND WEEPING HYSTERICALLY.

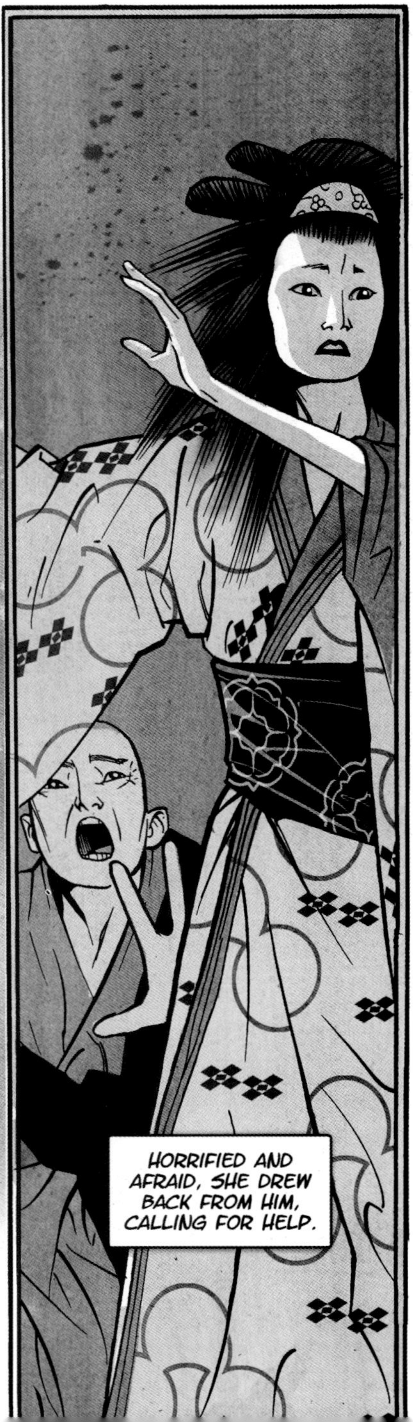
HORRIFIED AND AFRAID, SHE DREW BACK FROM HIM, CALLING FOR HELP.

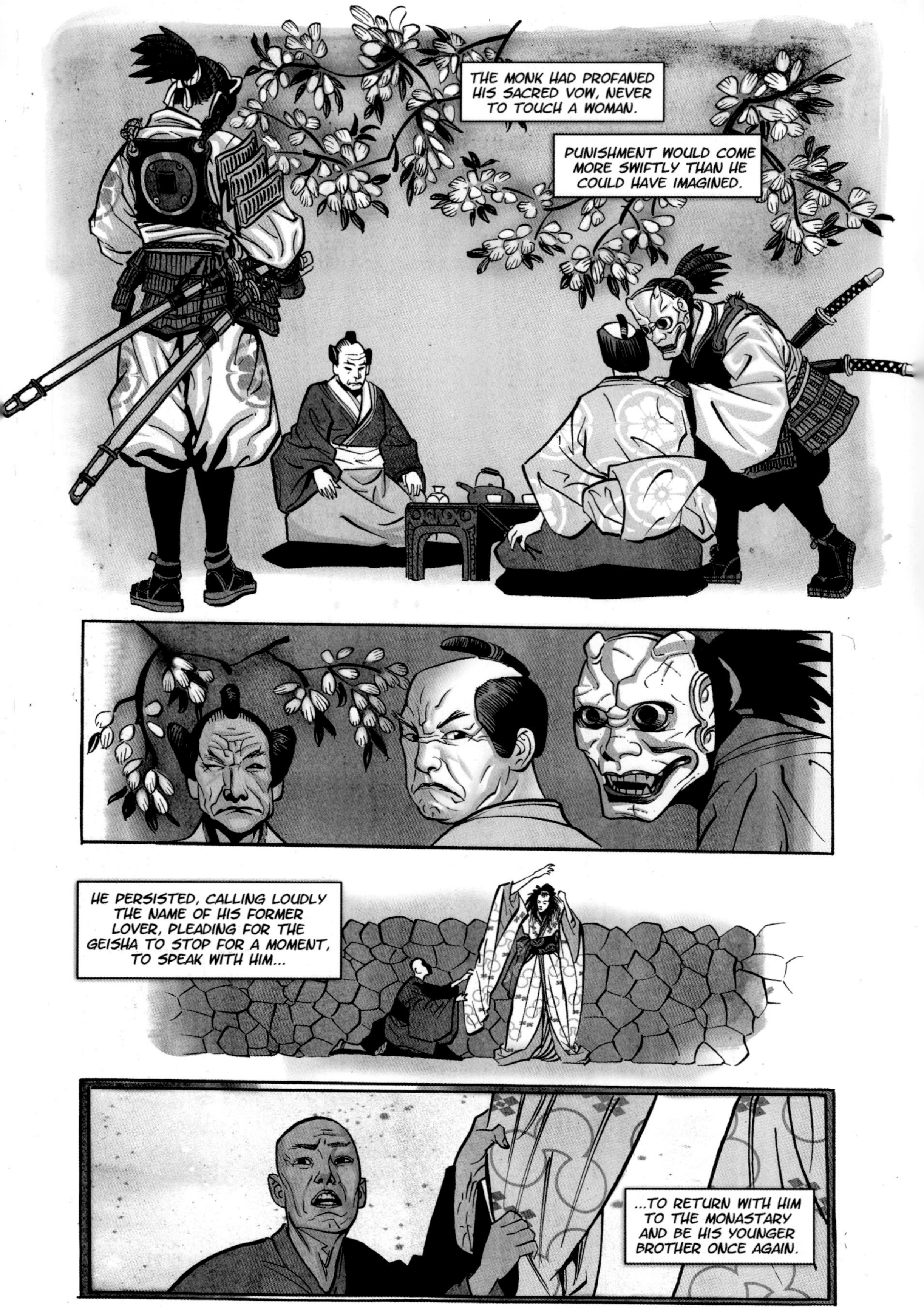

THE MONK HAD PROFANED HIS SACRED VOW, NEVER TO TOUCH A WOMAN.
PUNISHMENT WOULD COME MORE SWIFTLY THAN HE COULD HAVE IMAGINED.
HE PERSISTED, CALLING LOUDLY THE NAME OF HIS FORMER LOVER, PLEADING FOR THE GEISHA TO STOP FOR A MOMENT, TO SPEAK WITH HIM...
...TO RETURN WITH HIM TO THE MONASTARY AND BE HIS YOUNGER BROTHER ONCE AGAIN.

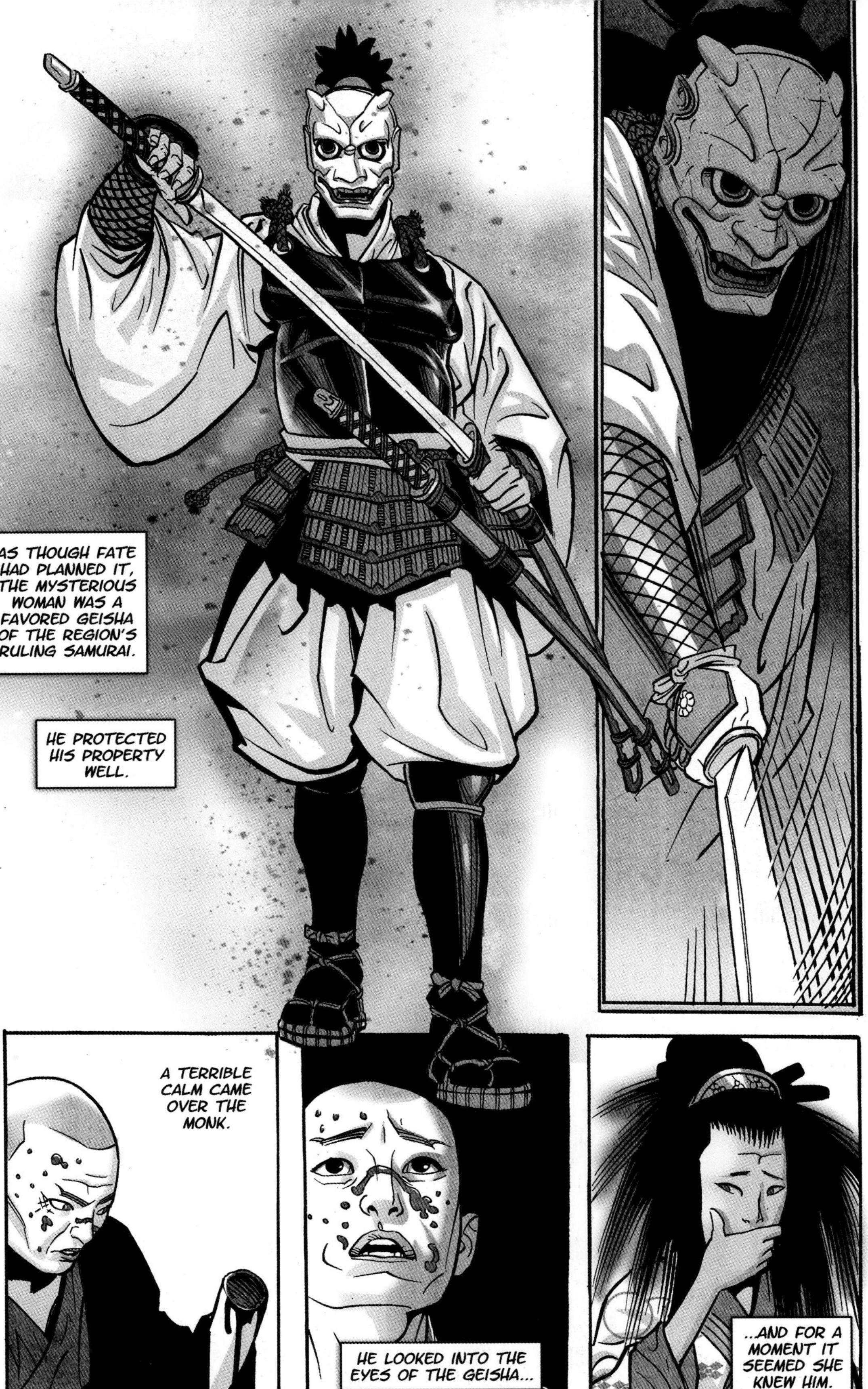
AS THOUGH FATE HAD PLANNED IT, THE MYSTERIOUS WOMAN WAS A FAVORED GEISHA OF THE REGION'S RULING SAMURAI.
HE PROTECTED HIS PROPERTY WELL.
A TERRIBLE CALM CAME OVER THE MONK.
HE LOOKED INTO THE EYES OF THE GEISHA...
...AND FOR A MOMENT IT SEEMED SHE KNEW HIM.

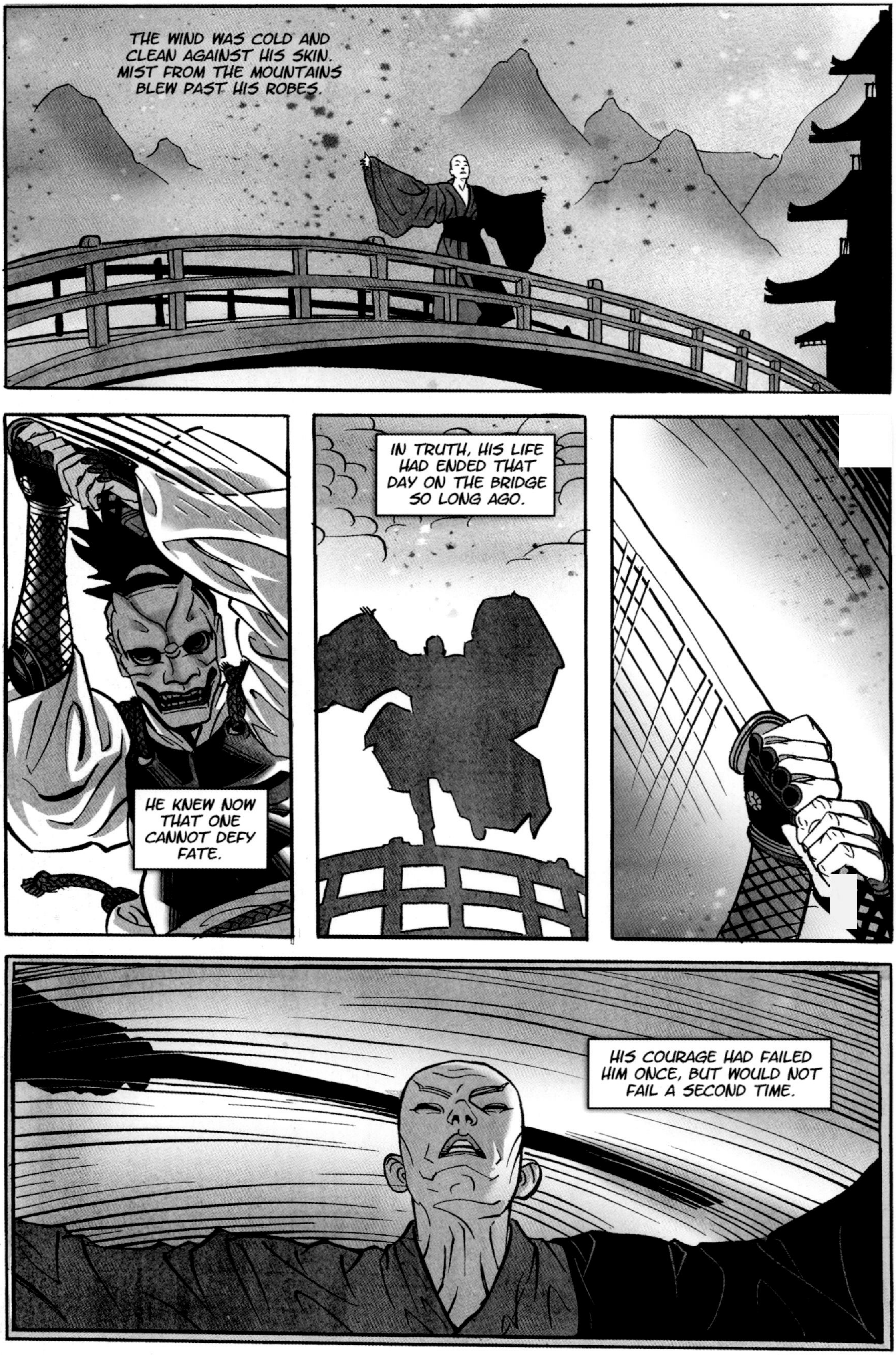
THE WIND WAS COLD AND CLEAN AGAINST HIS SKIN. MIST FROM THE MOUNTAINS BLEW PAST HIS ROBES.
HE KNEW NOW THAT ONE CANNOT DEFY FATE.
IN TRUTH, HIS LIFE HAD ENDED THAT DAY ON THE BRIDGE SO LONG AGO.
HIS COURAGE HAD FAILED HIM ONCE, BUT WOULD NOT FAIL A SECOND TIME.

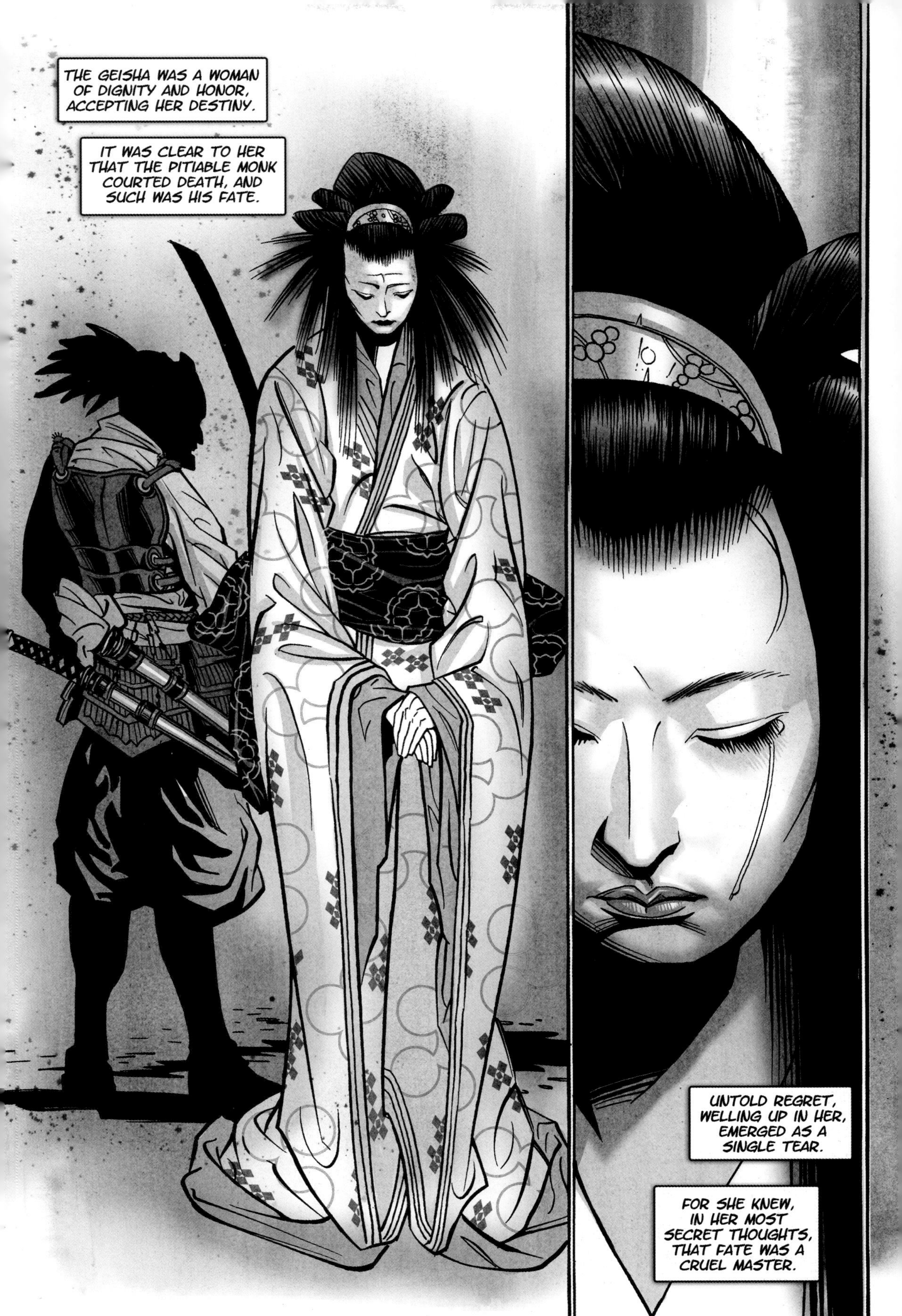
THE GEISHA WAS A WOMAN OF DIGNITY AND HONOR, ACCEPTING HER DESTINY.
IT WAS CLEAR TO HER THAT THE PITIABLE MONK COURTED DEATH, AND SUCH WAS HIS FATE.
UNTOLD REGRET, WELLING UP IN HER, EMERGED AS A SINGLE TEAR.
FOR SHE KNEW, IN HER MOST SECRET THOUGHTS, THAT FATE WAS A CRUEL MASTER.

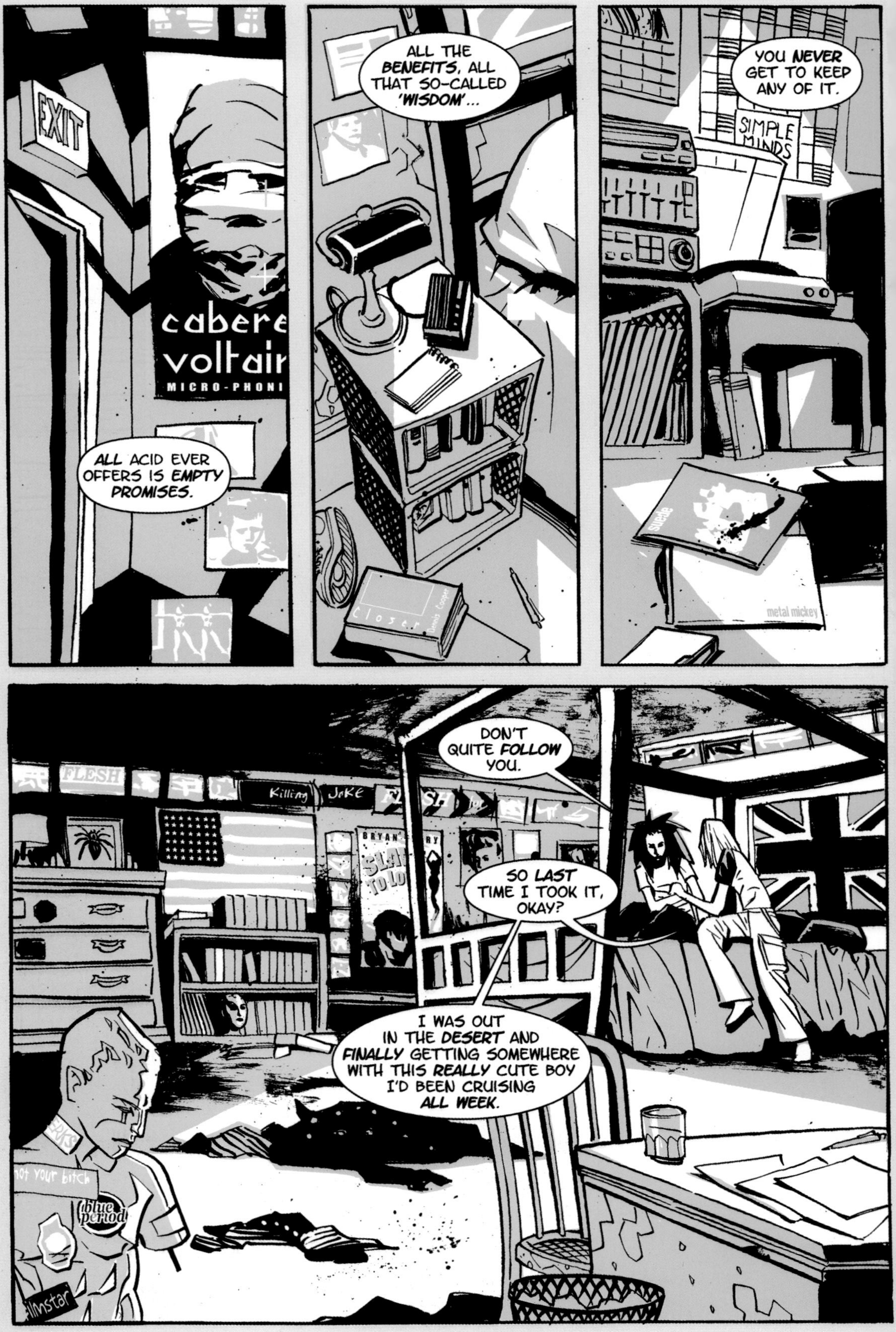
EXIT
cabere
voltair
MICRO-PHONI
ALL ACID EVER OFFERS IS EMPTY PROMISES.
ALL THE BENEFITS, ALL THAT SO-CALLED 'WISDOM'...
Closer
Dennis Cooper
YOU NEVER GET TO KEEP ANY OF IT.
SIMPLE MINDS
suede
metal mickey
FLESH
Killing JoKE
DON'T QUITE FOLLOW YOU.
SO LAST TIME I TOOK IT, OKAY?
I WAS OUT IN THE DESERT AND FINALLY GETTING SOMEWHERE WITH THIS REALLY CUTE BOY I'D BEEN CRUISING ALL WEEK.
not your bitch
blue period

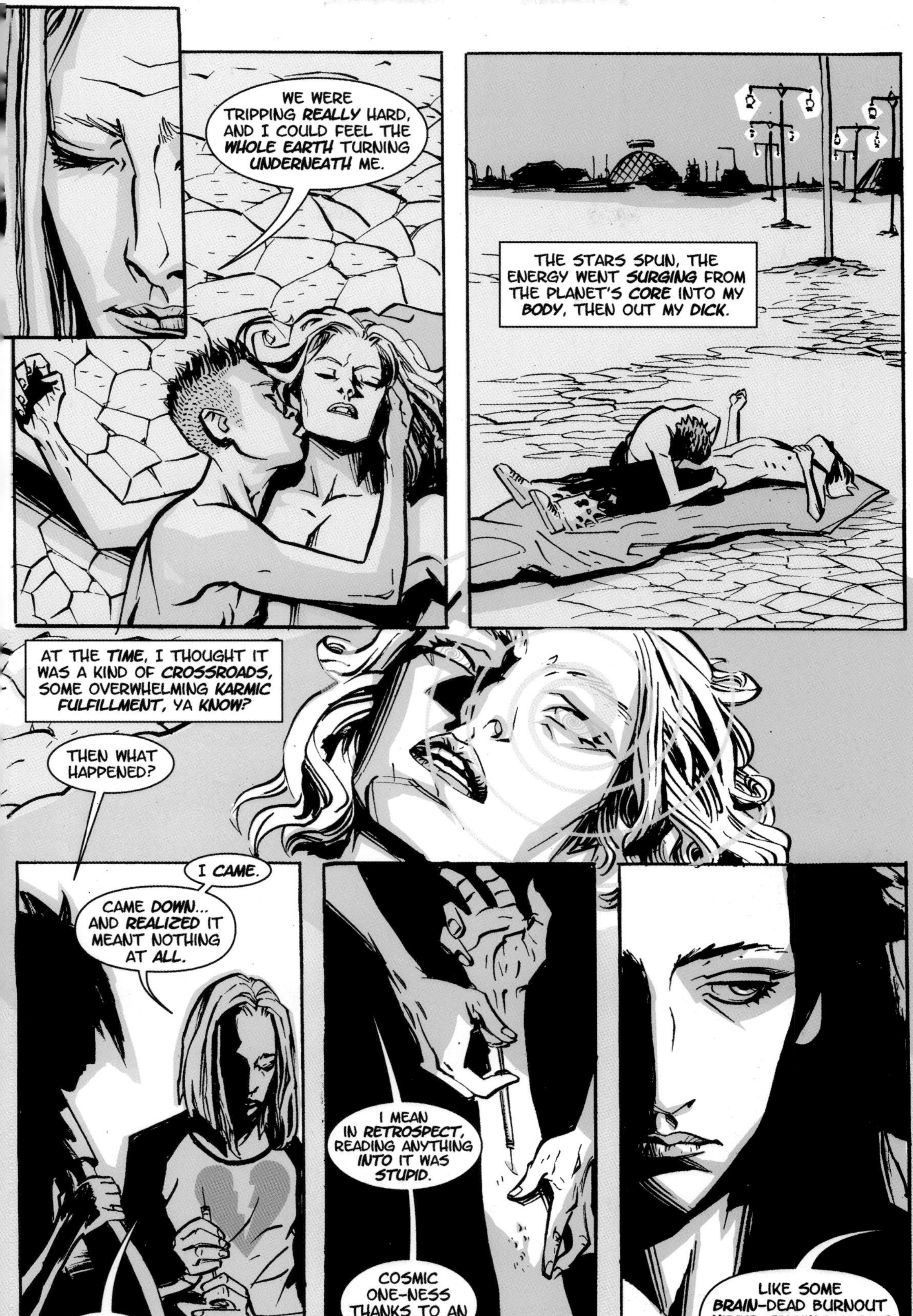
WE WERE TRIPPING REALLY HARD, AND I COULD FEEL THE WHOLE EARTH TURNING UNDERNEATH ME.
THE STARS SPUN, THE ENERGY WENT SURGING FROM THE PLANET'S CORE INTO MY BODY, THEN OUT MY DICK.
AT THE TIME, I THOUGHT IT WAS A KIND OF CROSSROADS, SOME OVERWHELMING KARMIC FULFILLMENT, YA KNOW?
THEN WHAT HAPPENED?
I CAME.
CAME DOWN... AND REALIZED IT MEANT NOTHING AT ALL.
MAYBE LESS THAN NOTHING.
I MEAN IN RETROSPECT, READING ANYTHING INTO IT WAS STUPID.
COSMIC ONE-NESS THANKS TO AN ACID TRIP?
LIKE SOME BRAIN-DEAD BURNOUT HIPPIE TALKING ABOUT HOW 'GREAT IT ALL WAS BACK THEN'.

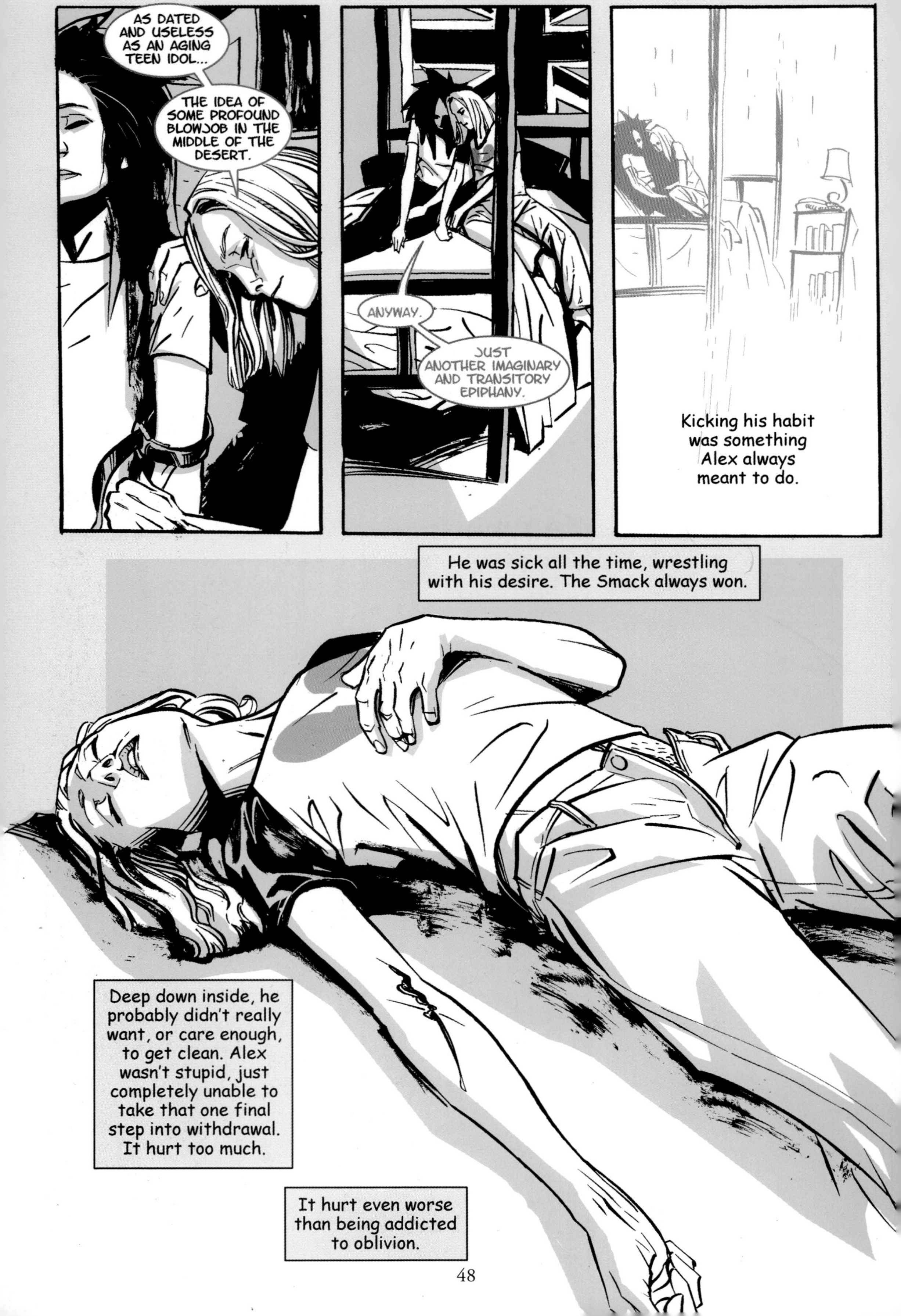
AS DATED AND USELESS AS AN AGING TEEN IDOL...
THE IDEA OF SOME PROFOUND BLOWJOB IN THE MIDDLE OF THE DESERT.
ANYWAY.
JUST ANOTHER IMAGINARY AND TRANSITORY EPIPHANY.
Kicking his habit was something Alex always meant to do.
He was sick all the time, wrestling with his desire. The Smack always won.
Deep down inside, he probably didn't really want, or care enough, to get clean. Alex wasn't stupid, just completely unable to take that one final step into withdrawal. It hurt too much.
It hurt even worse than being addicted to oblivion.

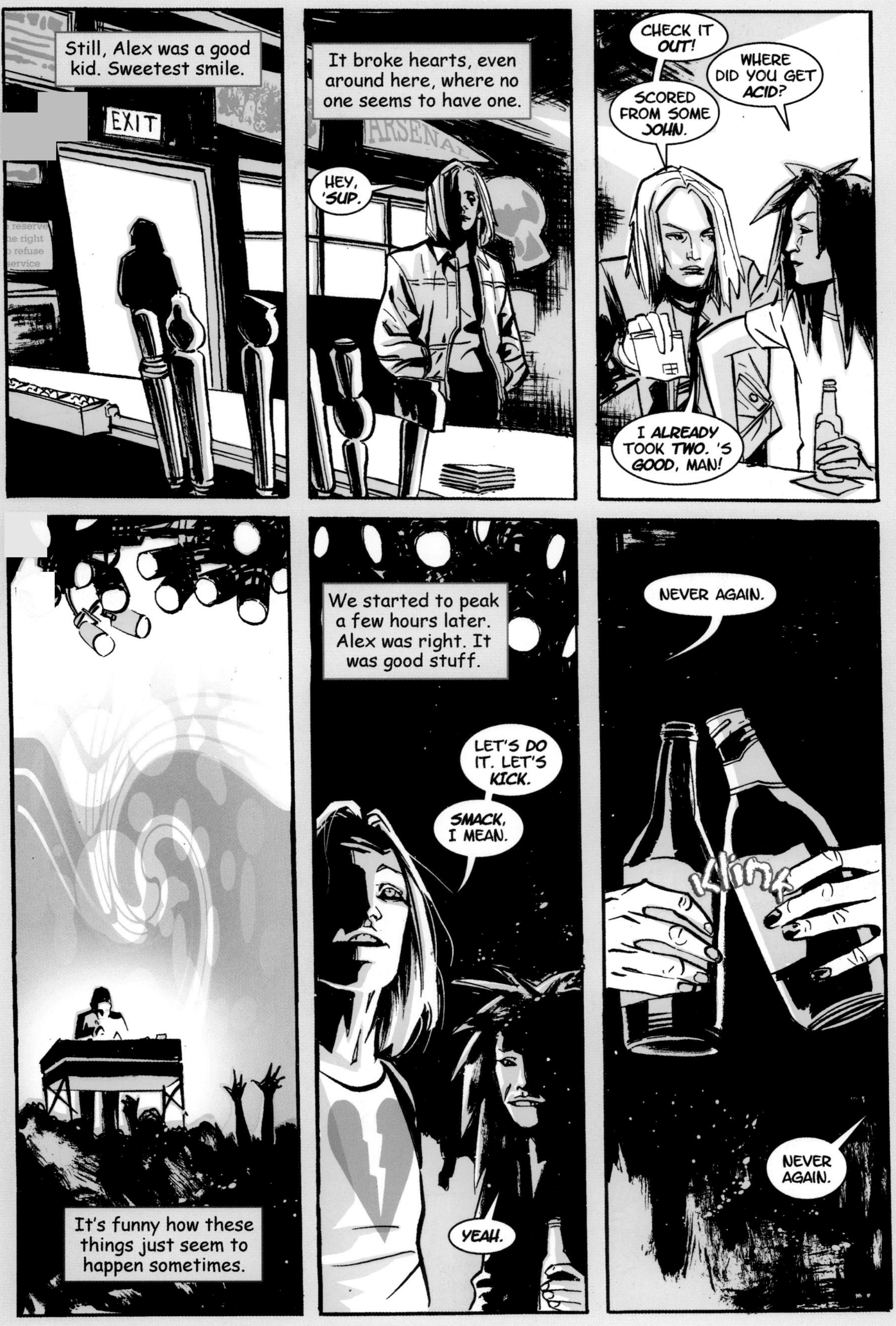
Still, Alex was a good kid. Sweetest smile.
EXIT
It broke hearts, even around here, where no one seems to have one.
ARSENAL
HEY, 'SUP.
CHECK IT OUT!
SCORED FROM SOME JOHN.
WHERE DID YOU GET ACID?
I ALREADY TOOK TWO. 'S GOOD, MAN!
It's funny how these things just seem to happen sometimes.
We started to peak a few hours later. Alex was right. It was good stuff.
LET'S DO IT. LET'S KICK.
SMACK, I MEAN.
YEAH.
NEVER AGAIN.
Klink
NEVER AGAIN.

We worked out our plan in a fever of desperate enthusiasm.

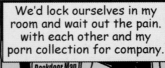

We'd lock ourselves in my room and wait out the pain. with each other and my porn collection for company.

Backdoor Man II
Laying Pipe
MO' BETTA BUTT

CELL SHOCKED

Our conviction was real in the way that only acid can make it.

The Damne
Phan ismogora

We were dead certain that we could and wanted to change our lives permanently.

Stop

I CAN'T JUST *SIT* HERE.

LET'S *GO* *SOMEWHERE*. GET A DRINK. *DANCE* OR SOMETHING.

I was still hallucinating around the edges, but his desperation was infectious.

It was Monday night. The pickings were slim...

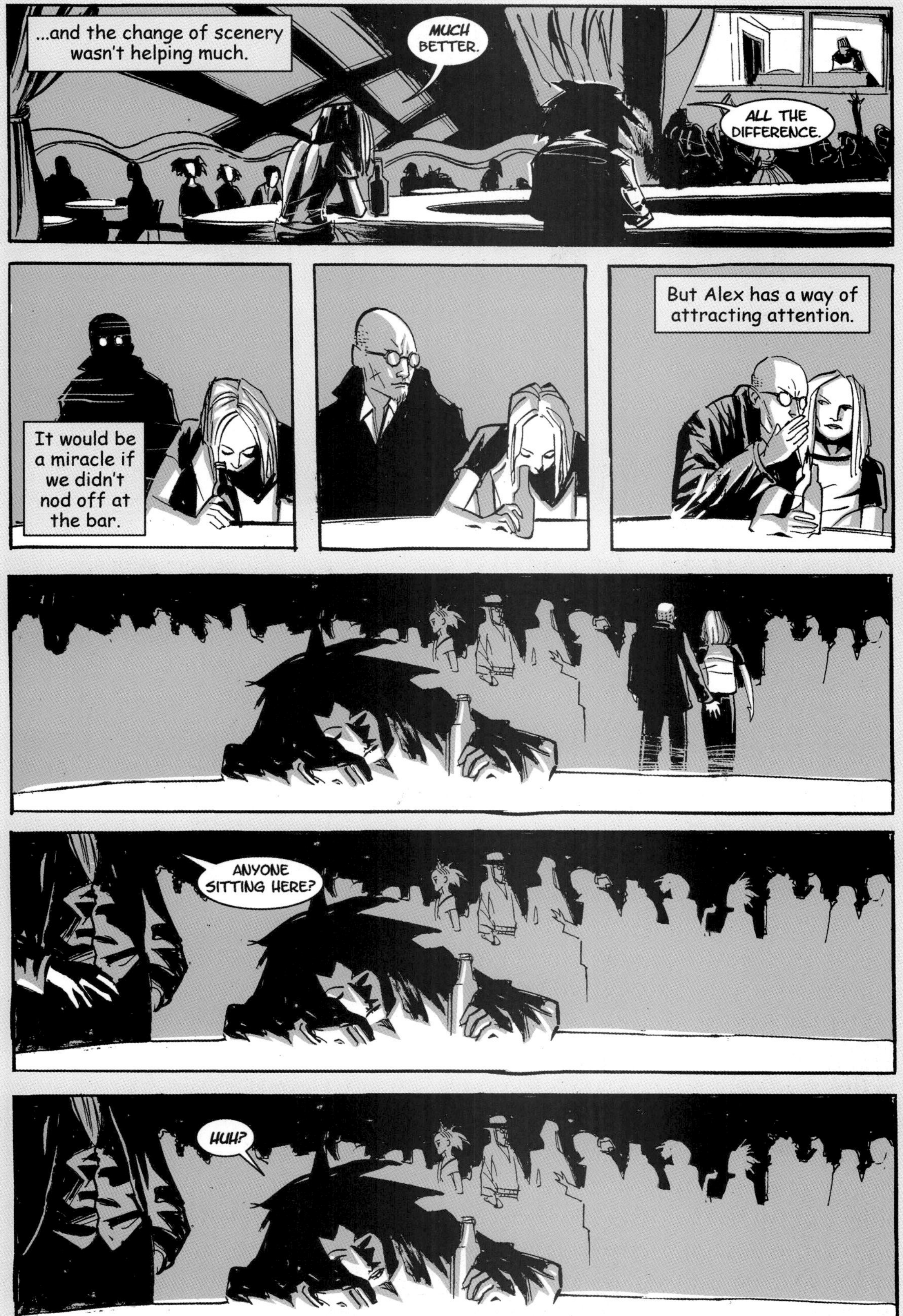
...and the change of scenery wasn't helping much.
MUCH BETTER.
ALL THE DIFFERENCE.
It would be a miracle if we didn't nod off at the bar.
But Alex has a way of attracting attention.
ANYONE SITTING HERE?
HUH?

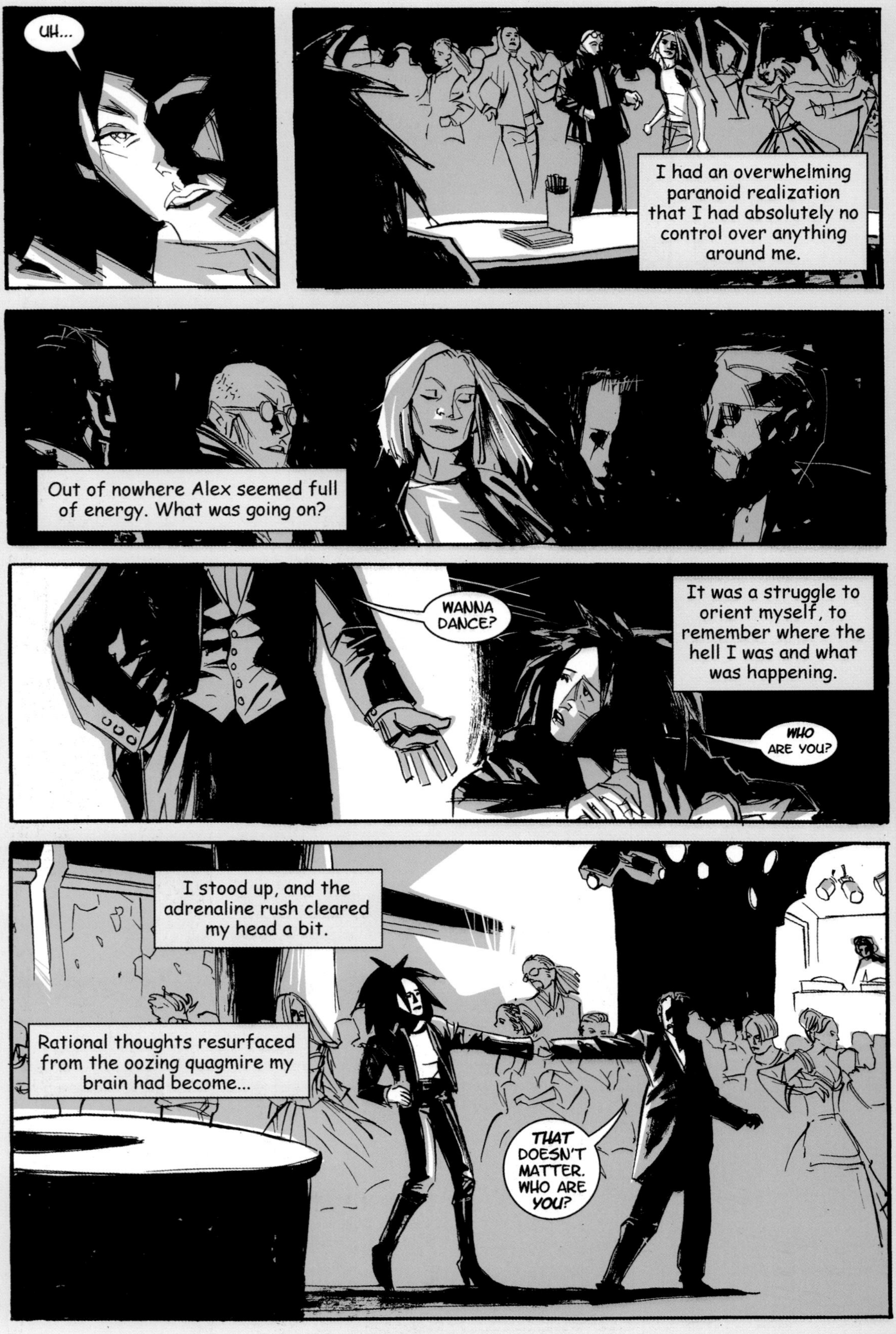
UH...
I had an overwhelming paranoid realization that I had absolutely no control over anything around me.
Out of nowhere Alex seemed full of energy. What was going on?
WANNA DANCE?
It was a struggle to orient myself, to remember where the hell I was and what was happening.
WHO ARE YOU?
I stood up, and the adrenaline rush cleared my head a bit.
Rational thoughts resurfaced from the oozing quagmire my brain had become...
THAT DOESN'T MATTER. WHO ARE YOU?

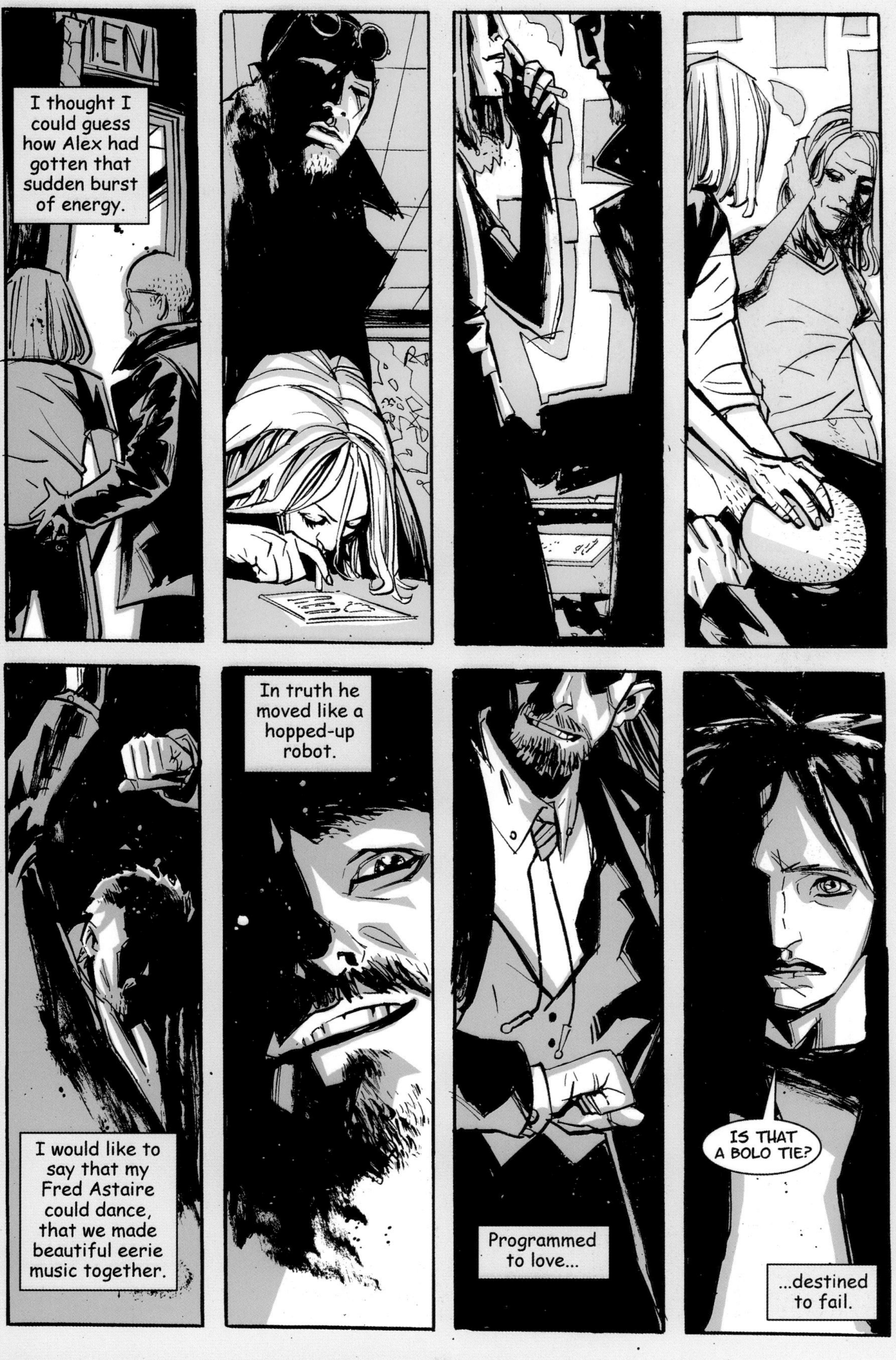
I thought I could guess how Alex had gotten that sudden burst of energy.
In truth he moved like a hopped-up robot.
I would like to say that my Fred Astaire could dance, that we made beautiful eerie music together.
Programmed to love...
IS THAT A BOLO TIE?
...destined to fail.

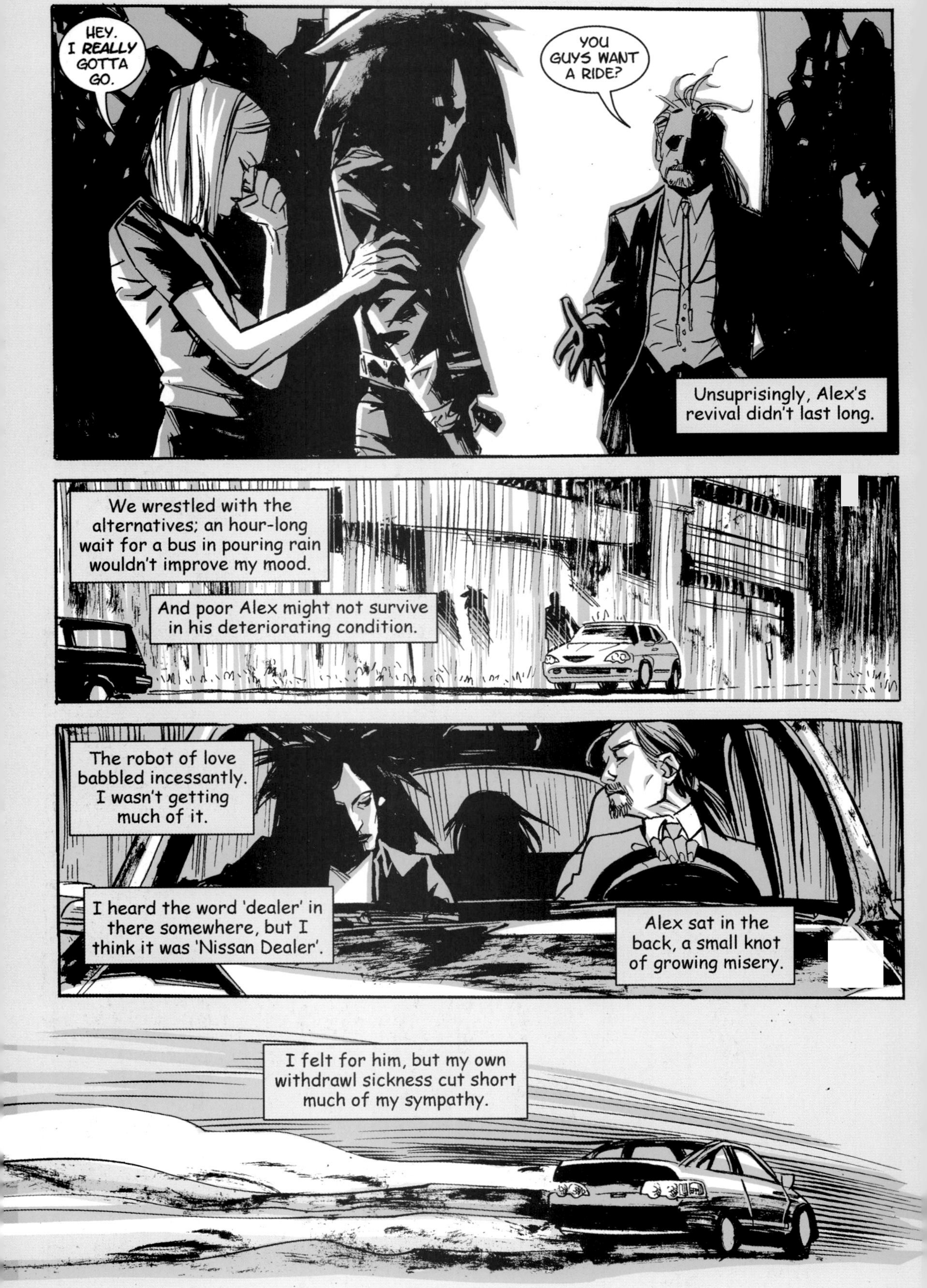
HEY. I REALLY GOTTA GO.
YOU GUYS WANT A RIDE?
Unsuprisingly, Alex's revival didn't last long.
We wrestled with the alternatives; an hour-long wait for a bus in pouring rain wouldn't improve my mood.
And poor Alex might not survive in his deteriorating condition.
The robot of love babbled incessantly. I wasn't getting much of it.
I heard the word 'dealer' in there somewhere, but I think it was 'Nissan Dealer'.
Alex sat in the back, a small knot of growing misery.
I felt for him, but my own withdrawl sickness cut short much of my sympathy.

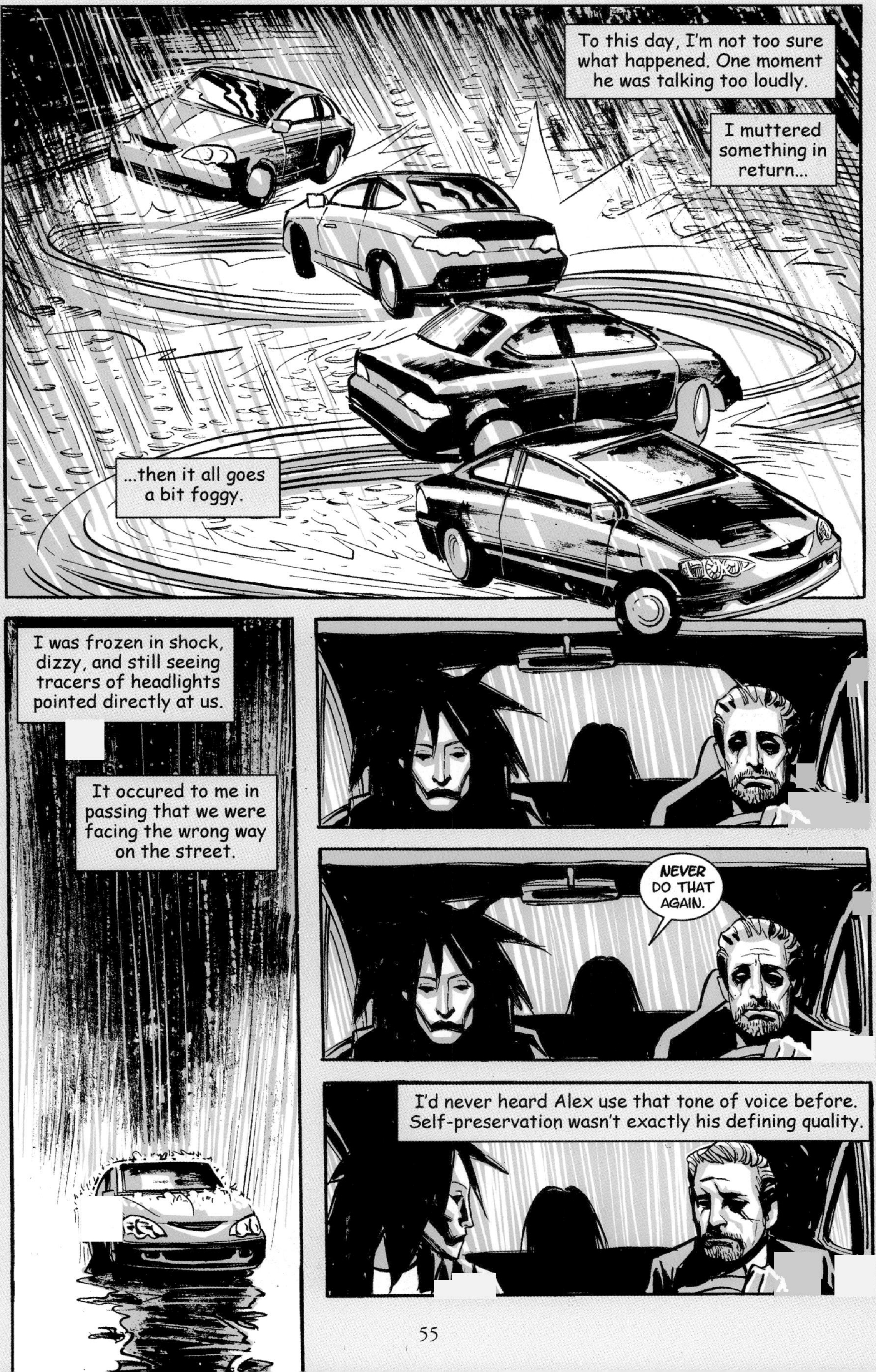
To this day, I'm not too sure what happened. One moment he was talking too loudly.
I muttered something in return...
...then it all goes a bit foggy.
I was frozen in shock, dizzy, and still seeing tracers of headlights pointed directly at us.
It occured to me in passing that we were facing the wrong way on the street.
NEVER DO THAT AGAIN.
I'd never heard Alex use that tone of voice before. Self-preservation wasn't exactly his defining quality.

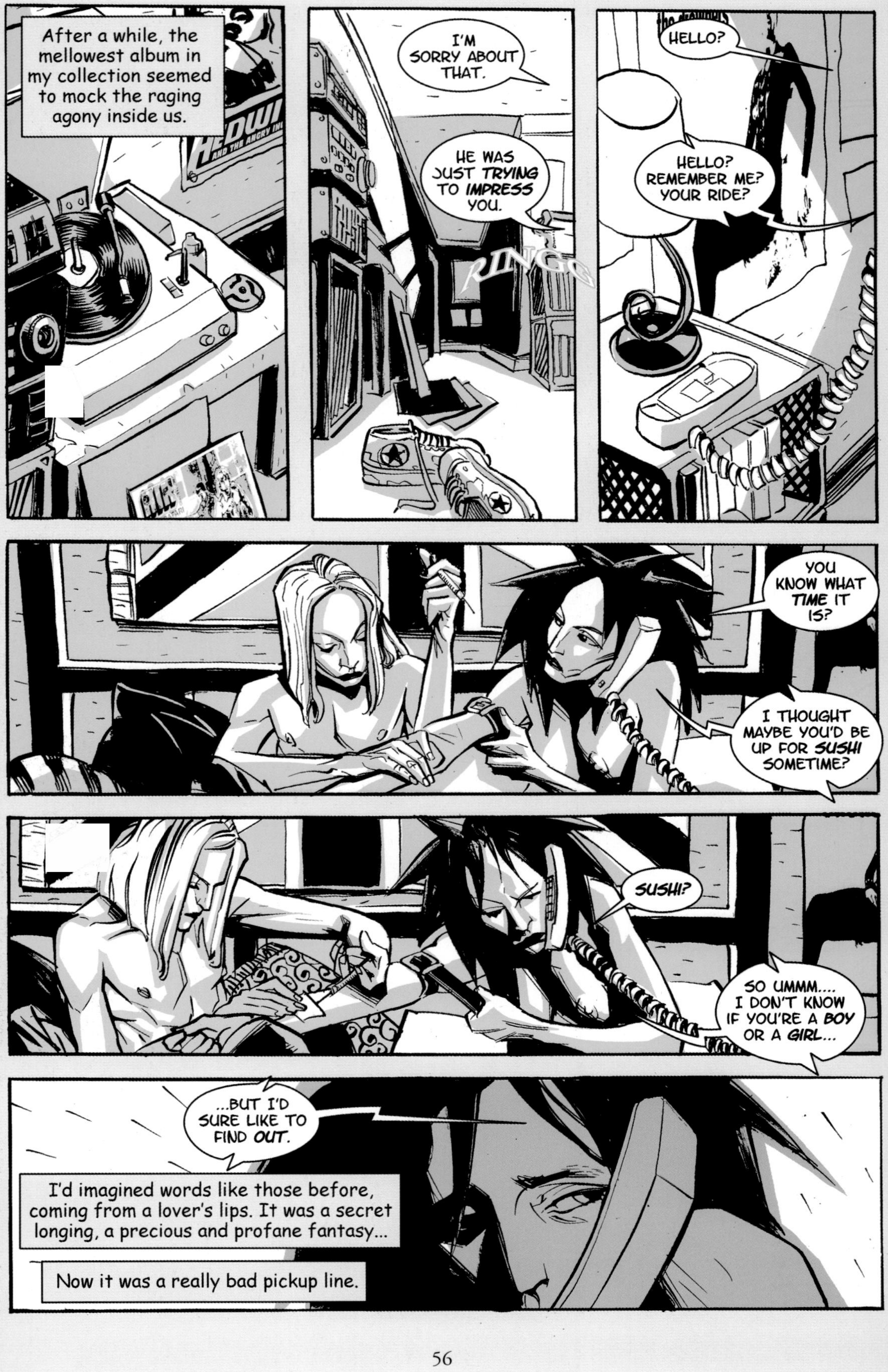
After a while, the mellowest album in my collection seemed to mock the raging agony inside us.
I'M SORRY ABOUT THAT.
HE WAS JUST TRYING TO IMPRESS YOU.
RINGG
HELLO?
HELLO? REMEMBER ME? YOUR RIDE?
YOU KNOW WHAT TIME IT IS?
I THOUGHT MAYBE YOU'D BE UP FOR SUSHI SOMETIME?
SUSHI?
SO UMMM.... I DON'T KNOW IF YOU'RE A BOY OR A GIRL...
...BUT I'D SURE LIKE TO FIND OUT.
I'd imagined words like those before, coming from a lover's lips. It was a secret longing, a precious and profane fantasy...
Now it was a really bad pickup line.

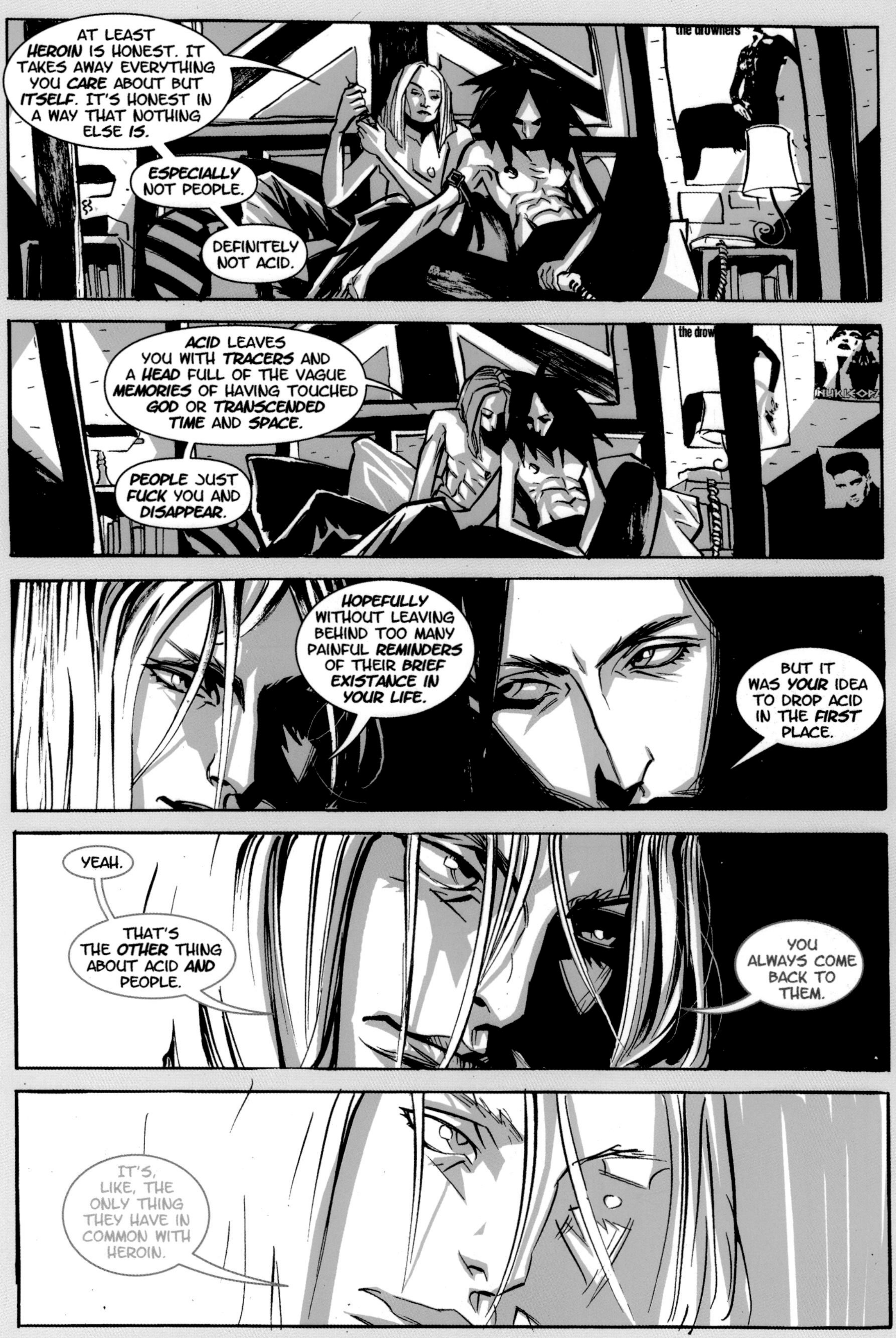
AT LEAST HEROIN IS HONEST. IT TAKES AWAY EVERYTHING YOU CARE ABOUT BUT ITSELF. IT'S HONEST IN A WAY THAT NOTHING ELSE IS.
ESPECIALLY NOT PEOPLE.
DEFINITELY NOT ACID.
the drowners
ACID LEAVES YOU WITH TRACERS AND A HEAD FULL OF THE VAGUE MEMORIES OF HAVING TOUCHED GOD OR TRANSCENDED TIME AND SPACE.
PEOPLE JUST FUCK YOU AND DISAPPEAR.
HOPEFULLY WITHOUT LEAVING BEHIND TOO MANY PAINFUL REMINDERS OF THEIR BRIEF EXISTANCE IN YOUR LIFE.
BUT IT WAS YOUR IDEA TO DROP ACID IN THE FIRST PLACE.
YEAH.
THAT'S THE OTHER THING ABOUT ACID AND PEOPLE.
YOU ALWAYS COME BACK TO THEM.
IT'S, LIKE, THE ONLY THING THEY HAVE IN COMMON WITH HEROIN.

chapter 3

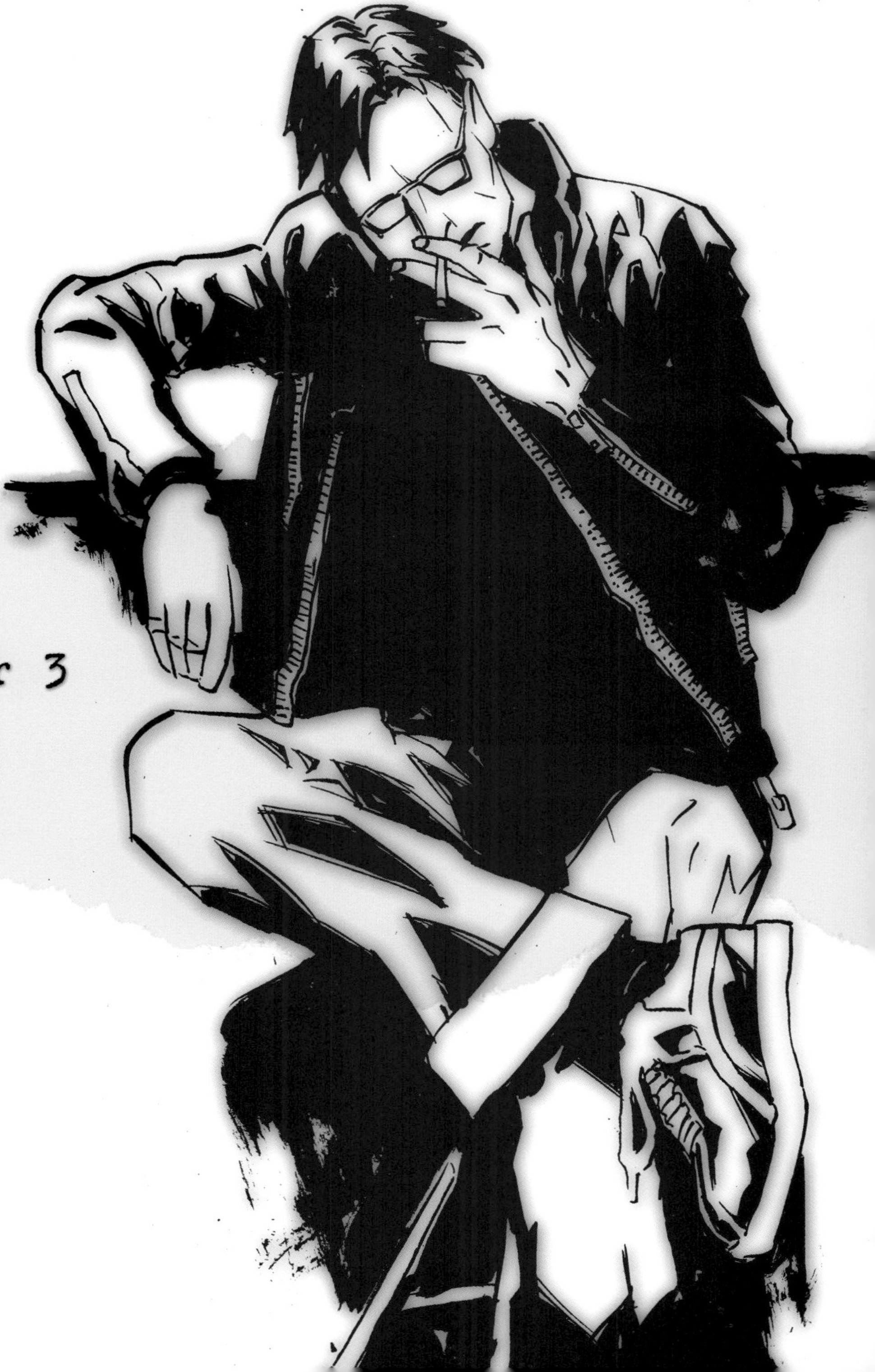

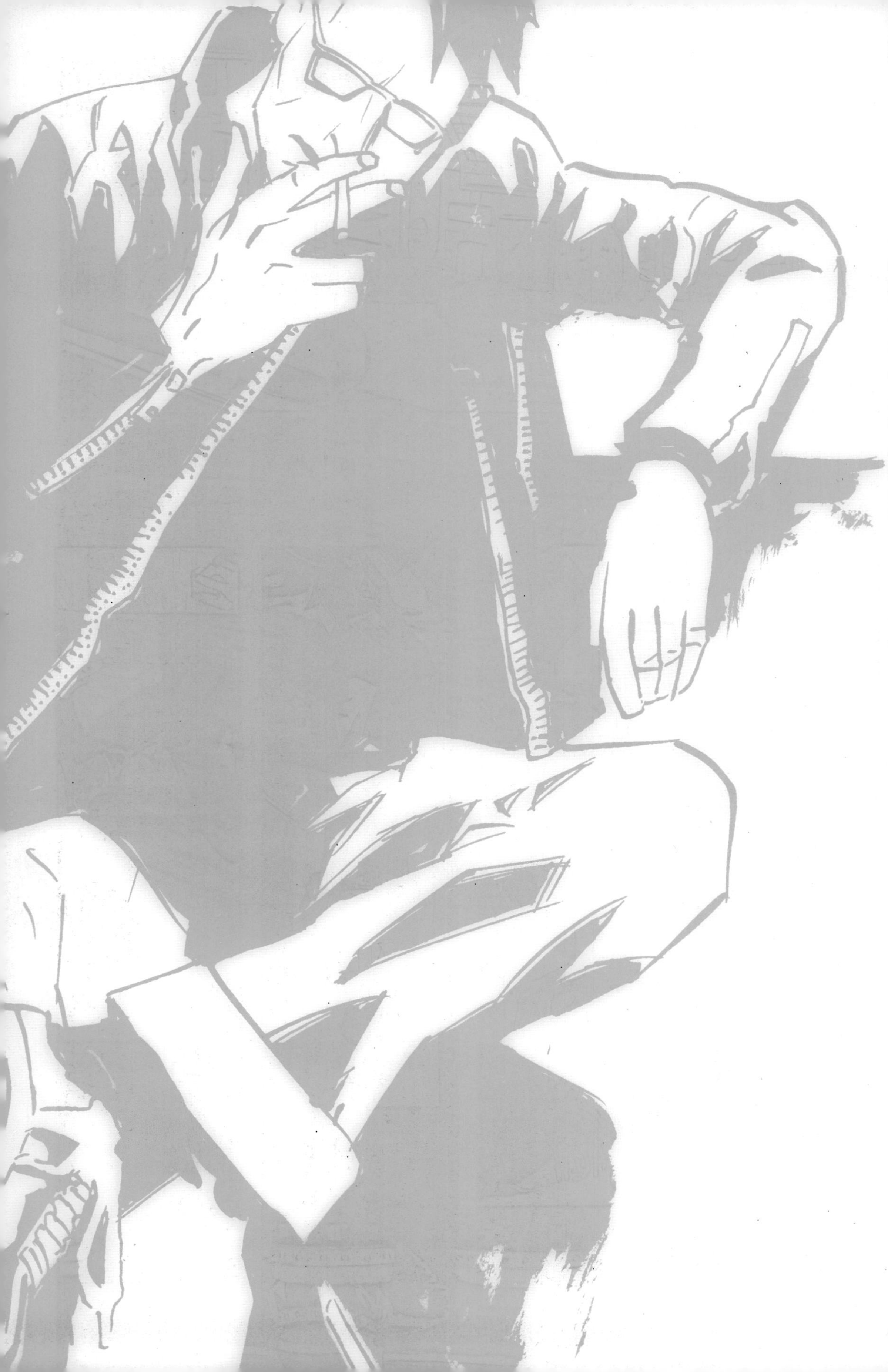

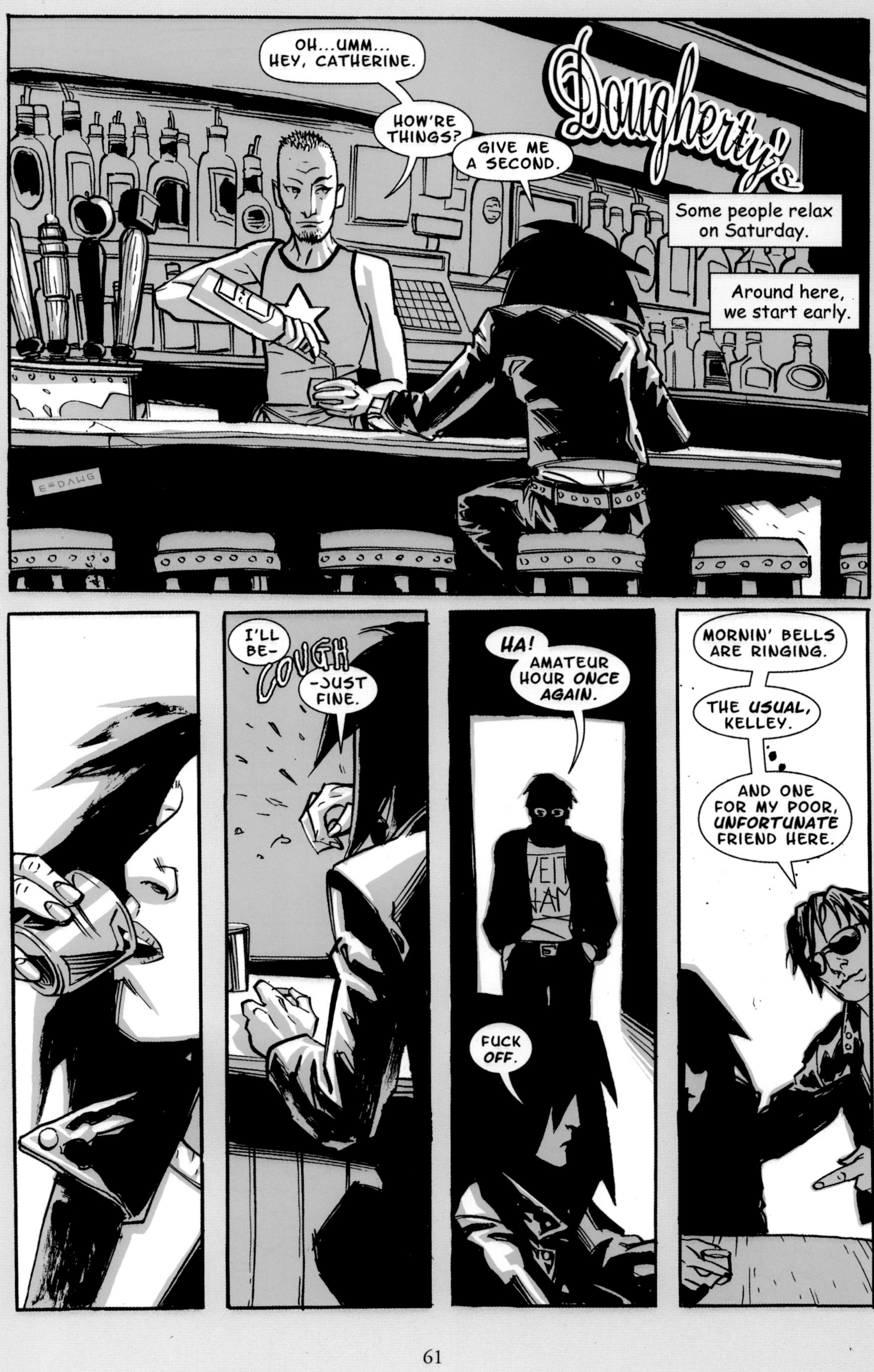
OH...UMM...
HEY, CATHERINE.
HOW'RE THINGS?
GIVE ME A SECOND.
Dougherty's
Some people relax on Saturday.
Around here, we start early.
E#DAWG
I'LL BE-
COUGH
-JUST FINE.
HA! AMATEUR HOUR ONCE AGAIN.
FUCK OFF.
MORNIN' BELLS ARE RINGING.
THE USUAL, KELLEY.
AND ONE FOR MY POOR, UNFORTUNATE FRIEND HERE.

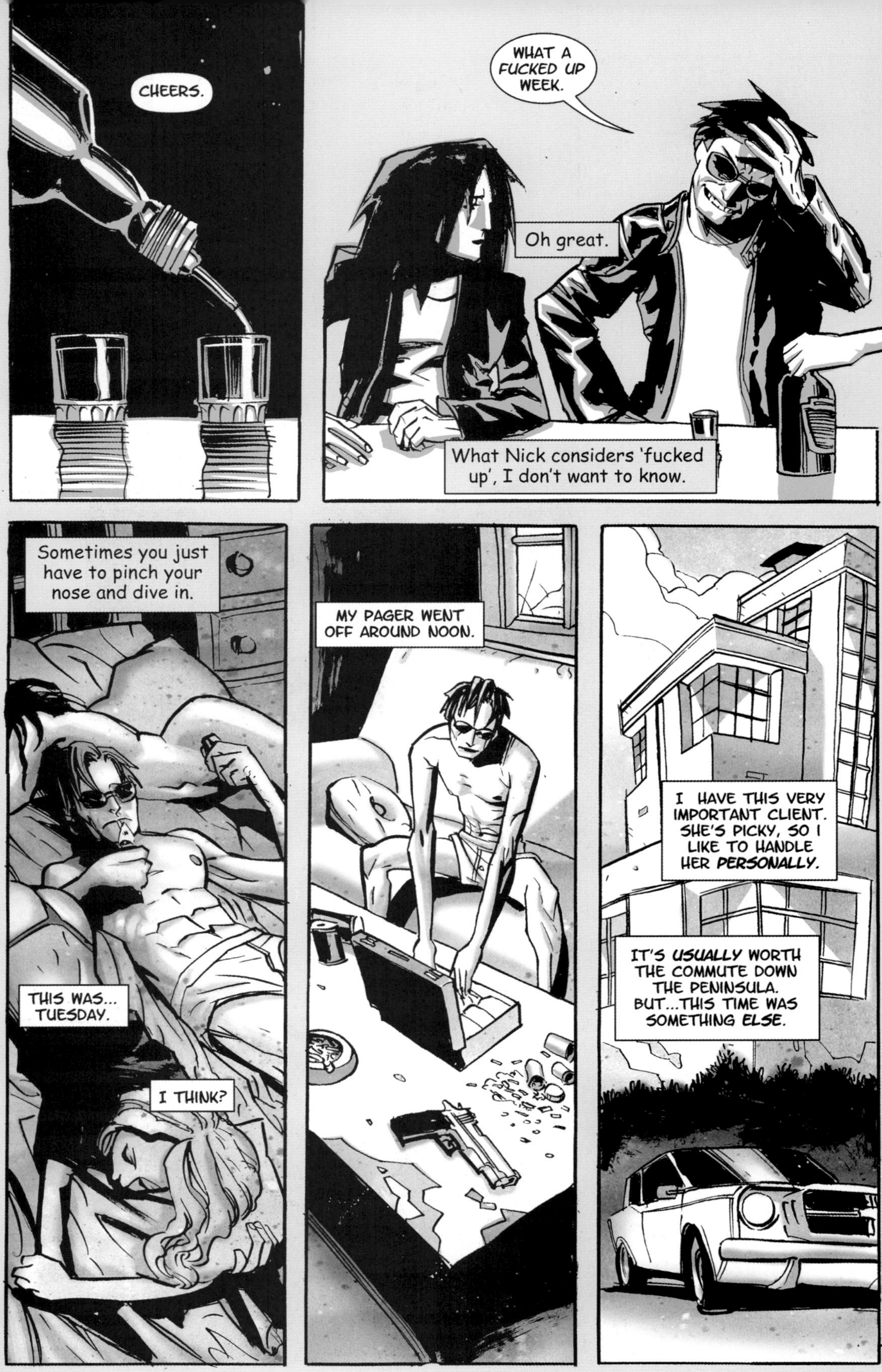
CHEERS.
WHAT A FUCKED UP WEEK.
Oh great.
What Nick considers 'fucked up', I don't want to know.
Sometimes you just have to pinch your nose and dive in.
THIS WAS... TUESDAY.
I THINK?
MY PAGER WENT OFF AROUND NOON.
I HAVE THIS VERY IMPORTANT CLIENT. SHE'S PICKY, SO I LIKE TO HANDLE HER PERSONALLY.
IT'S USUALLY WORTH THE COMMUTE DOWN THE PENINSULA. BUT...THIS TIME WAS SOMETHING ELSE.

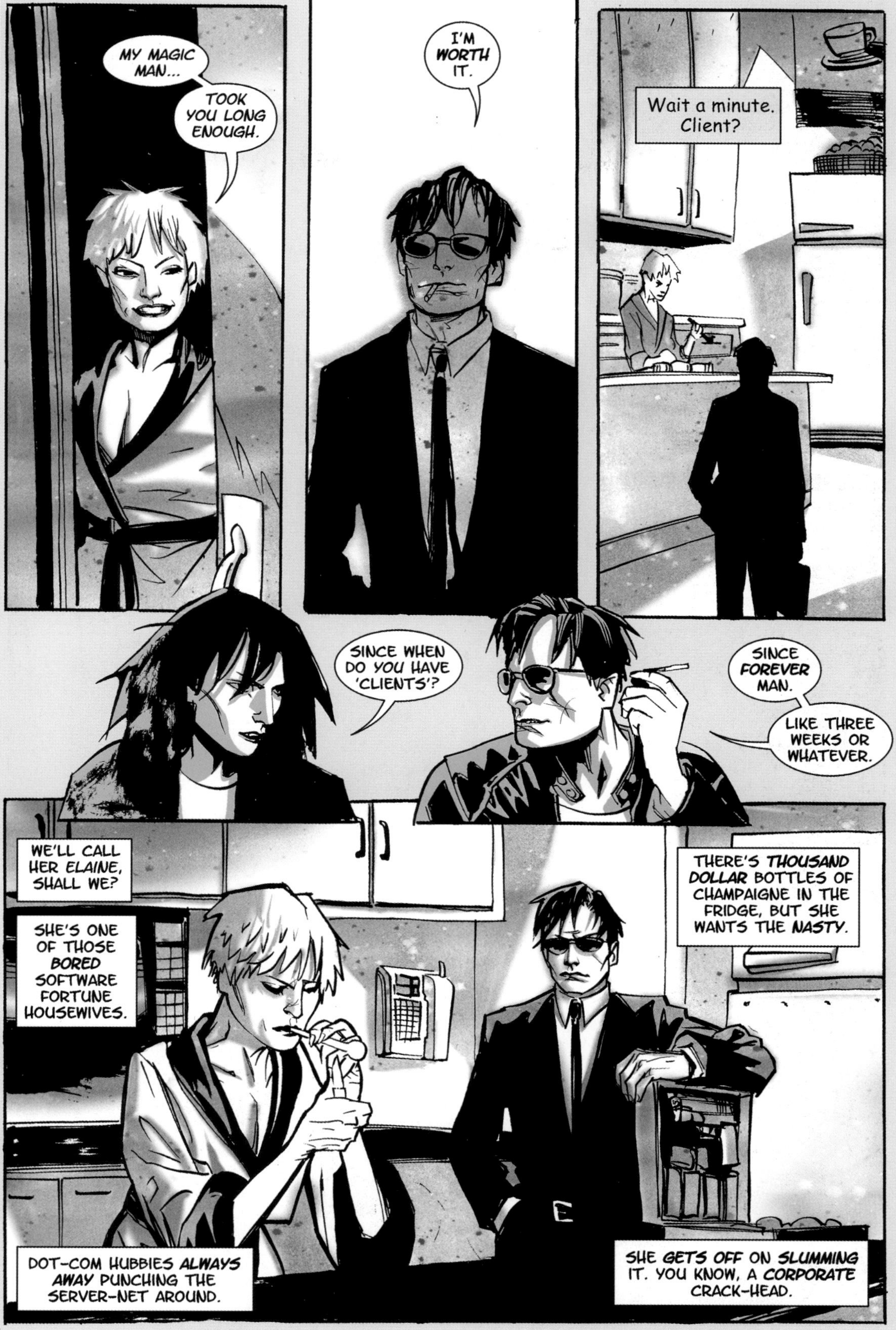

MY MAGIC MAN...
TOOK YOU LONG ENOUGH.
I'M WORTH IT.
Wait a minute. Client?
SINCE WHEN DO YOU HAVE 'CLIENTS'?
SINCE FOREVER MAN.
LIKE THREE WEEKS OR WHATEVER.
WE'LL CALL HER ELAINE, SHALL WE?
SHE'S ONE OF THOSE BORED SOFTWARE FORTUNE HOUSEWIVES.
DOT-COM HUBBIES ALWAYS AWAY PUNCHING THE SERVER-NET AROUND.
THERE'S THOUSAND DOLLAR BOTTLES OF CHAMPAIGNE IN THE FRIDGE, BUT SHE WANTS THE NASTY.
SHE GETS OFF ON SLUMMING IT. YOU KNOW, A CORPORATE CRACK-HEAD.

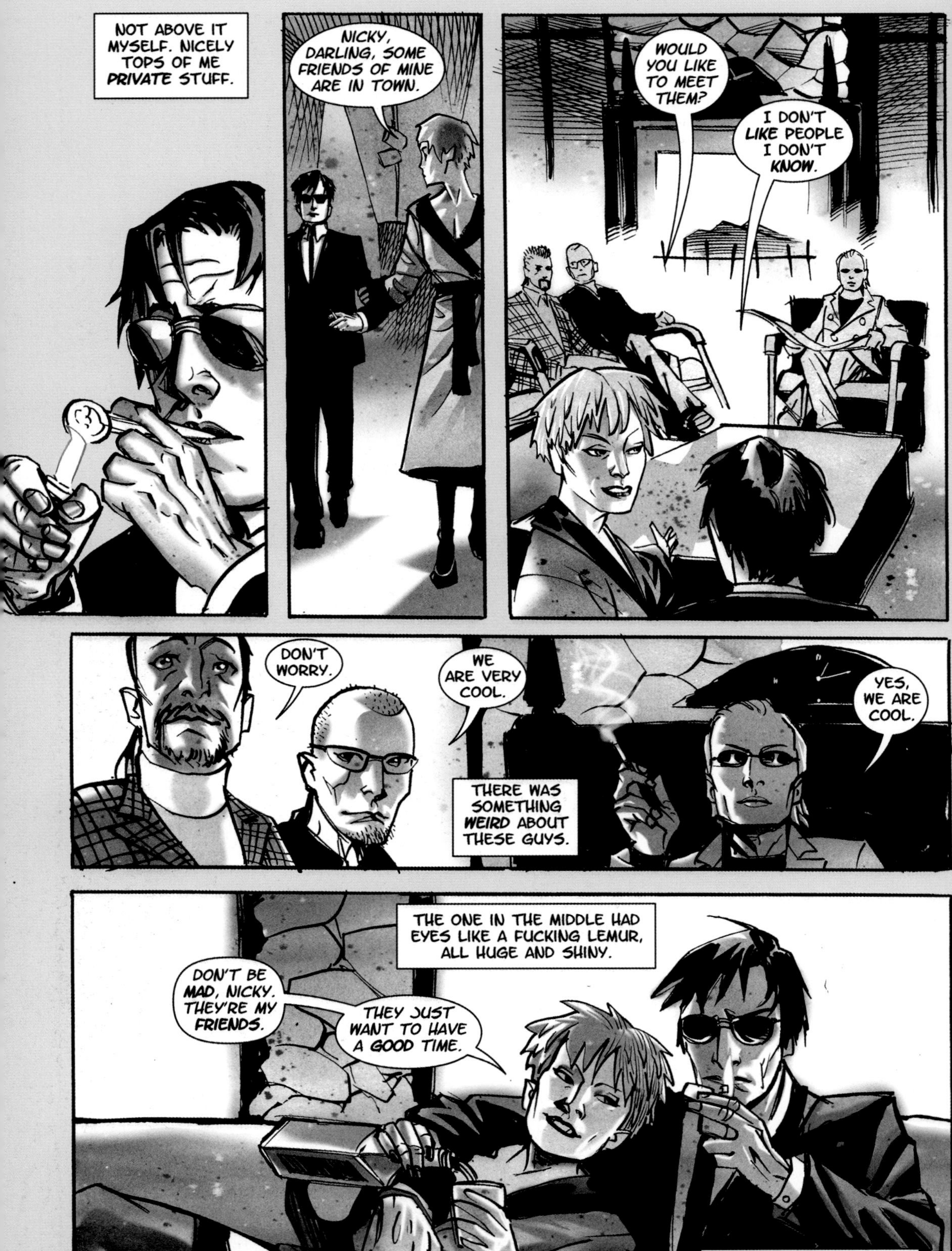
NOT ABOVE IT MYSELF. NICELY TOPS OF ME PRIVATE STUFF.
NICKY, DARLING, SOME FRIENDS OF MINE ARE IN TOWN.
WOULD YOU LIKE TO MEET THEM?
I DON'T LIKE PEOPLE I DON'T KNOW.
DON'T WORRY.
WE ARE VERY COOL.
THERE WAS SOMETHING WEIRD ABOUT THESE GUYS.
YES, WE ARE COOL.
THE ONE IN THE MIDDLE HAD EYES LIKE A FUCKING LEMUR, ALL HUGE AND SHINY.
DON'T BE MAD, NICKY. THEY'RE MY FRIENDS.
THEY JUST WANT TO HAVE A GOOD TIME.
THEY KEPT LOOKING AT ME LIKE THEY WANTED SOMETHING.

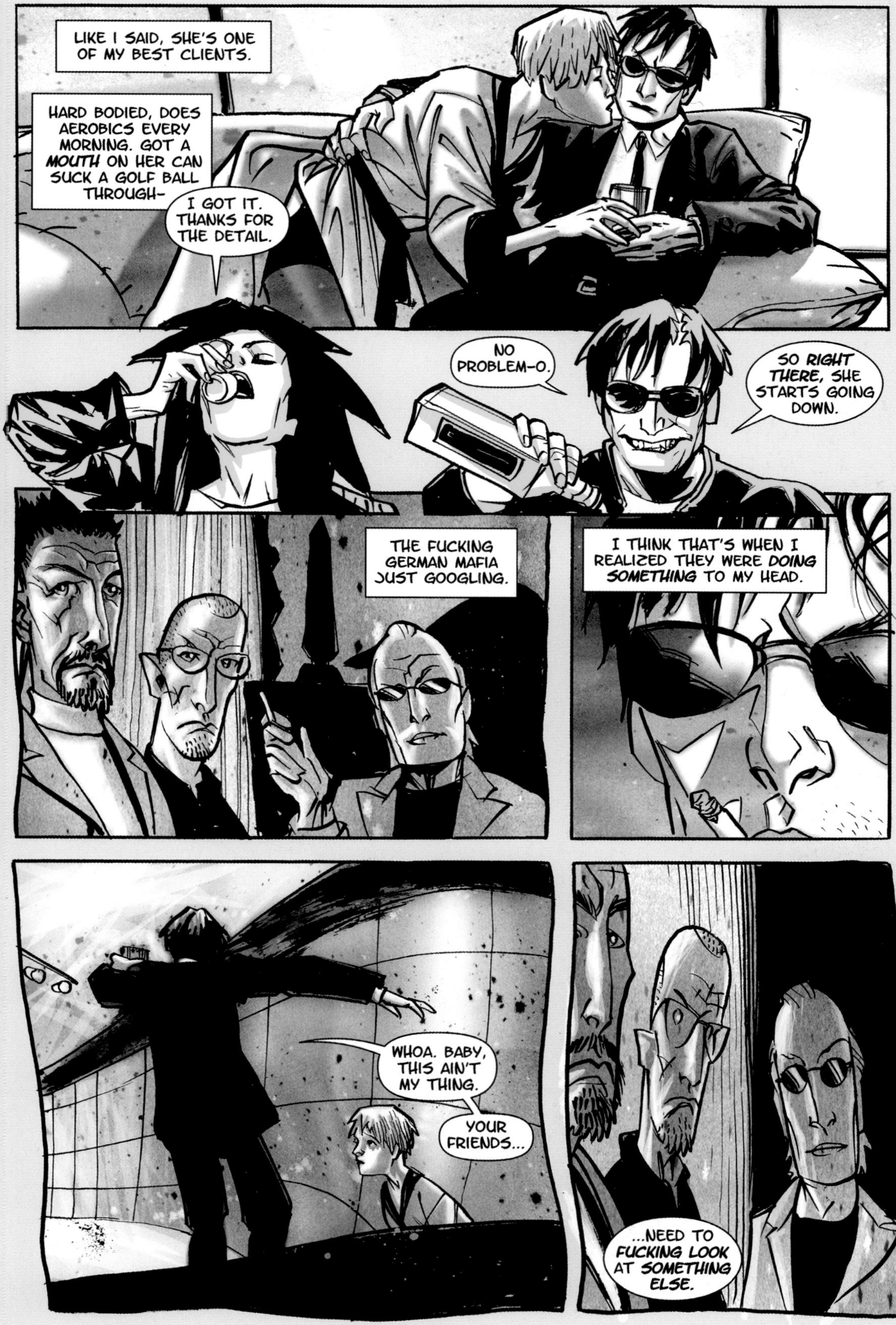
LIKE I SAID, SHE'S ONE OF MY BEST CLIENTS.
HARD BODIED, DOES AEROBICS EVERY MORNING. GOT A MOUTH ON HER CAN SUCK A GOLF BALL THROUGH-
I GOT IT. THANKS FOR THE DETAIL.
NO PROBLEM-O.
SO RIGHT THERE, SHE STARTS GOING DOWN.
THE FUCKING GERMAN MAFIA JUST GOOGLING.
I THINK THAT'S WHEN I REALIZED THEY WERE DOING SOMETHING TO MY HEAD.
WHOA. BABY, THIS AIN'T MY THING.
YOUR FRIENDS...
...NEED TO FUCKING LOOK AT SOMETHING ELSE.

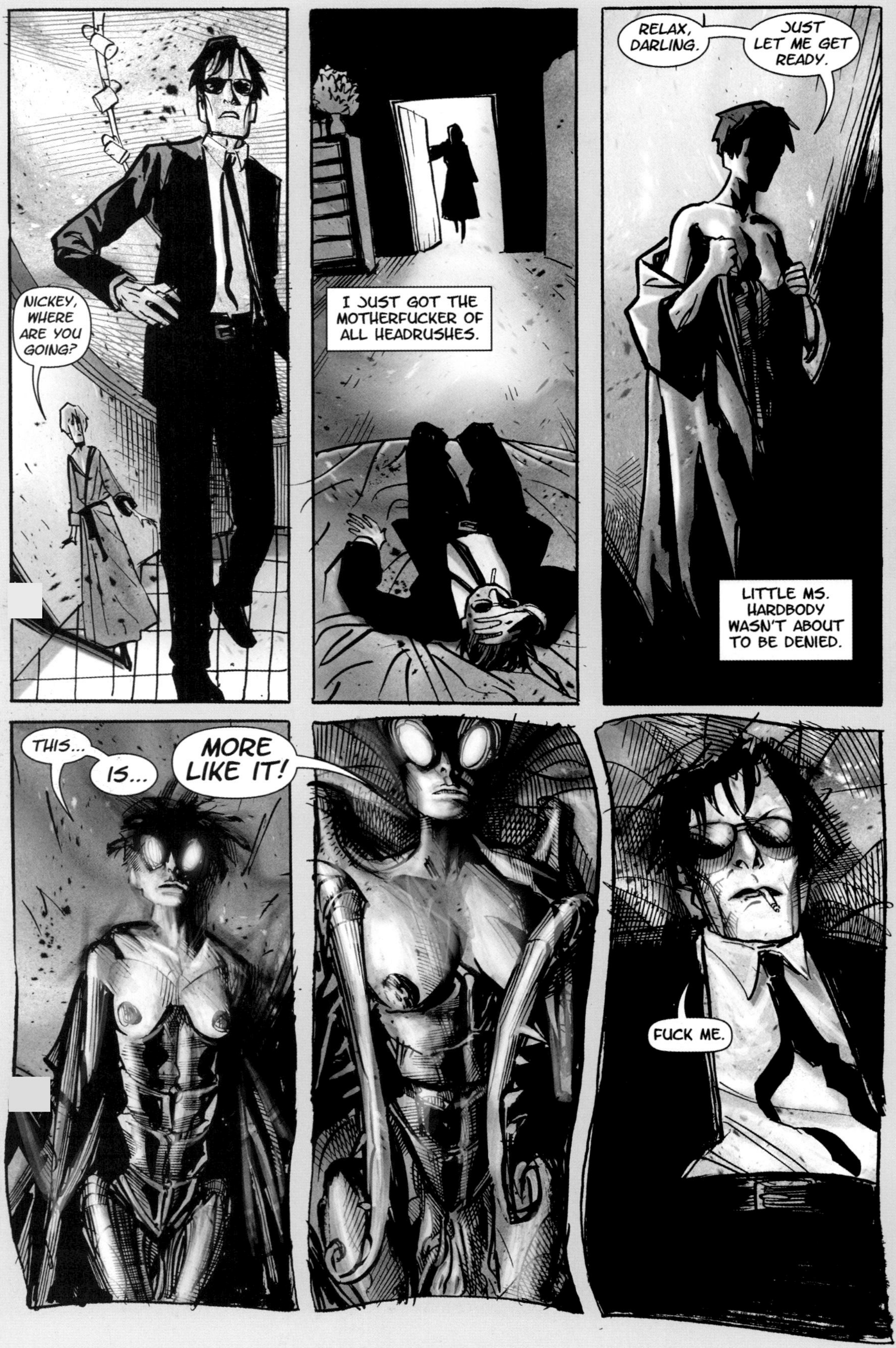
NICKEY, WHERE ARE YOU GOING?
I JUST GOT THE MOTHERFUCKER OF ALL HEADRUSHES.
RELAX, DARLING.
JUST LET ME GET READY.
LITTLE MS. HARDBODY WASN'T ABOUT TO BE DENIED.
THIS...
IS...
MORE LIKE IT!
FUCK ME.

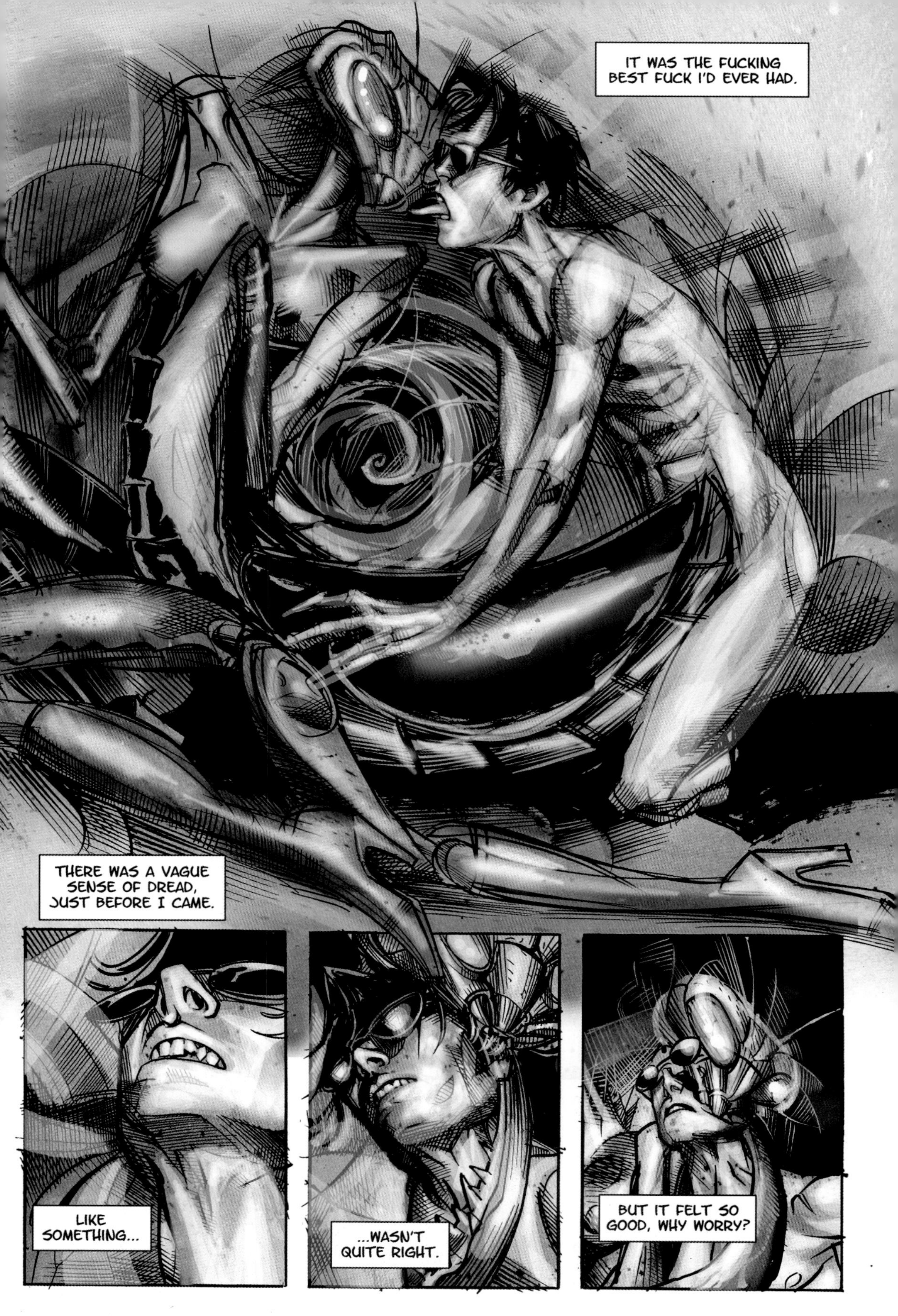
IT WAS THE FUCKING BEST FUCK I'D EVER HAD.
THERE WAS A VAGUE SENSE OF DREAD, JUST BEFORE I CAME.
LIKE SOMETHING...
...WASN'T QUITE RIGHT.
BUT IT FELT SO GOOD, WHY WORRY?

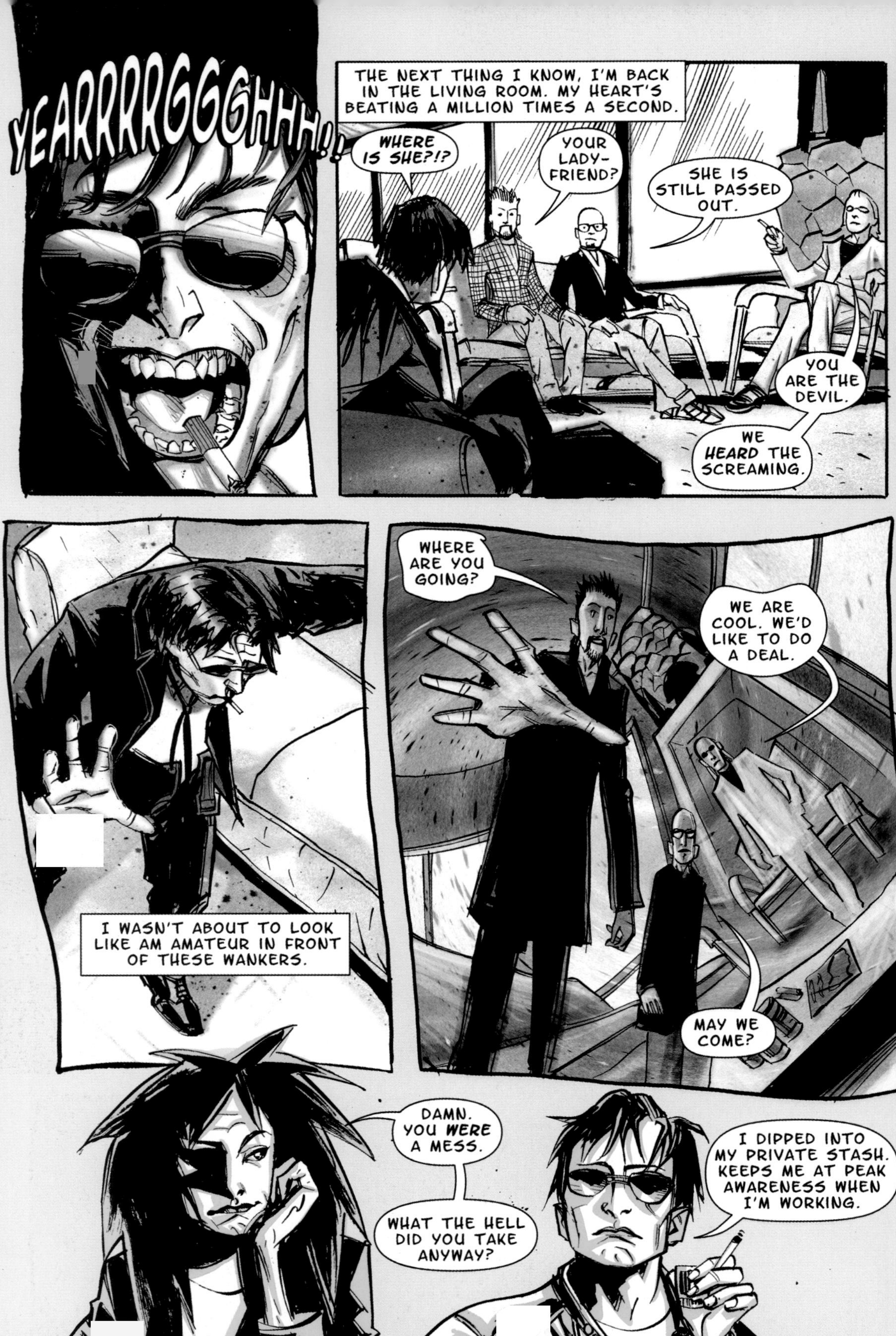
YEARRRRGGGHHH!!
THE NEXT THING I KNOW, I'M BACK IN THE LIVING ROOM. MY HEART'S BEATING A MILLION TIMES A SECOND.
WHERE IS SHE?!?
YOUR LADY-FRIEND?
SHE IS STILL PASSED OUT.
YOU ARE THE DEVIL.
WE HEARD THE SCREAMING.
I WASN'T ABOUT TO LOOK LIKE AM AMATEUR IN FRONT OF THESE WANKERS.
WHERE ARE YOU GOING?
WE ARE COOL. WE'D LIKE TO DO A DEAL.
MAY WE COME?
DAMN. YOU WERE A MESS.
WHAT THE HELL DID YOU TAKE ANYWAY?
I DIPPED INTO MY PRIVATE STASH. KEEPS ME AT PEAK AWARENESS WHEN I'M WORKING.

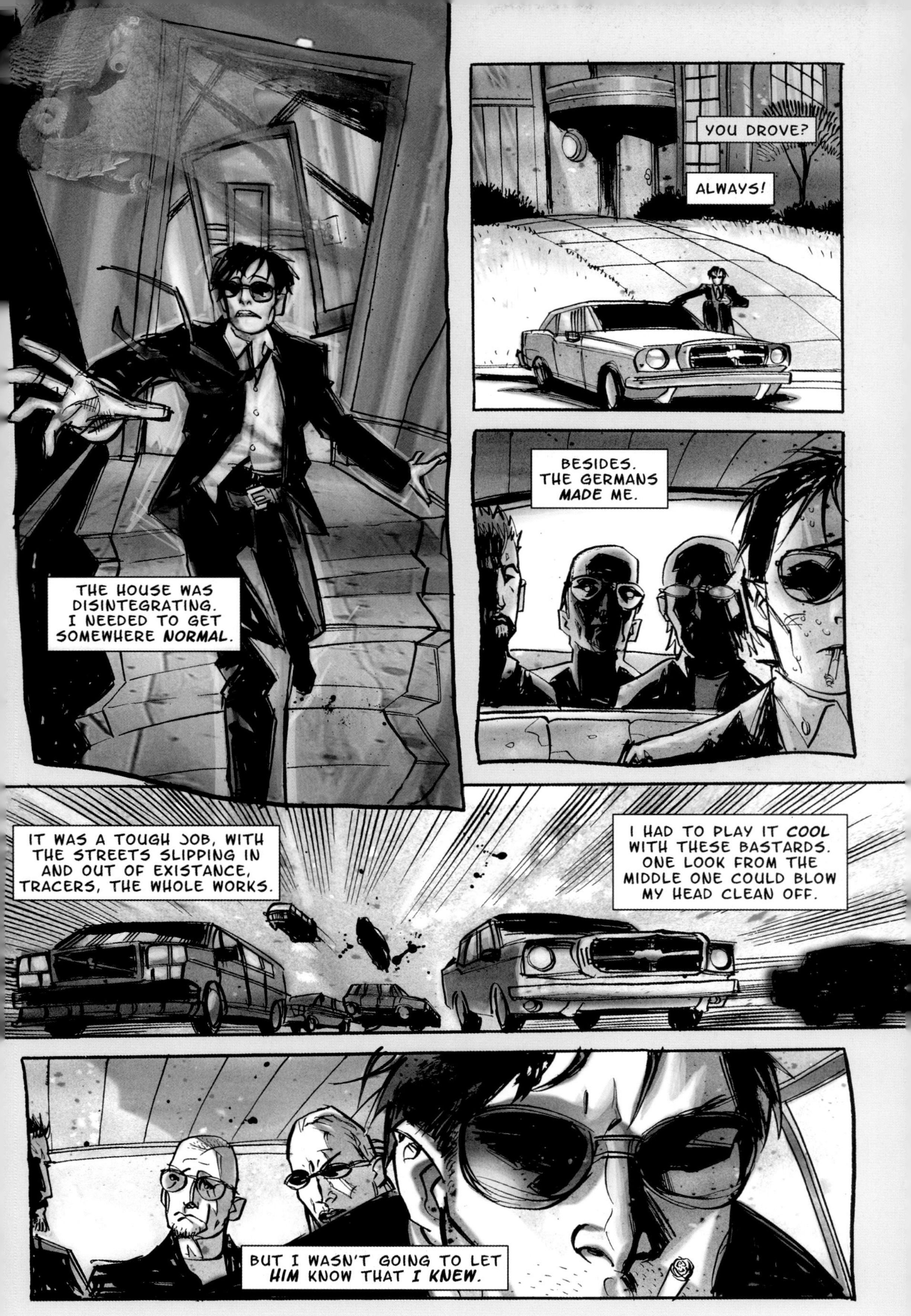
THE HOUSE WAS DISINTEGRATING. I NEEDED TO GET SOMEWHERE NORMAL.
YOU DROVE?
ALWAYS!
BESIDES. THE GERMANS MADE ME.
IT WAS A TOUGH JOB, WITH THE STREETS SLIPPING IN AND OUT OF EXISTANCE, TRACERS, THE WHOLE WORKS.
I HAD TO PLAY IT COOL WITH THESE BASTARDS. ONE LOOK FROM THE MIDDLE ONE COULD BLOW MY HEAD CLEAN OFF.
BUT I WASN'T GOING TO LET HIM KNOW THAT I KNEW.

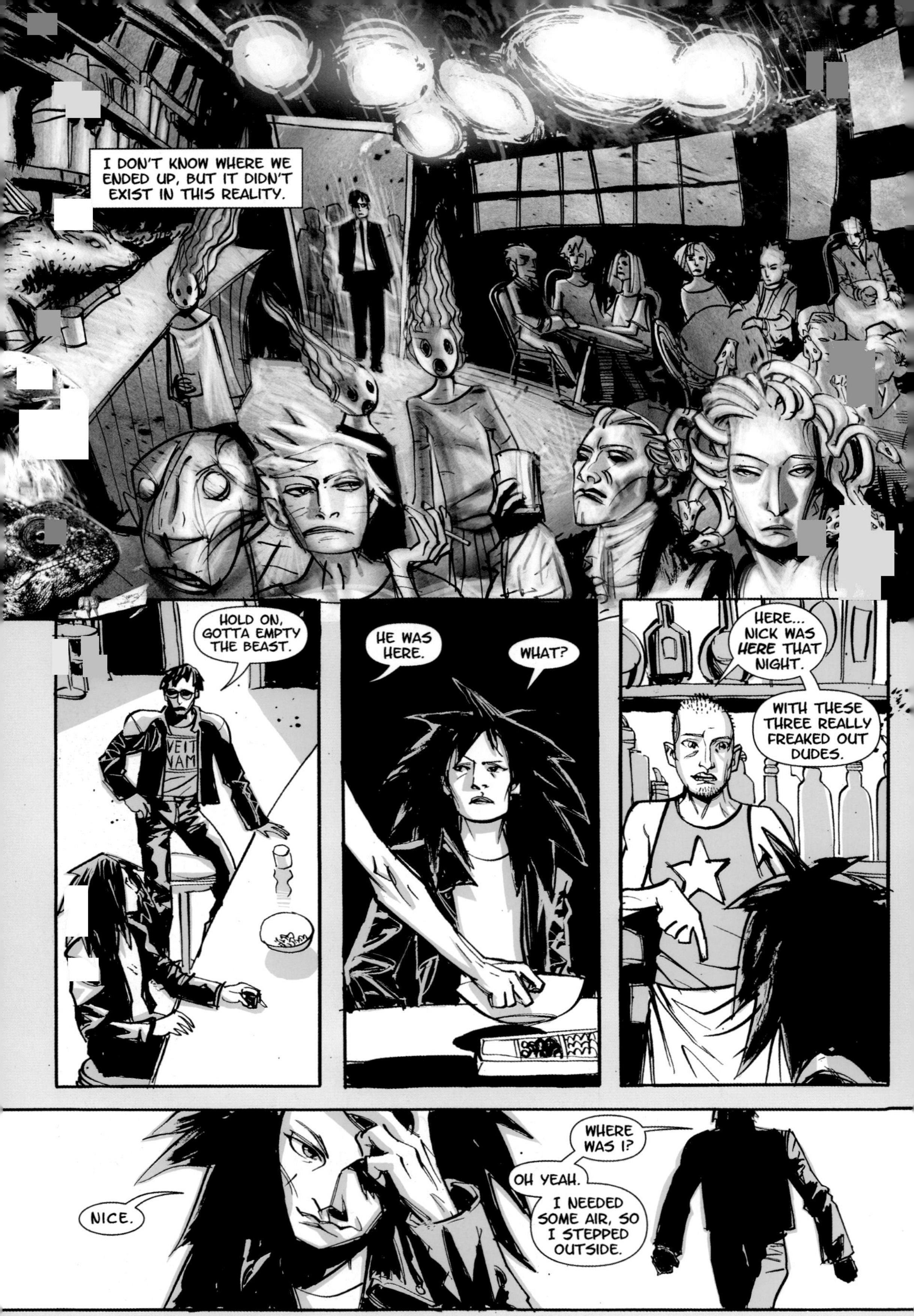

I DON'T KNOW WHERE WE ENDED UP, BUT IT DIDN'T EXIST IN THIS REALITY.
HOLD ON, GOTTA EMPTY THE BEAST.
VEIT NAM
HE WAS HERE.
WHAT?
HERE... NICK WAS HERE THAT NIGHT.
WITH THESE THREE REALLY FREAKED OUT DUDES.
NICE.
WHERE WAS I?
OH YEAH.
I NEEDED SOME AIR, SO I STEPPED OUTSIDE.

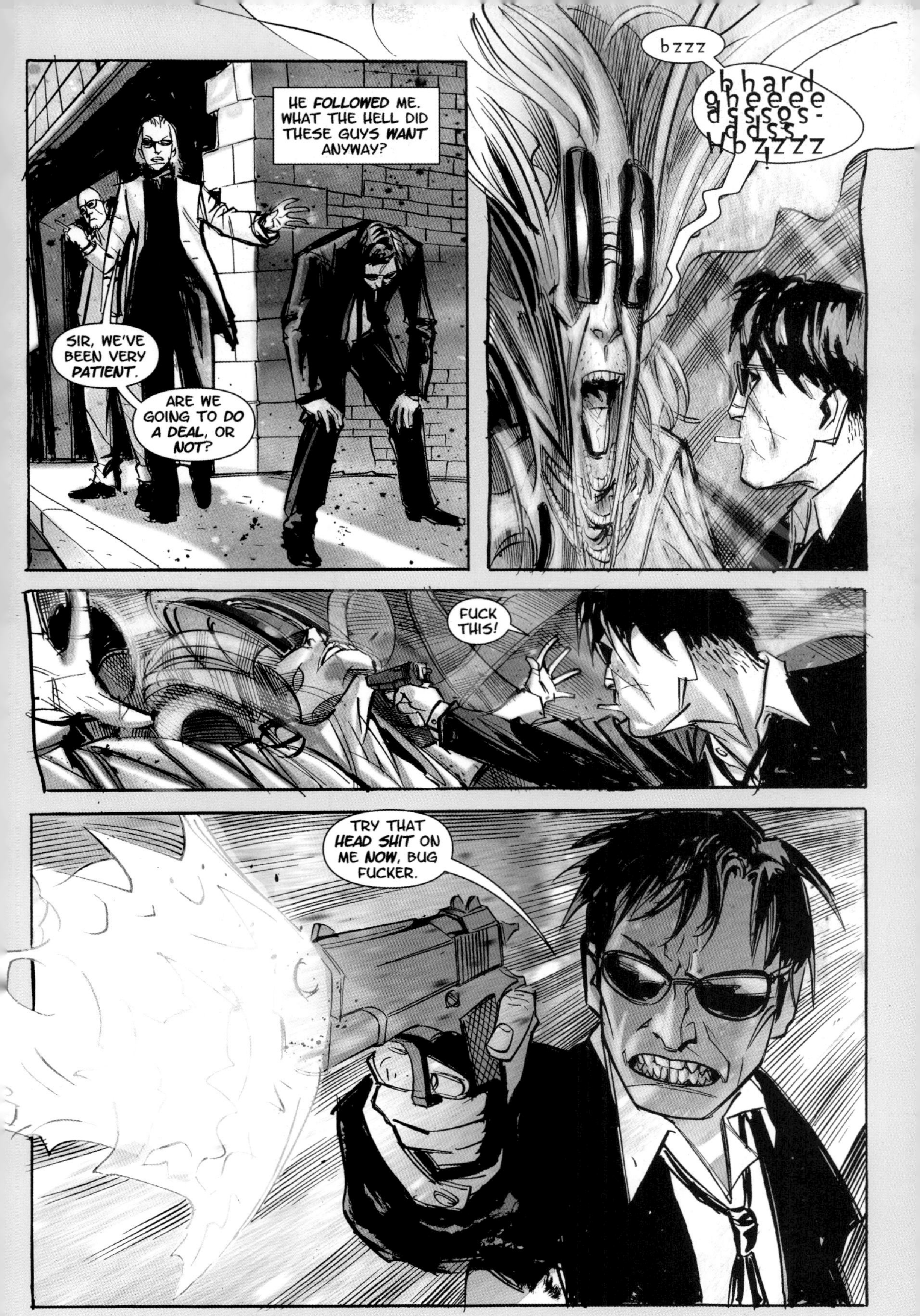
HE FOLLOWED ME. WHAT THE HELL DID THESE GUYS WANT ANYWAY?
SIR, WE'VE BEEN VERY PATIENT.
ARE WE GOING TO DO A DEAL, OR NOT?
bzzz
bhard gheeeee asssos- ddss, hbzzzz !
FUCK THIS!
TRY THAT HEAD SHIT ON ME NOW, BUG FUCKER.

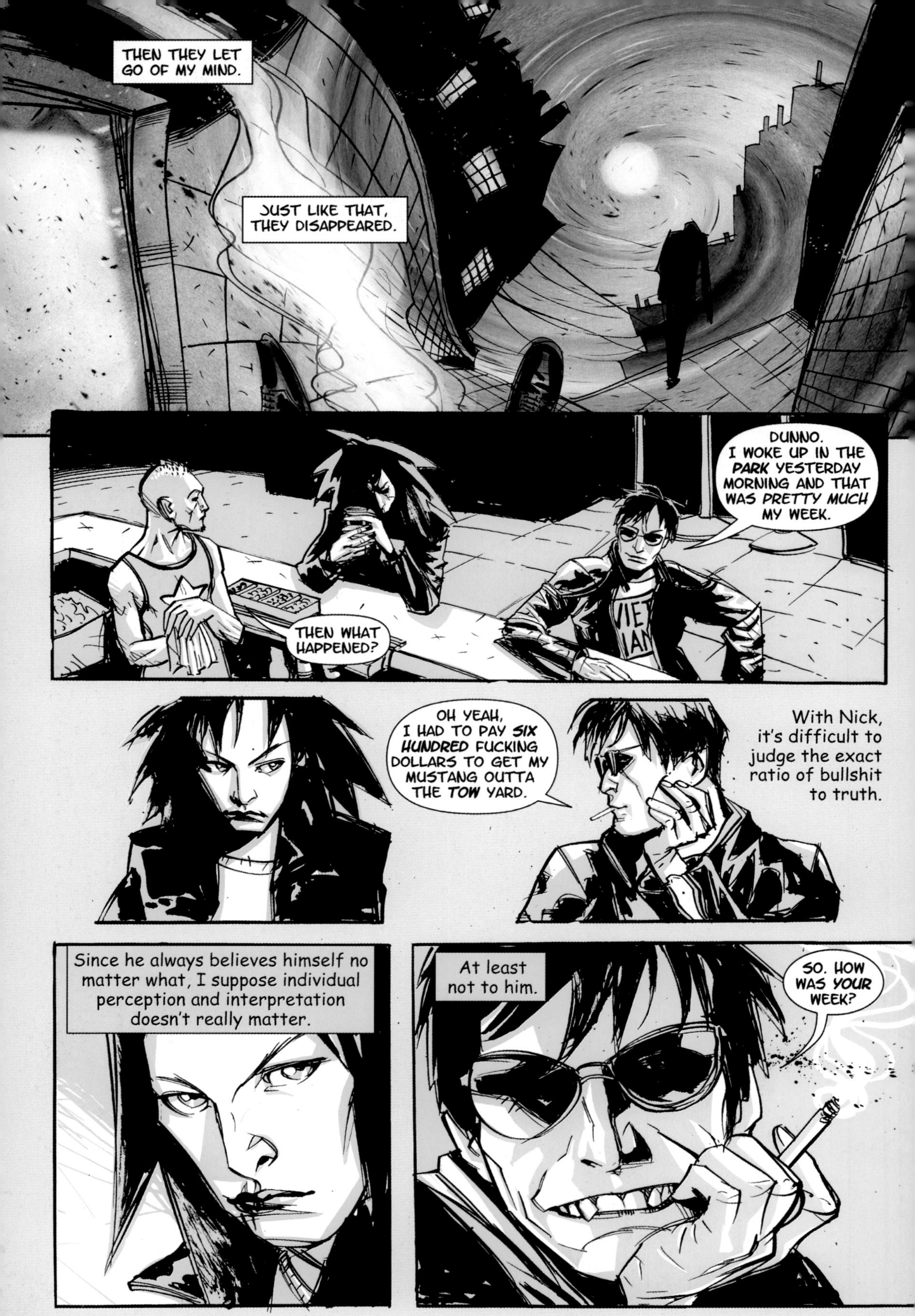
THEN THEY LET GO OF MY MIND.
JUST LIKE THAT, THEY DISAPPEARED.
DUNNO. I WOKE UP IN THE PARK YESTERDAY MORNING AND THAT WAS PRETTY MUCH MY WEEK.
THEN WHAT HAPPENED?
OH YEAH, I HAD TO PAY SIX HUNDRED FUCKING DOLLARS TO GET MY MUSTANG OUTTA THE TOW YARD.
With Nick, it's difficult to judge the exact ratio of bullshit to truth.
Since he always believes himself no matter what, I suppose individual perception and interpretation doesn't really matter.
At least not to him.
SO. HOW WAS YOUR WEEK?

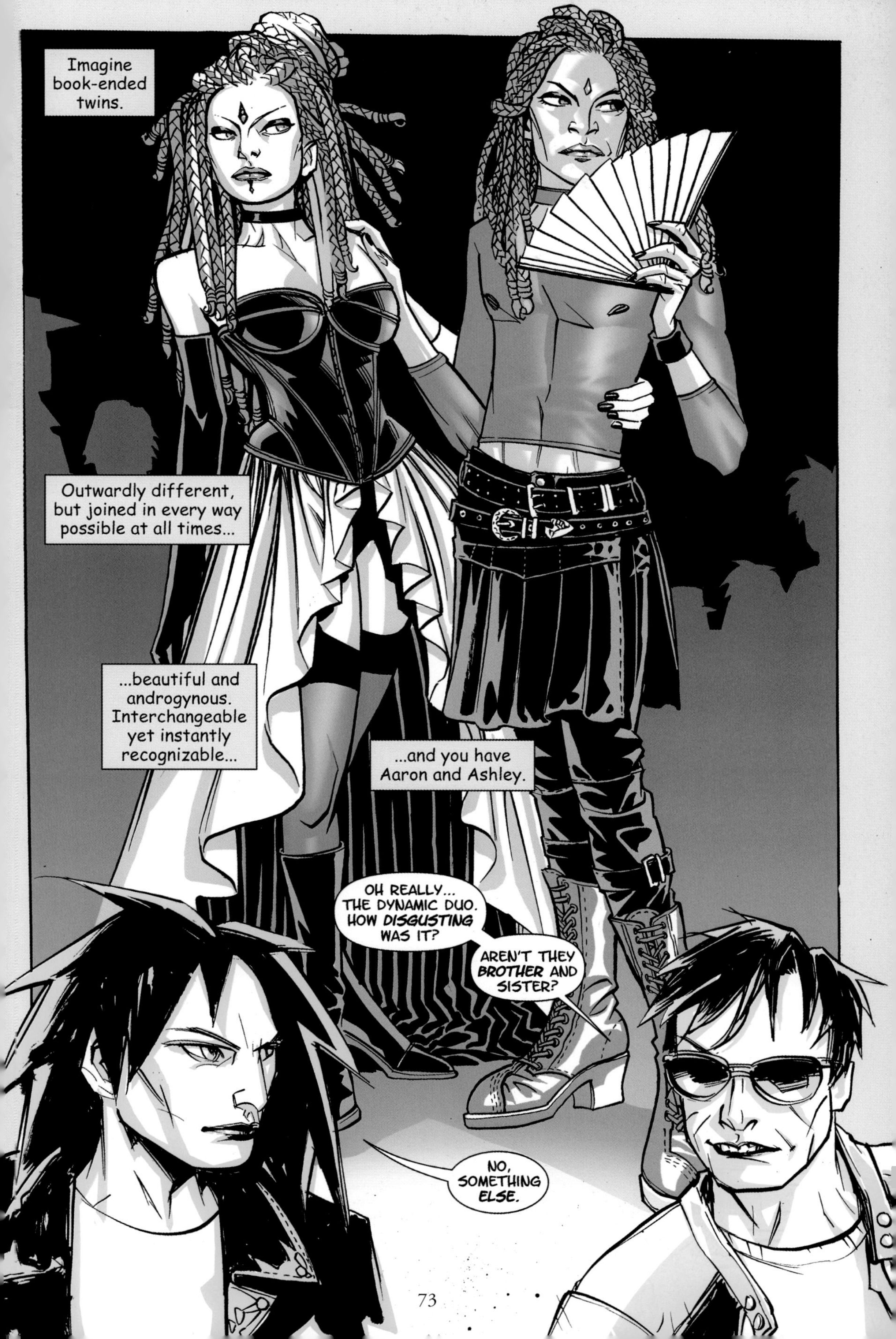
Imagine book-ended twins.
Outwardly different, but joined in every way possible at all times...
...beautiful and androgynous. Interchangeable yet instantly recognizable...
...and you have Aaron and Ashley.
OH REALLY... THE DYNAMIC DUO. HOW DISGUSTING WAS IT?
AREN'T THEY BROTHER AND SISTER?
NO, SOMETHING ELSE.

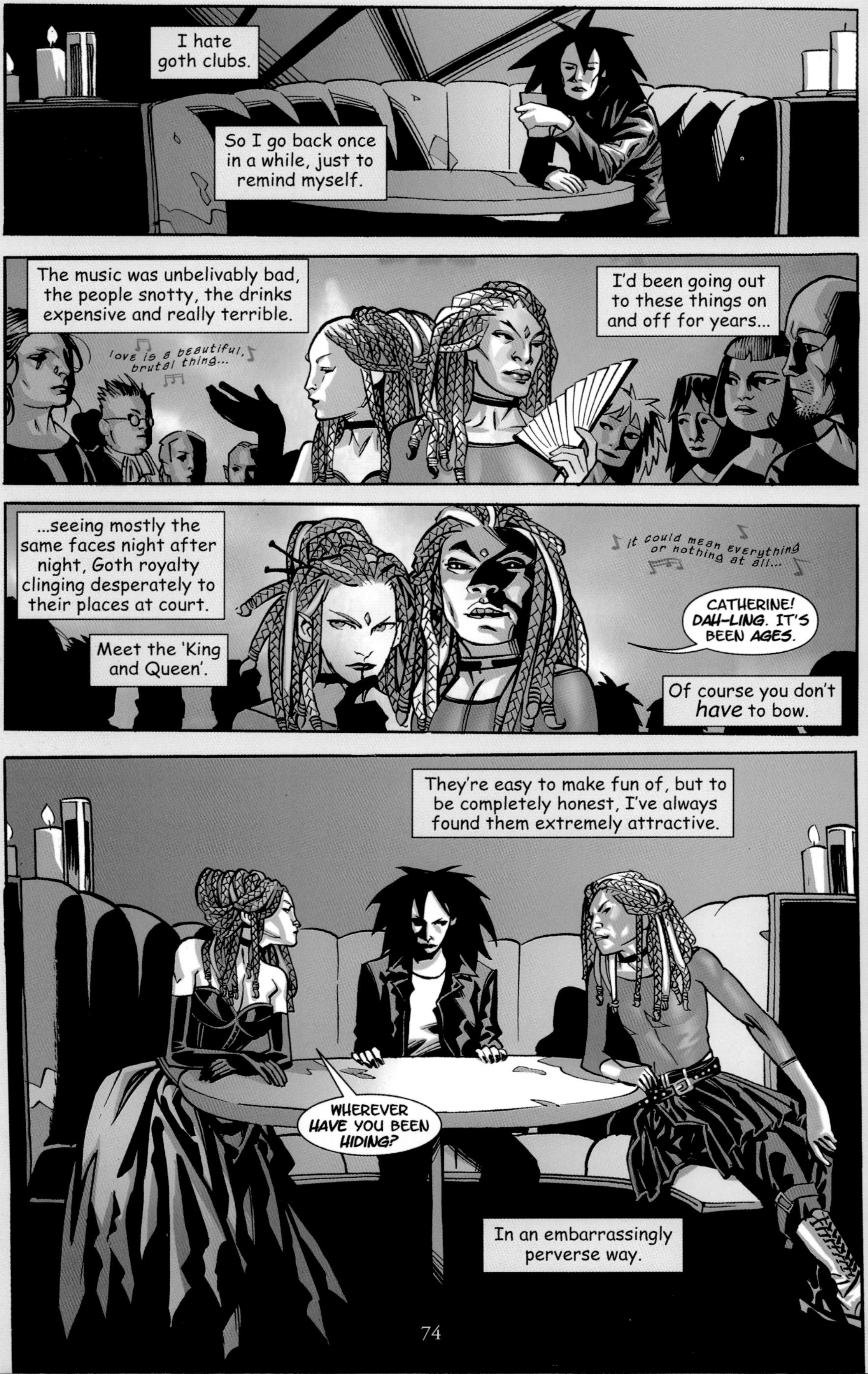

I hate goth clubs.
So I go back once in a while, just to remind myself.
The music was unbelivably bad, the people snotty, the drinks expensive and really terrible.
love is a beautiful, brutal thing...
I'd been going out to these things on and off for years...
...seeing mostly the same faces night after night, Goth royalty clinging desperately to their places at court.
Meet the 'King and Queen'.
it could mean everything or nothing at all...
CATHERINE! DAH-LING. IT'S BEEN AGES.
Of course you don't have to bow.
They're easy to make fun of, but to be completely honest, I've always found them extremely attractive.
WHEREVER HAVE YOU BEEN HIDING?
In an embarrassingly perverse way.

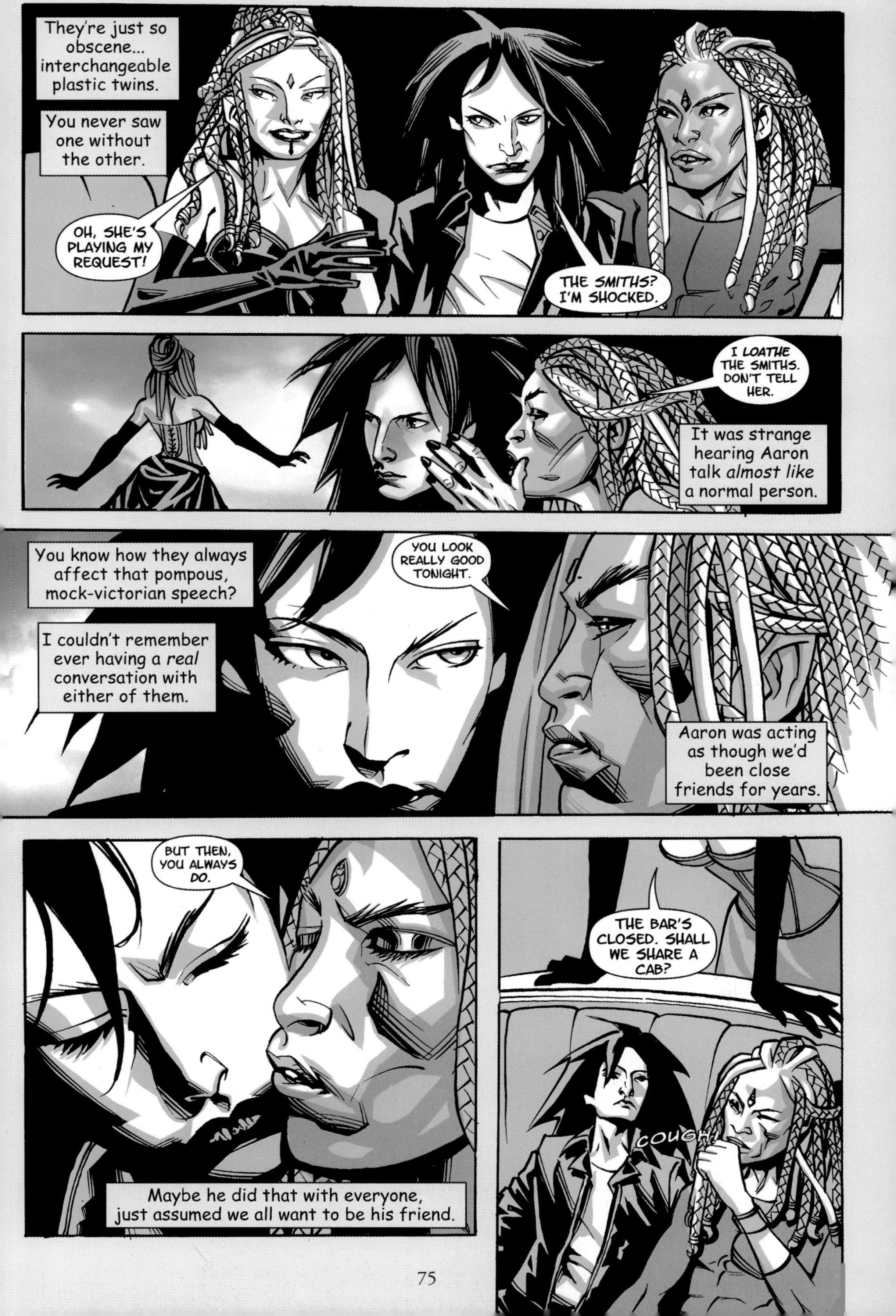
They're just so obscene... interchangeable plastic twins.
You never saw one without the other.
OH, SHE'S PLAYING MY REQUEST!
THE SMITHS? I'M SHOCKED.
I *LOATHE* THE SMITHS. DON'T TELL HER.
It was strange hearing Aaron talk *almost like* a normal person.
You know how they always affect that pompous, mock-victorian speech?
I couldn't remember ever having a *real* conversation with either of them.
YOU LOOK REALLY GOOD TONIGHT.
Aaron was acting as though we'd been close friends for years.
BUT THEN, YOU ALWAYS DO.
Maybe he did that with everyone, just assumed we all want to be his friend.
THE BAR'S CLOSED. SHALL WE SHARE A CAB?
COUGH!

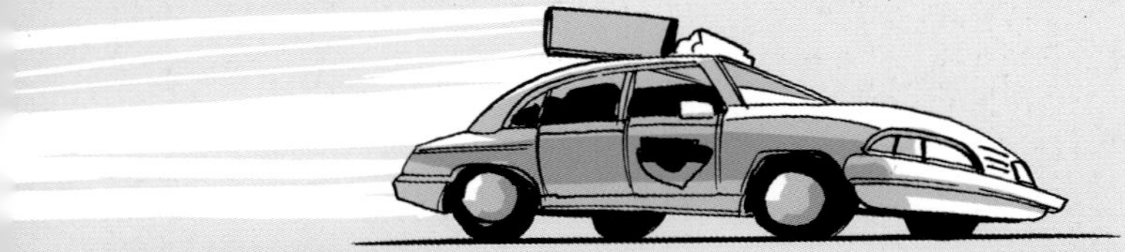

It was one of those blurry half-remembered cab rides, all drunken laughter as we were pushed against one another on those tight, fast turns.

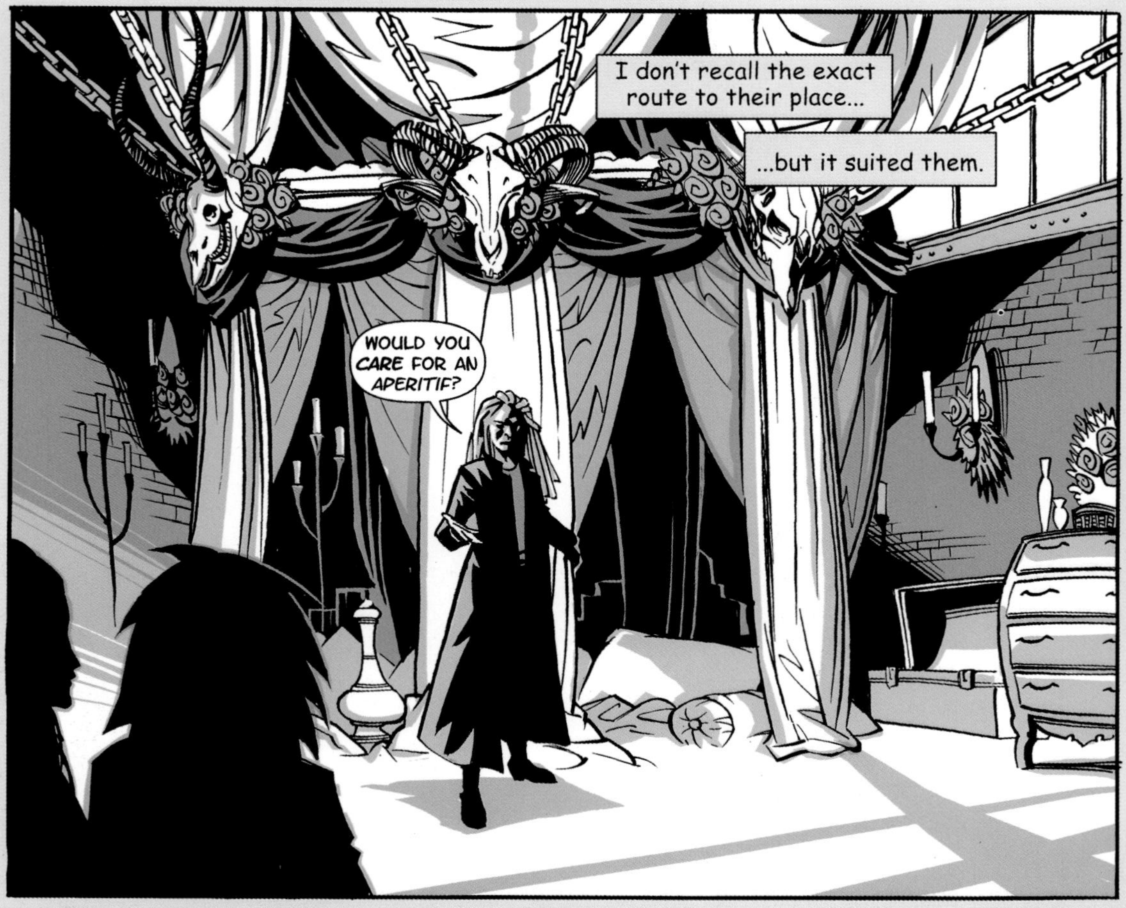
I don't recall the exact route to their place...
...but it suited them.
WOULD YOU CARE FOR AN APERITIF?

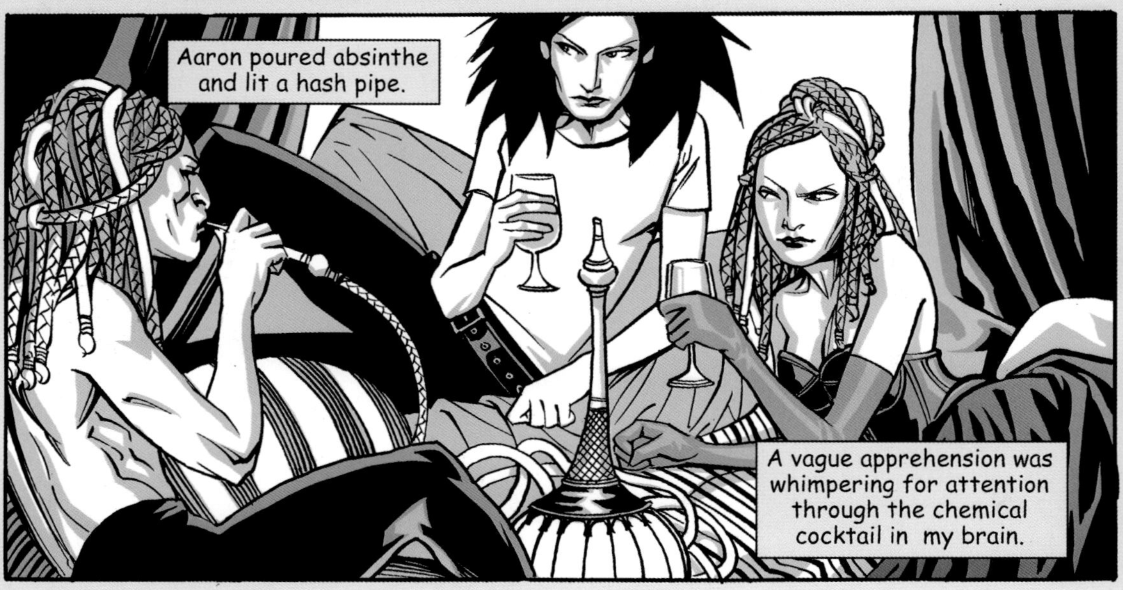
Aaron poured absinthe and lit a hash pipe.
A vague apprehension was whimpering for attention through the chemical cocktail in my brain.

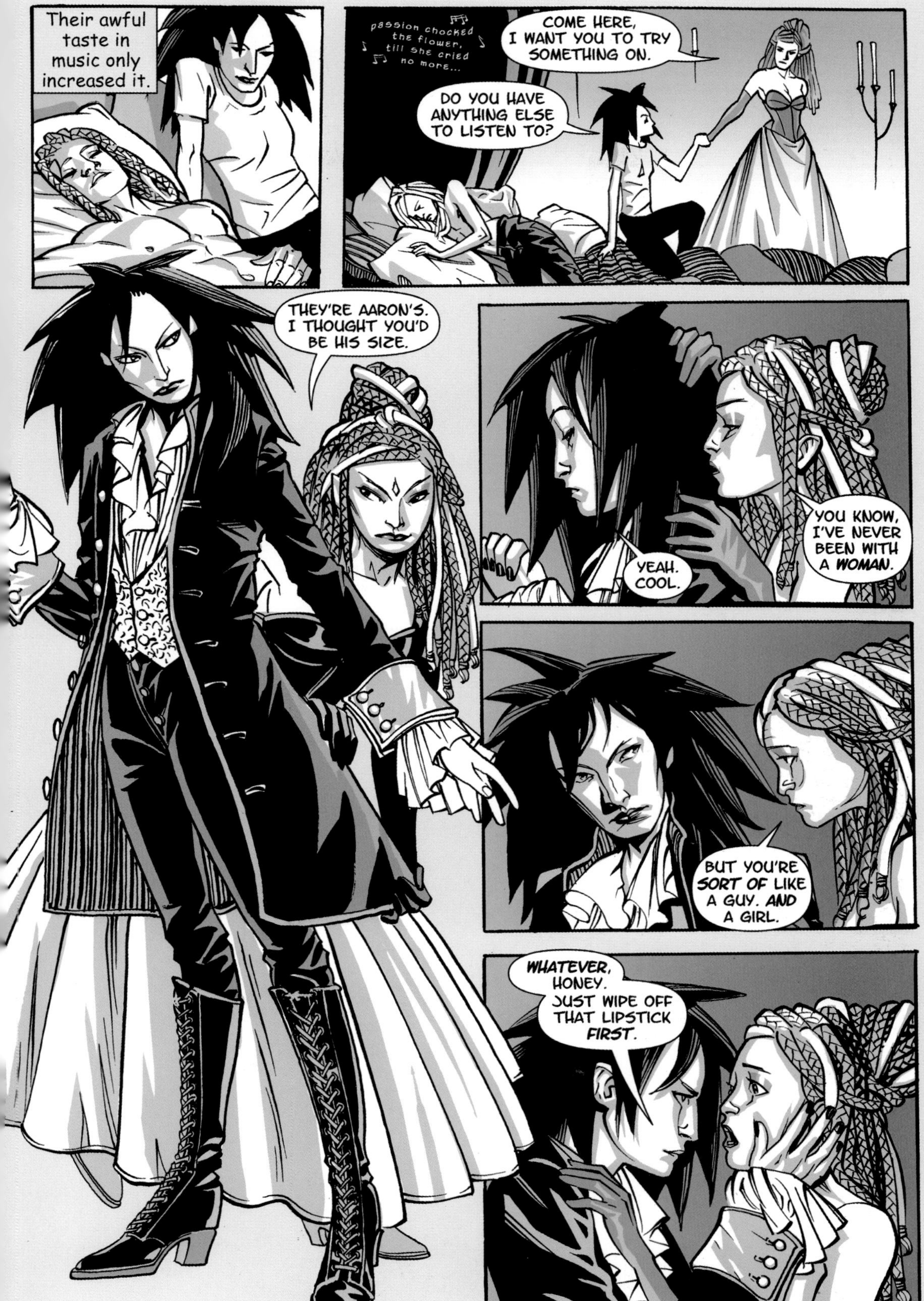

Their awful taste in music only increased it.
passion chocked the flower, till she cried no more...
COME HERE, I WANT YOU TO TRY SOMETHING ON.
DO YOU HAVE ANYTHING ELSE TO LISTEN TO?
THEY'RE AARON'S. I THOUGHT YOU'D BE HIS SIZE.
YOU KNOW, I'VE NEVER BEEN WITH A *WOMAN*.
YEAH. COOL.
BUT YOU'RE *SORT OF* LIKE A GUY. *AND* A GIRL.
WHATEVER, HONEY. JUST WIPE OFF THAT LIPSTICK *FIRST*.

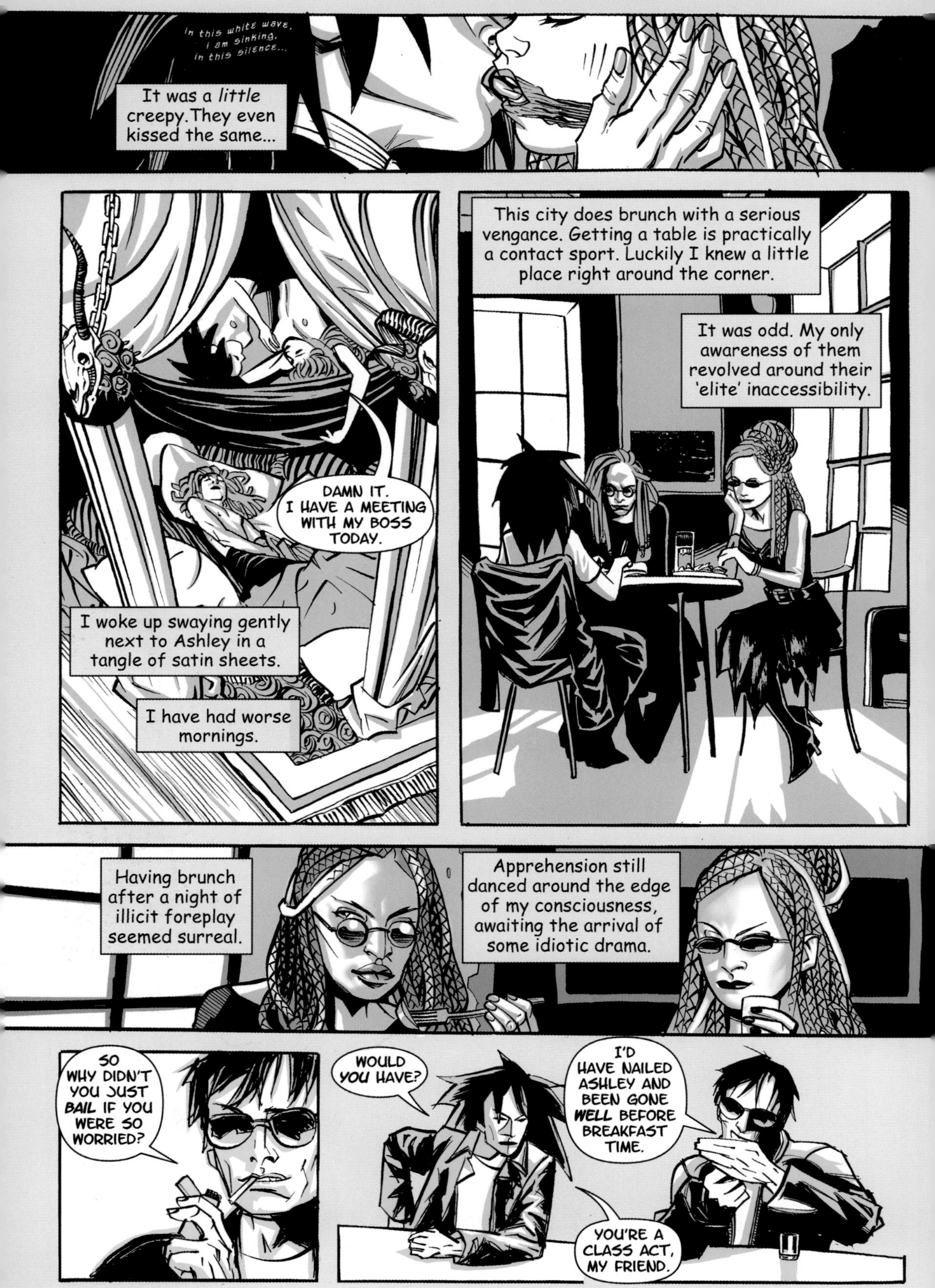
in this white wave,
i am sinking,
in this silence...
It was a *little* creepy. They even kissed the same...
I woke up swaying gently next to Ashley in a tangle of satin sheets.
DAMN IT. I HAVE A MEETING WITH MY BOSS TODAY.
I have had worse mornings.
This city does brunch with a serious vengance. Getting a table is practically a contact sport. Luckily I knew a little place right around the corner.
It was odd. My only awareness of them revolved around their 'elite' inaccessibility.
Having brunch after a night of illicit foreplay seemed surreal.
Apprehension still danced around the edge of my consciousness, awaiting the arrival of some idiotic drama.
SO WHY DIDN'T YOU JUST **BAIL** IF YOU WERE SO WORRIED?
WOULD ***YOU*** HAVE?
I'D HAVE NAILED ASHLEY AND BEEN GONE ***WELL*** BEFORE BREAKFAST TIME.
YOU'RE A CLASS ACT, MY FRIEND.

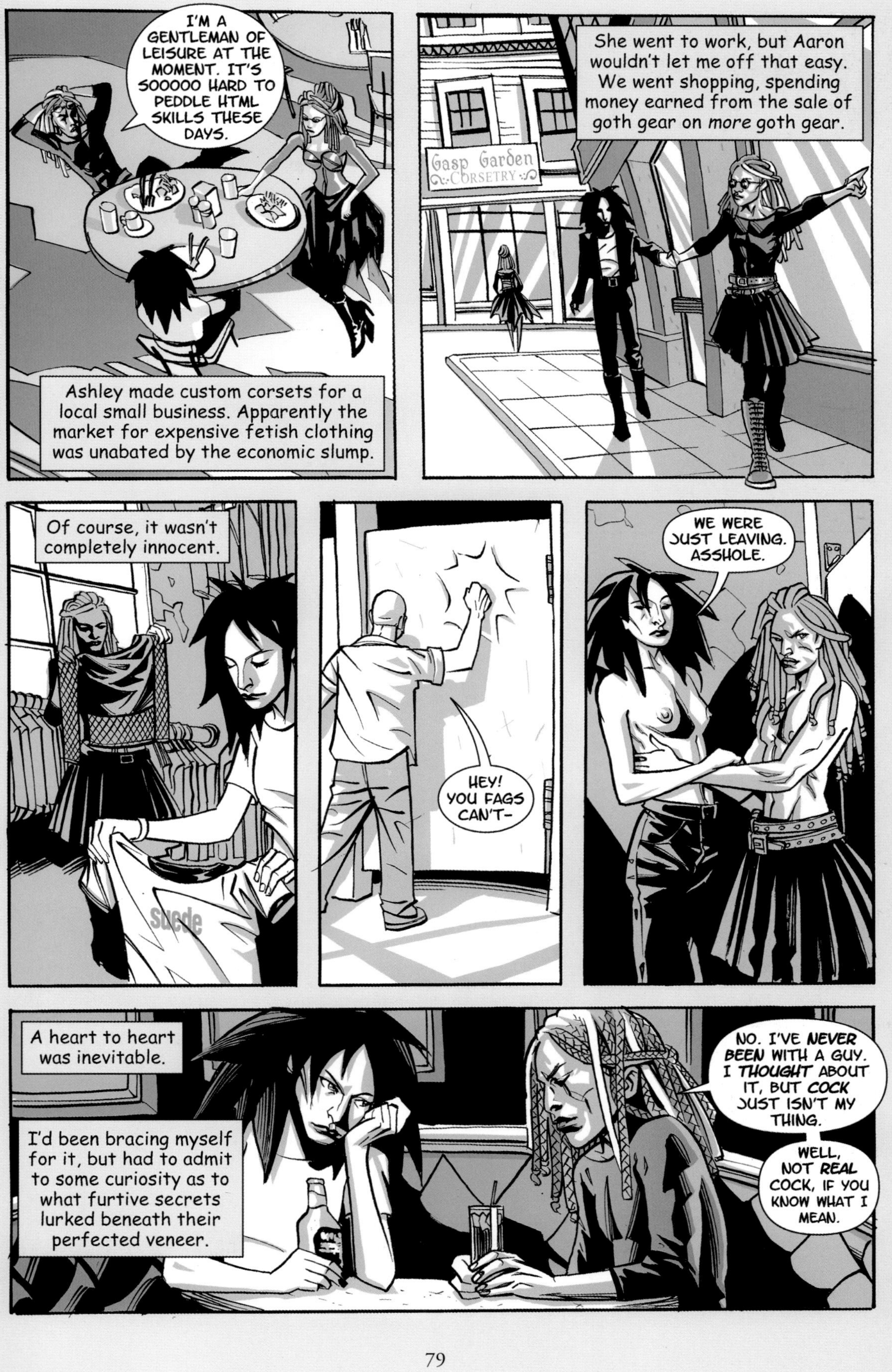
I'M A GENTLEMAN OF LEISURE AT THE MOMENT. IT'S SOOOOO HARD TO PEDDLE HTML SKILLS THESE DAYS.
Ashley made custom corsets for a local small business. Apparently the market for expensive fetish clothing was unabated by the economic slump.
She went to work, but Aaron wouldn't let me off that easy. We went shopping, spending money earned from the sale of goth gear on *more* goth gear.
Gasp Garden Corsetry
Of course, it wasn't completely innocent.
suede
HEY! YOU FAGS CAN'T-
WE WERE JUST LEAVING. ASSHOLE.
A heart to heart was inevitable.
I'd been bracing myself for it, but had to admit to some curiosity as to what furtive secrets lurked beneath their perfected veneer.
NO. I'VE **NEVER BEEN** WITH A GUY. I **THOUGHT** ABOUT IT, BUT **COCK** JUST ISN'T MY THING.
WELL, NOT **REAL** COCK, IF YOU KNOW WHAT I MEAN.

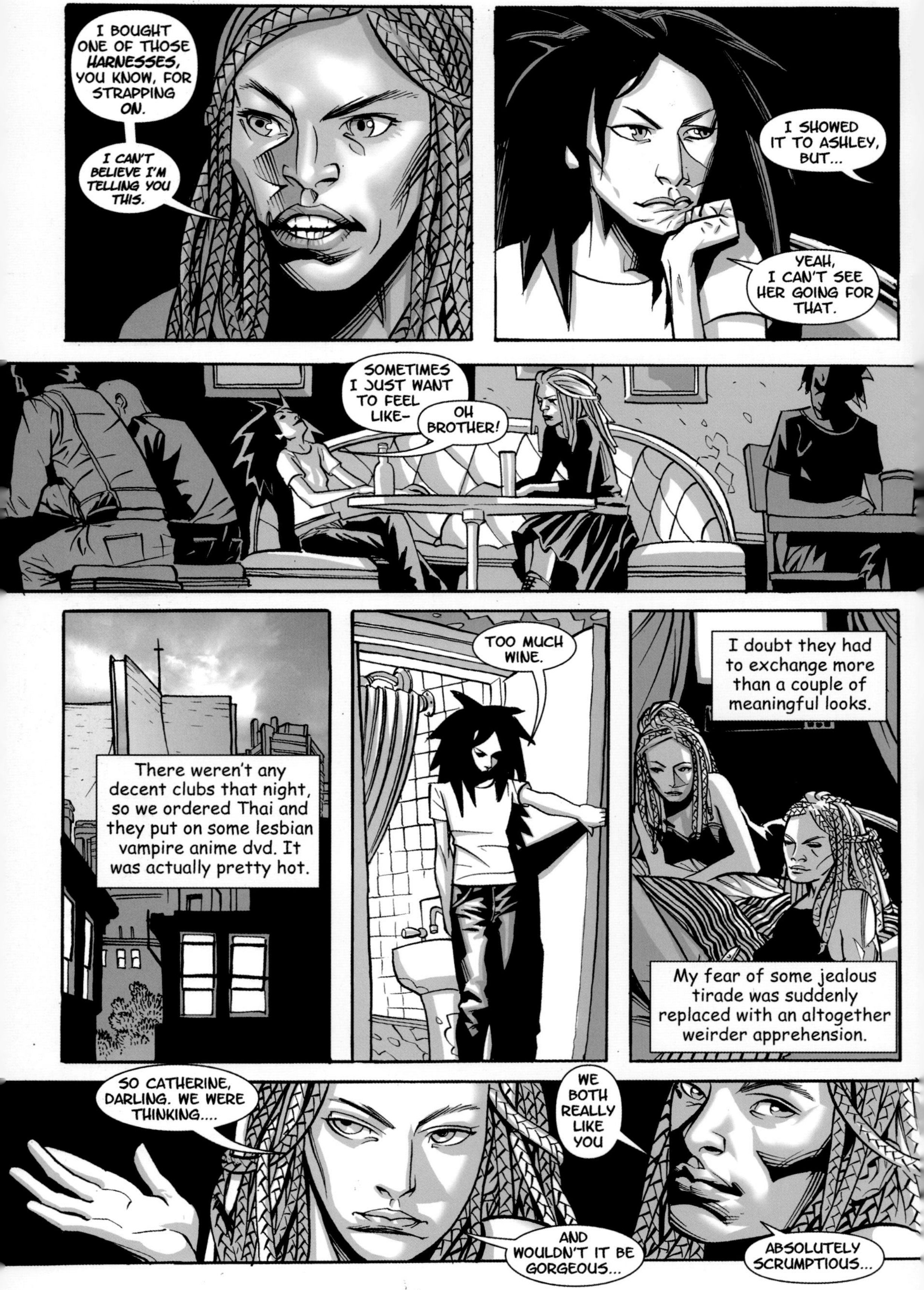
I BOUGHT ONE OF THOSE HARNESSES, YOU KNOW, FOR STRAPPING ON.
I CAN'T BELIEVE I'M TELLING YOU THIS.
I SHOWED IT TO ASHLEY, BUT...
YEAH, I CAN'T SEE HER GOING FOR THAT.
SOMETIMES I JUST WANT TO FEEL LIKE-
OH BROTHER!
There weren't any decent clubs that night, so we ordered Thai and they put on some lesbian vampire anime dvd. It was actually pretty hot.
TOO MUCH WINE.
I doubt they had to exchange more than a couple of meaningful looks.
My fear of some jealous tirade was suddenly replaced with an altogether weirder apprehension.
SO CATHERINE, DARLING. WE WERE THINKING....
WE BOTH REALLY LIKE YOU
AND WOULDN'T IT BE GORGEOUS...
ABSOLUTELY SCRUMPTIOUS...

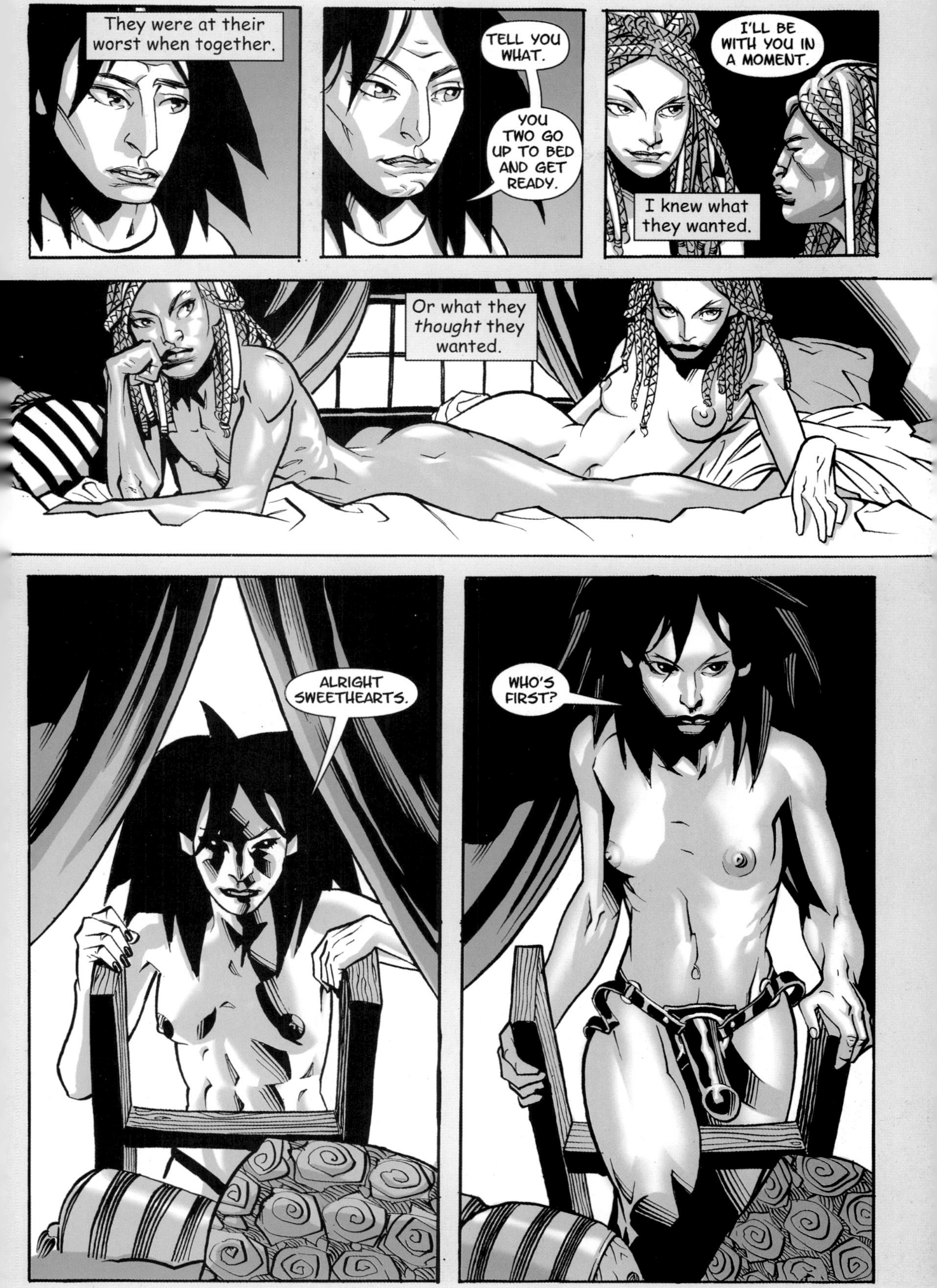
They were at their worst when together.
TELL YOU WHAT.
YOU TWO GO UP TO BED AND GET READY.
I'LL BE WITH YOU IN A MOMENT.
I knew what they wanted.
Or what they *thought* they wanted.
ALRIGHT SWEETHEARTS.
WHO'S FIRST?

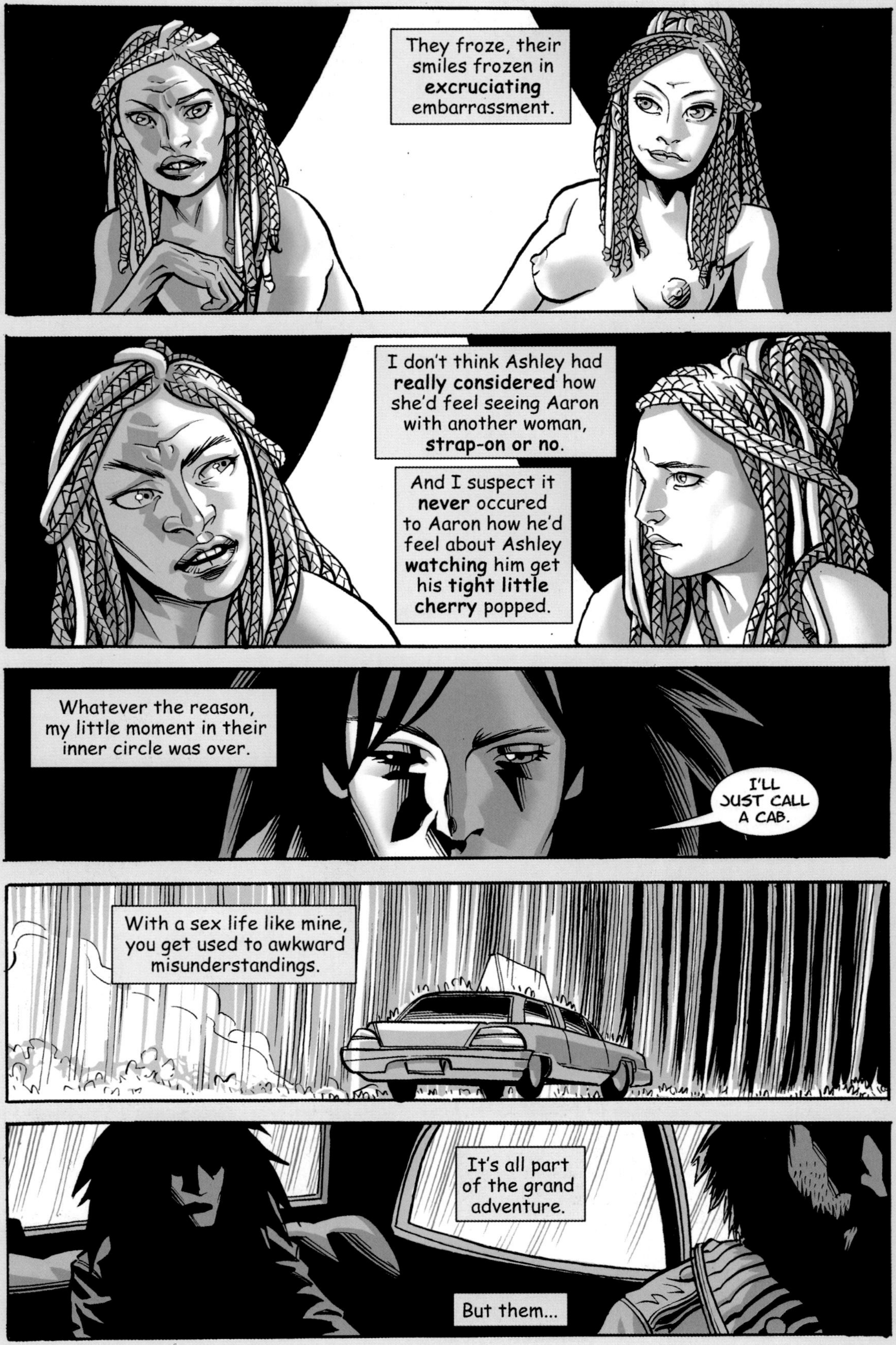
They froze, their smiles frozen in **excruciating** embarrassment.
I don't think Ashley had **really considered** how she'd feel seeing Aaron with another woman, **strap-on or no**.
And I suspect it **never** occured to Aaron how he'd feel about Ashley **watching** him get his **tight little cherry** popped.
Whatever the reason, my little moment in their inner circle was over.
I'LL JUST CALL A CAB.
With a sex life like mine, you get used to awkward misunderstandings.
It's all part of the grand adventure.
But them...

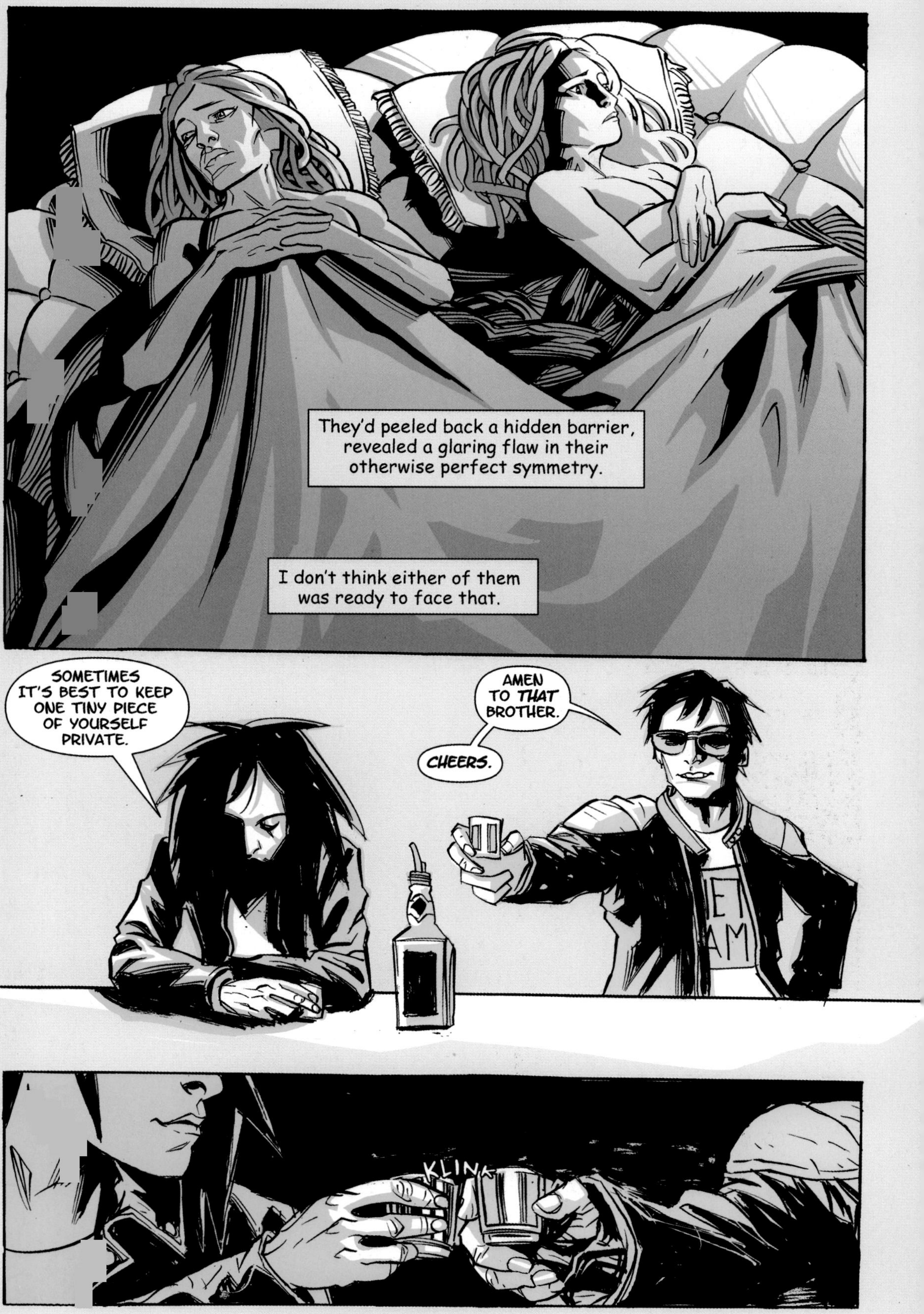
They'd peeled back a hidden barrier, revealed a glaring flaw in their otherwise perfect symmetry.
I don't think either of them was ready to face that.
SOMETIMES IT'S BEST TO KEEP ONE TINY PIECE OF YOURSELF PRIVATE.
AMEN TO *THAT* BROTHER.
CHEERS.
KLINK

chapter 4

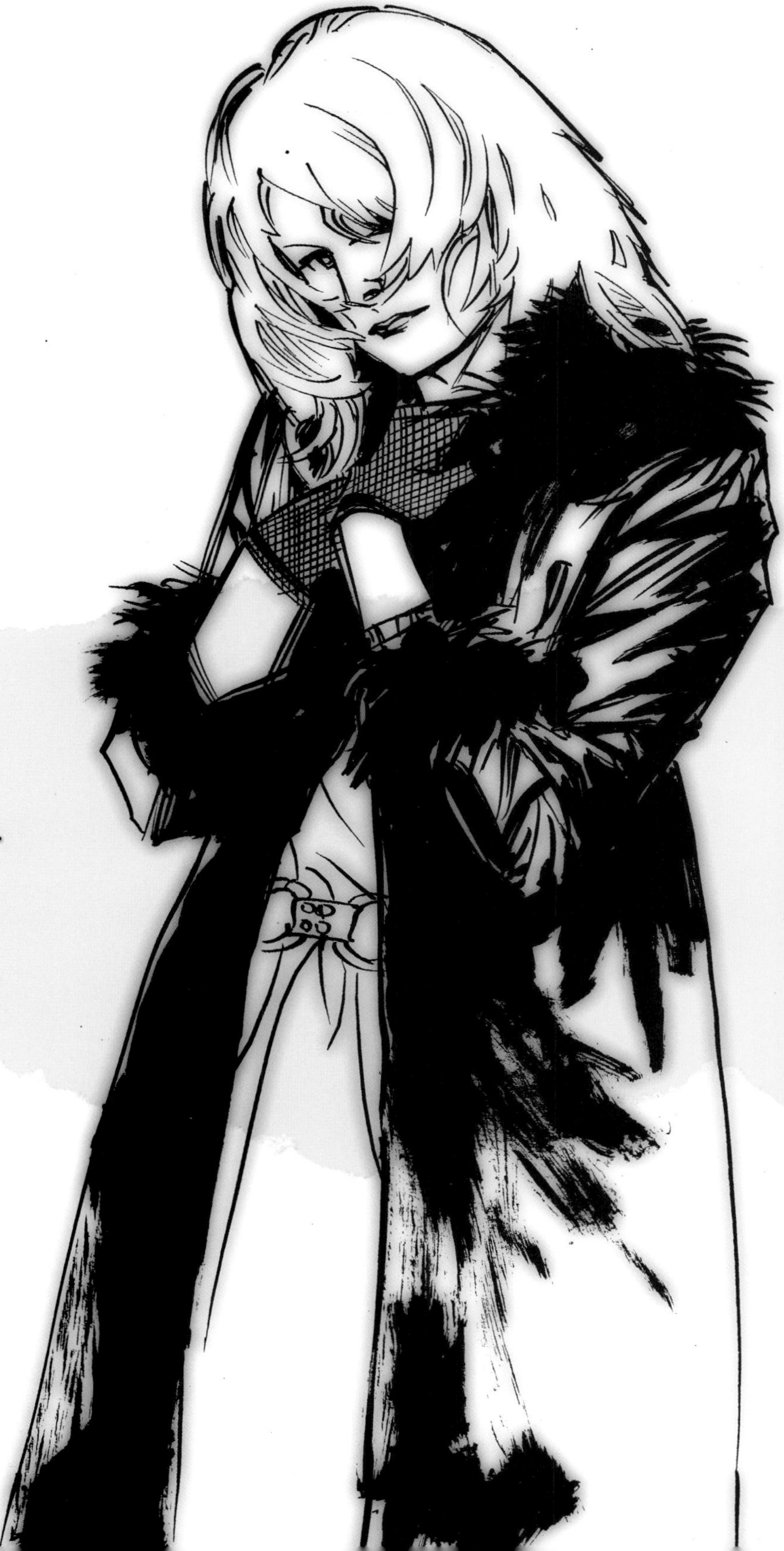

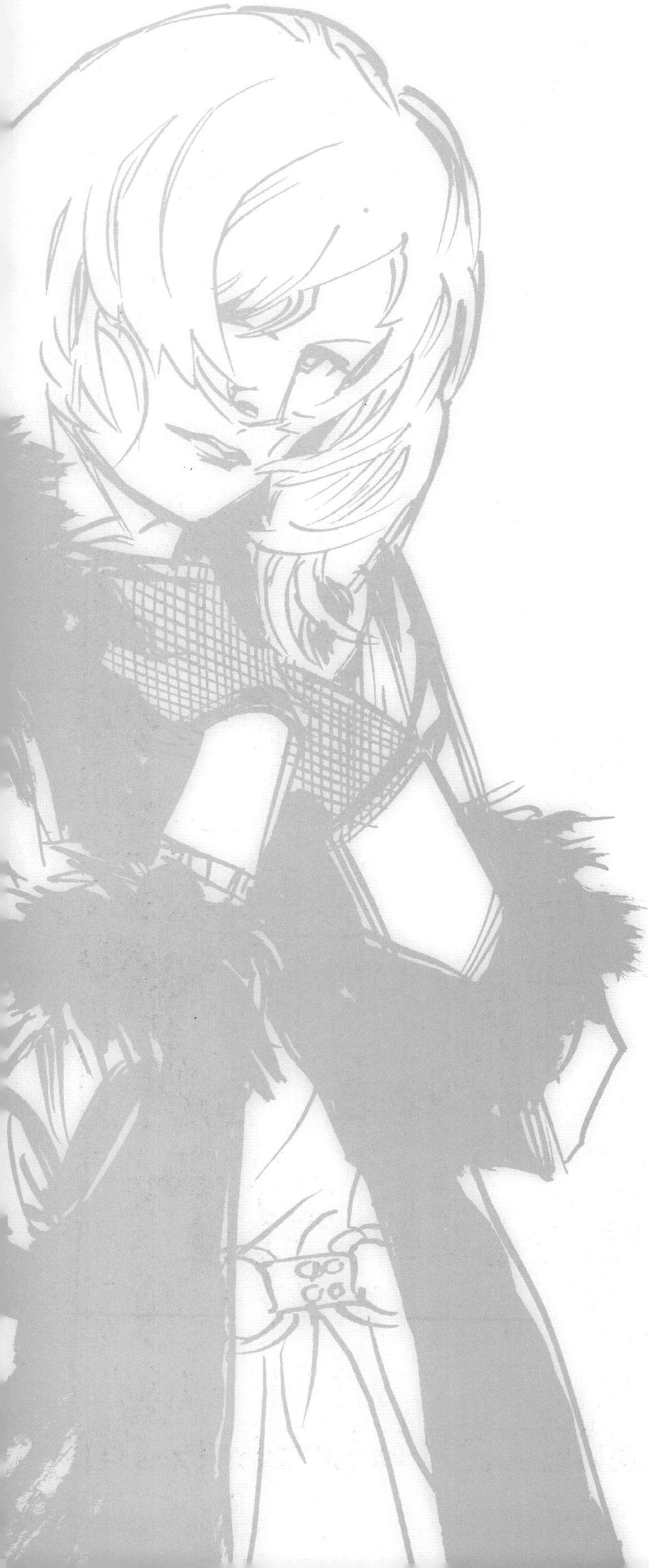

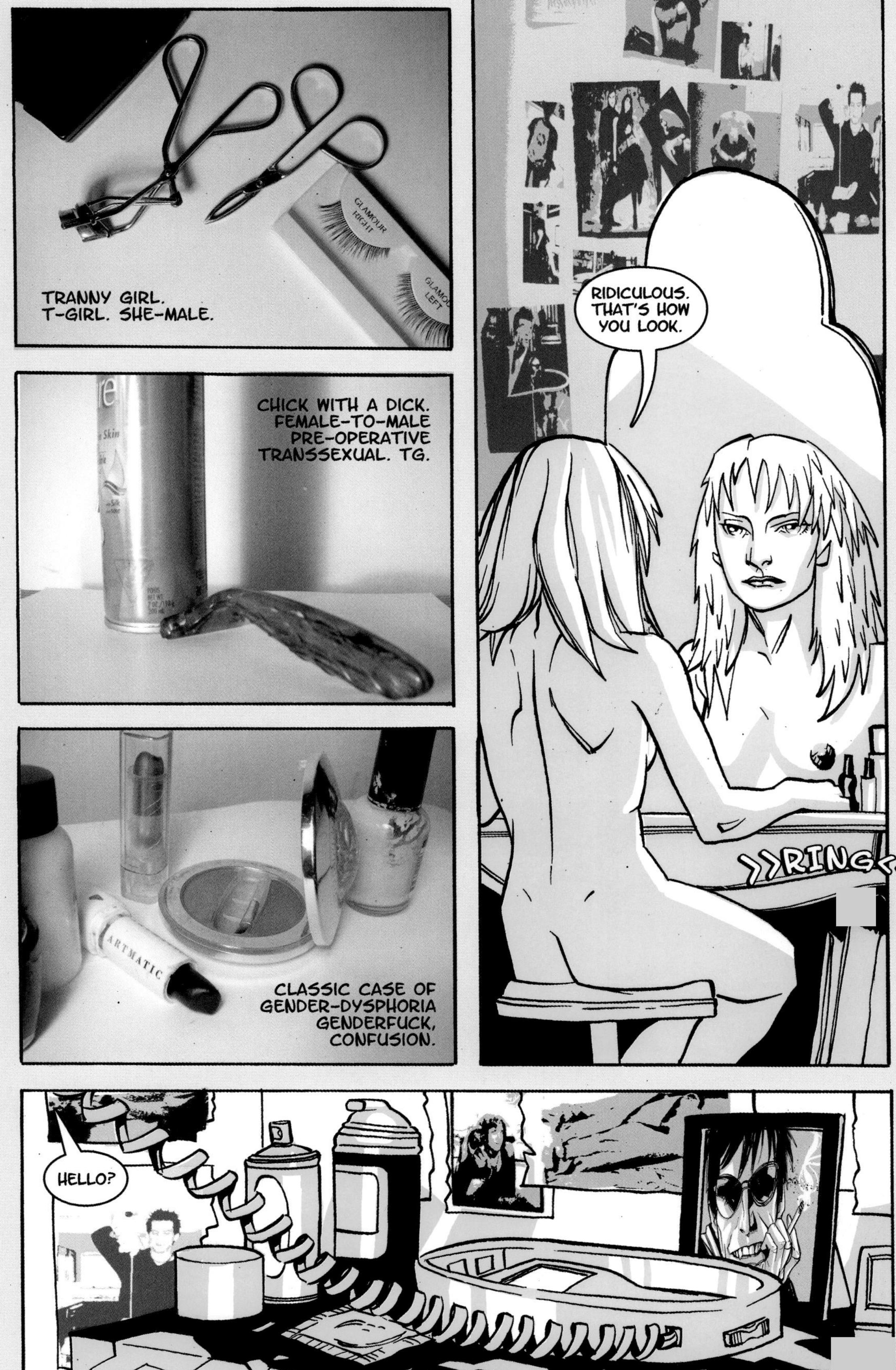
GLAMOUR RIGHT
GLAMOUR LEFT
TRANNY GIRL.
T-GIRL. SHE-MALE.
CHICK WITH A DICK.
FEMALE-TO-MALE
PRE-OPERATIVE
TRANSSEXUAL. TG.
ARTMATIC
CLASSIC CASE OF
GENDER-DYSPHORIA
GENDERFUCK,
CONFUSION.
RIDICULOUS.
THAT'S HOW
YOU LOOK.
>>RING<<
HELLO?

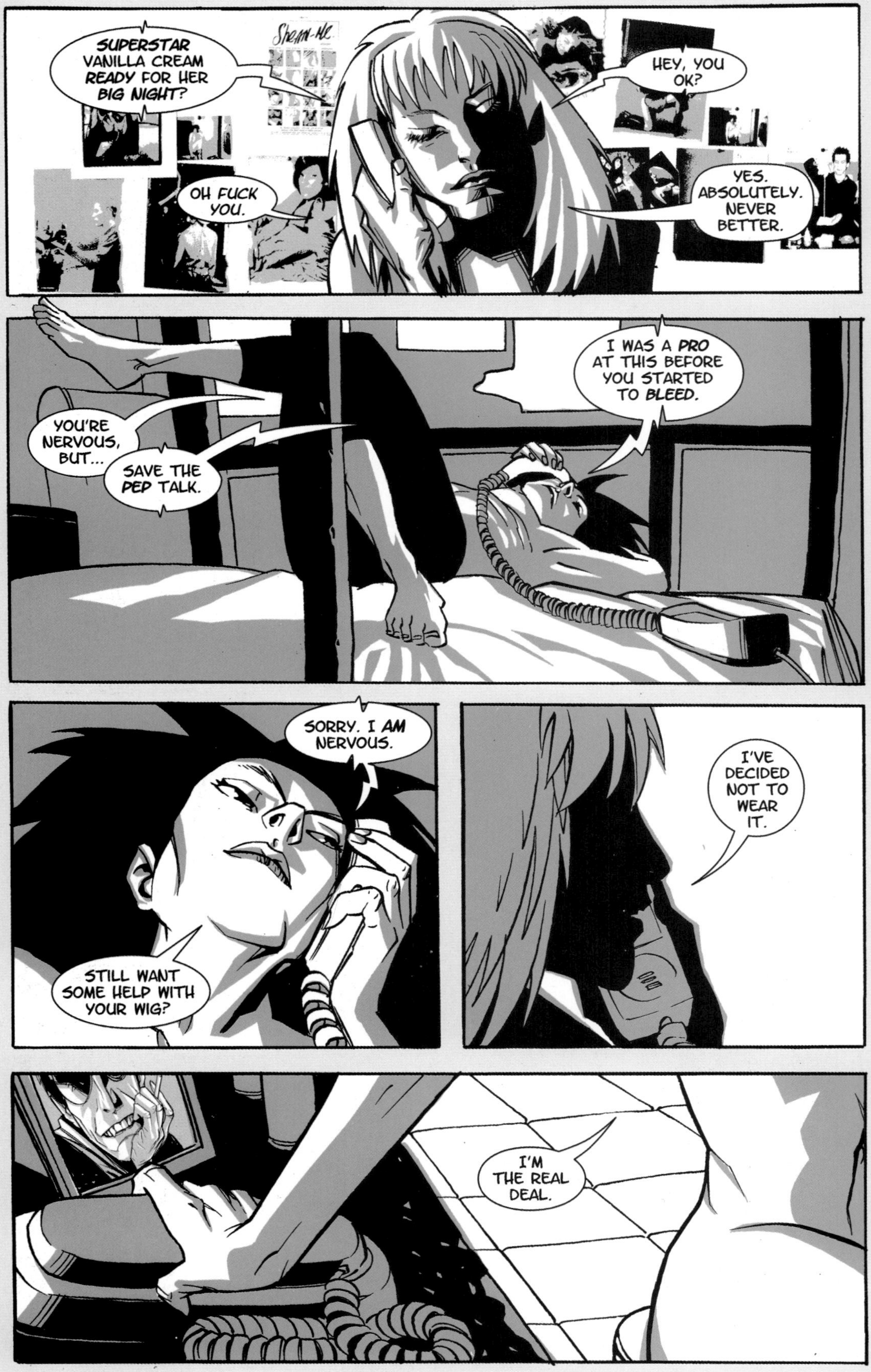
SUPERSTAR VANILLA CREAM READY FOR HER BIG NIGHT?
OH FUCK YOU.
HEY, YOU OK?
YES. ABSOLUTELY. NEVER BETTER.
YOU'RE NERVOUS, BUT...
SAVE THE PEP TALK.
I WAS A PRO AT THIS BEFORE YOU STARTED TO BLEED.
SORRY. I AM NERVOUS.
STILL WANT SOME HELP WITH YOUR WIG?
I'VE DECIDED NOT TO WEAR IT.
I'M THE REAL DEAL.

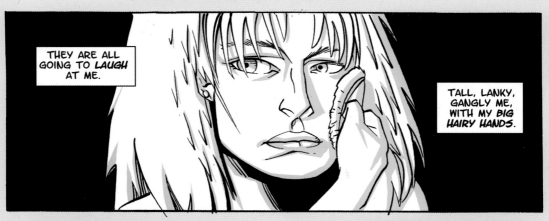

THEY ARE ALL GOING TO *LAUGH* AT ME.

TALL, LANKY, GANGLY ME, WITH MY *BIG HAIRY HANDS.*

THEY SAY IT'S THE HANDS THAT *'GIVE AWAY'* A TRANSSEXUAL.

THIS IS NOT TRUE; IT'S MOSTLY IN THE ATTITUDE.

THE PERFECT *DREAM-DATE* DIVALICIOUS SUPERSTAR

WALK INTO EVERY SITUATION LIKE YOU *OWN* IT,

EVERY BAR, BATHROOM, AND HORRIBLE HOTEL *KNOWING* YOU ARE THE *ULTIMATE UNDISCOVERED LIE,*

AND THE WORLD'S YOURS.

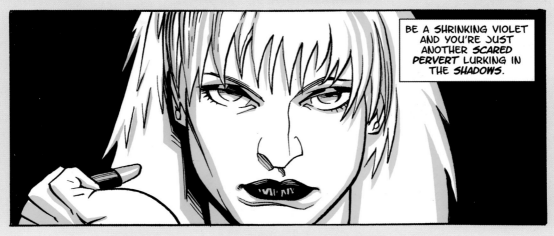

BE A SHRINKING VIOLET AND YOU'RE JUST ANOTHER *SCARED PERVERT* LURKING IN THE *SHADOWS.*

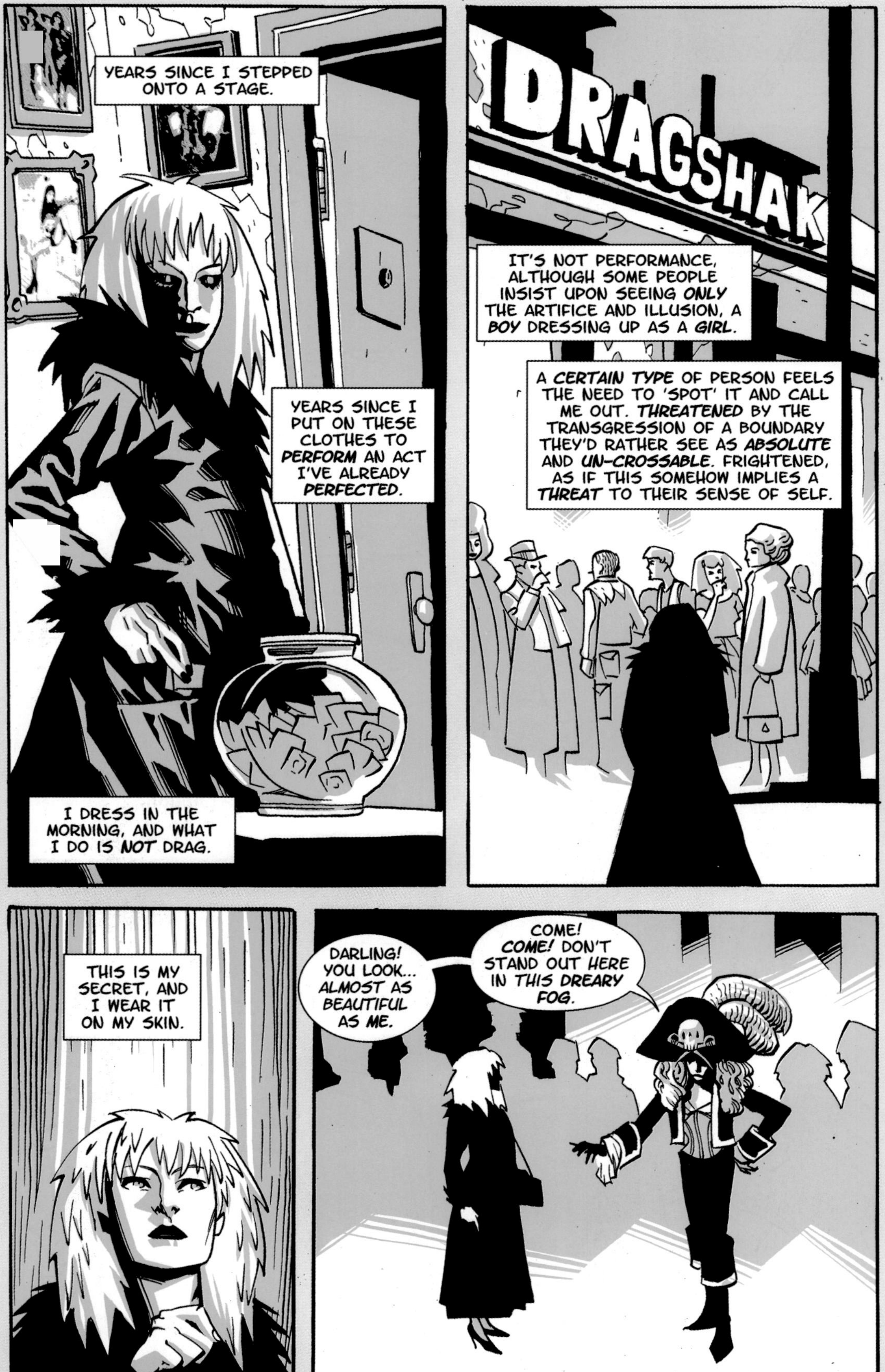
YEARS SINCE I STEPPED ONTO A STAGE.
YEARS SINCE I PUT ON THESE CLOTHES TO PERFORM AN ACT I'VE ALREADY PERFECTED.
I DRESS IN THE MORNING, AND WHAT I DO IS NOT DRAG.
DRAGSHAK
IT'S NOT PERFORMANCE, ALTHOUGH SOME PEOPLE INSIST UPON SEEING ONLY THE ARTIFICE AND ILLUSION, A BOY DRESSING UP AS A GIRL.
A CERTAIN TYPE OF PERSON FEELS THE NEED TO 'SPOT' IT AND CALL ME OUT. THREATENED BY THE TRANSGRESSION OF A BOUNDARY THEY'D RATHER SEE AS ABSOLUTE AND UN-CROSSABLE. FRIGHTENED, AS IF THIS SOMEHOW IMPLIES A THREAT TO THEIR SENSE OF SELF.
THIS IS MY SECRET, AND I WEAR IT ON MY SKIN.
DARLING! YOU LOOK... ALMOST AS BEAUTIFUL AS ME.
COME! COME! DON'T STAND OUT HERE IN THIS DREARY FOG.

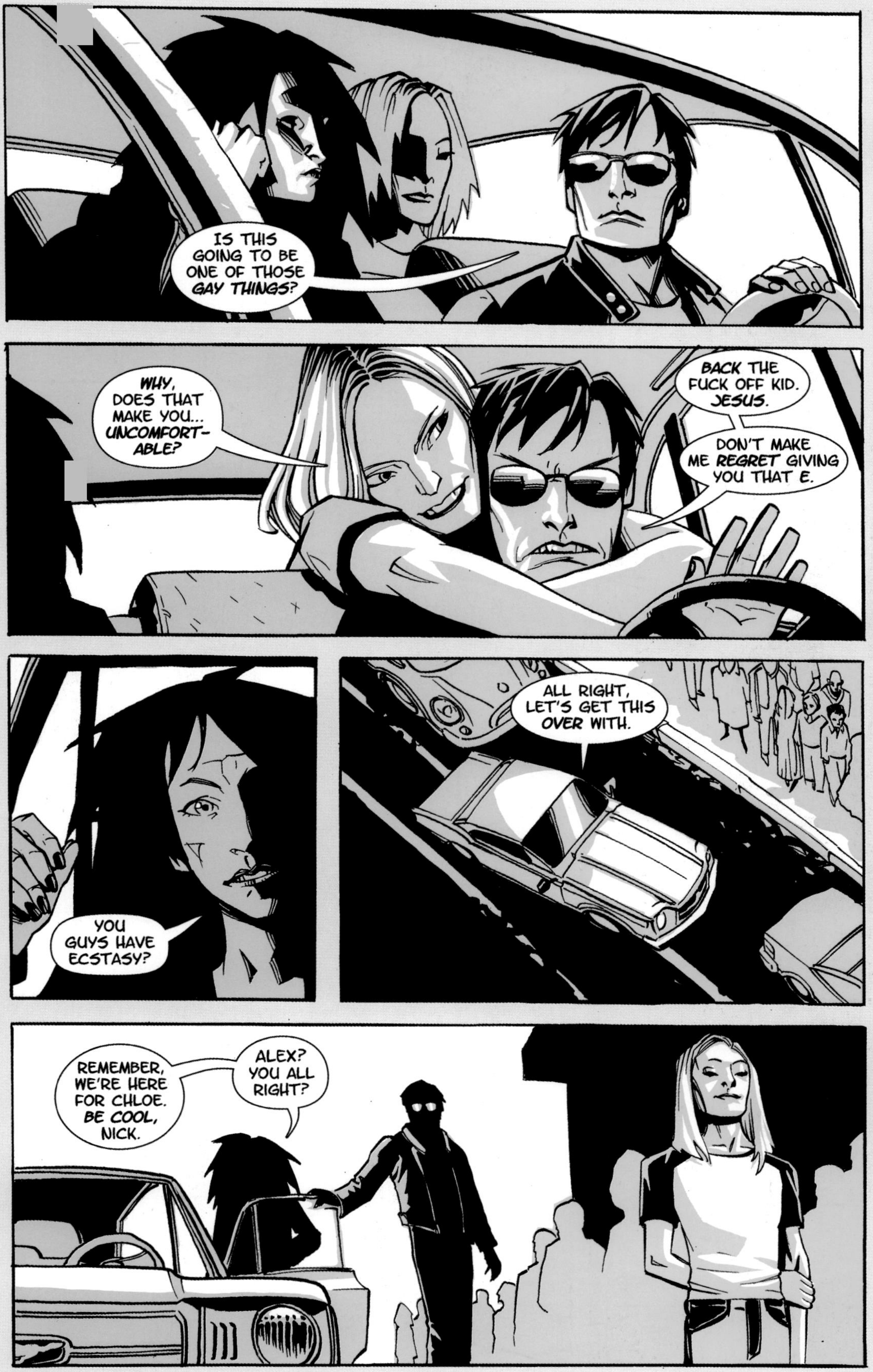
IS THIS GOING TO BE ONE OF THOSE GAY THINGS?
WHY, DOES THAT MAKE YOU... UNCOMFORT-ABLE?
BACK THE FUCK OFF KID. JESUS.
DON'T MAKE ME REGRET GIVING YOU THAT E.
YOU GUYS HAVE ECSTASY?
ALL RIGHT, LET'S GET THIS OVER WITH.
REMEMBER, WE'RE HERE FOR CHLOE. BE COOL, NICK.
ALEX? YOU ALL RIGHT?

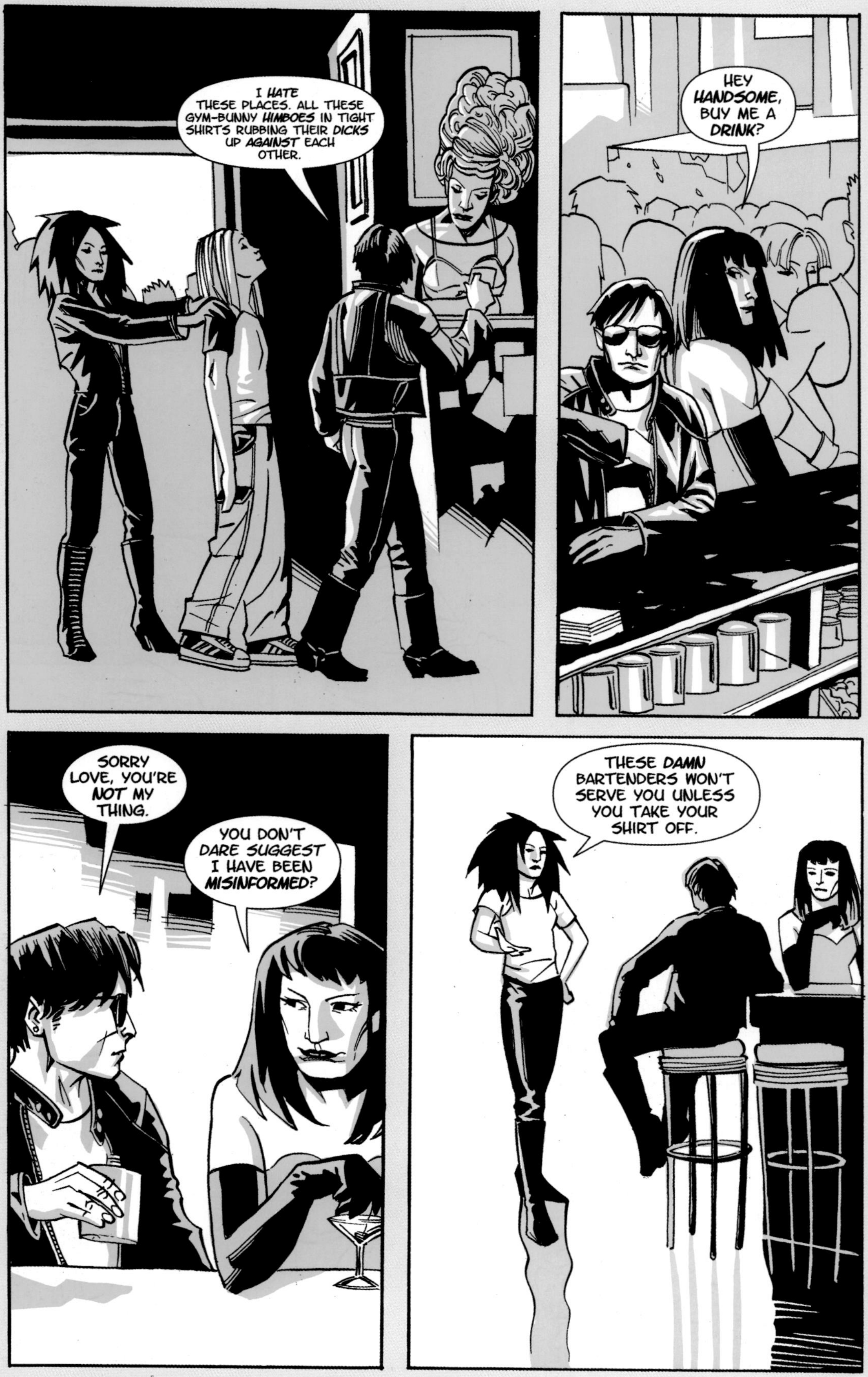
I HATE THESE PLACES. ALL THESE GYM-BUNNY HIMBOES IN TIGHT SHIRTS RUBBING THEIR DICKS UP AGAINST EACH OTHER.
HEY HANDSOME, BUY ME A DRINK?
SORRY LOVE, YOU'RE NOT MY THING.
YOU DON'T DARE SUGGEST I HAVE BEEN MISINFORMED?
THESE DAMN BARTENDERS WON'T SERVE YOU UNLESS YOU TAKE YOUR SHIRT OFF.

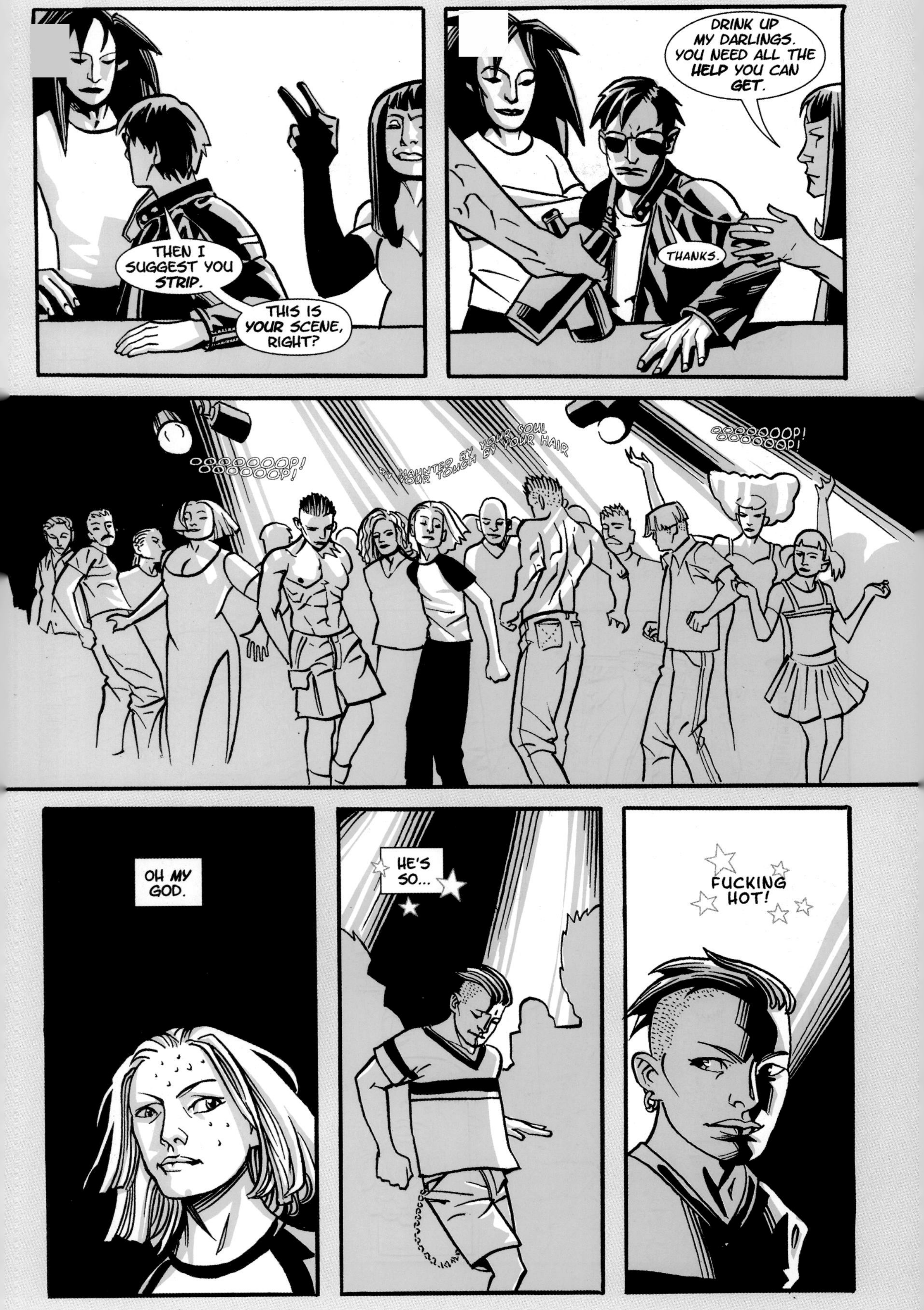
THEN I SUGGEST YOU STRIP.
THIS IS YOUR SCENE, RIGHT?
DRINK UP MY DARLINGS. YOU NEED ALL THE HELP YOU CAN GET.
THANKS.
OOOOOOOOP! OOOOOOOP!
HAUNTED BY YOUR SOUL
YOUR TOUCH BY YOUR HAIR
OOOOOOOOP! OOOOOOOP!
OH MY GOD.
HE'S SO...
FUCKING HOT!

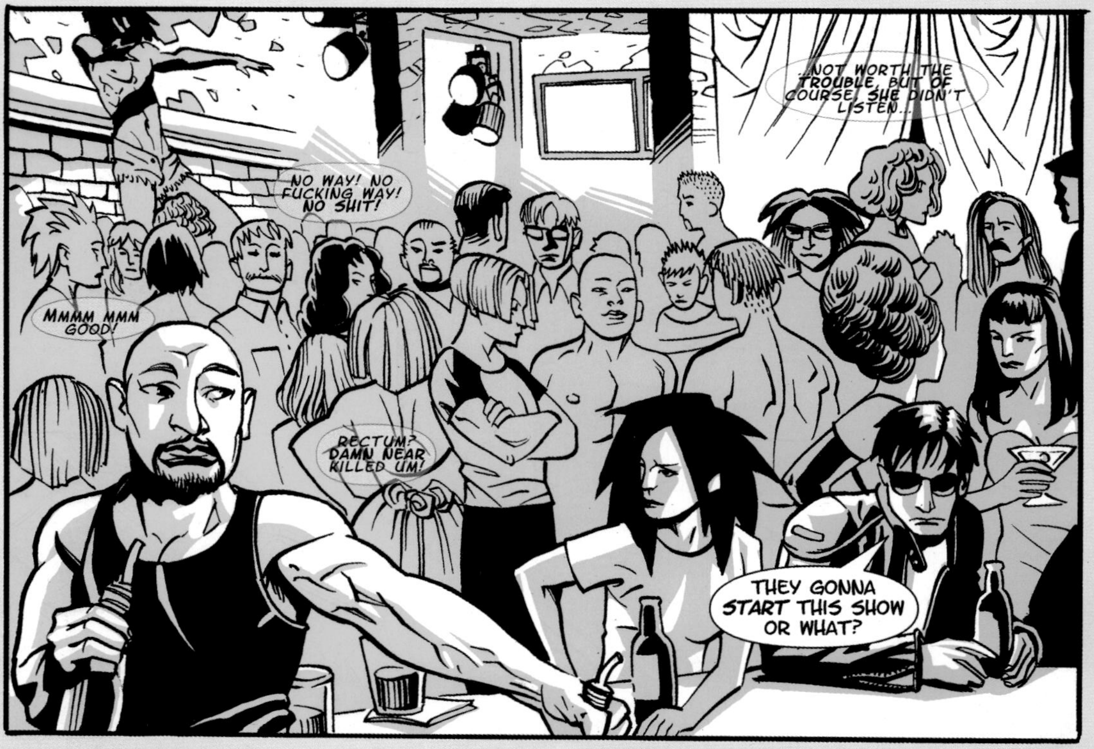
...NOT WORTH THE TROUBLE, BUT OF COURSE, SHE DIDN'T LISTEN...
NO WAY! NO FUCKING WAY! NO SHIT!
MMMM MMM GOOD!
RECTUM? DAMN NEAR KILLED UM!
THEY GONNA START THIS SHOW OR WHAT?

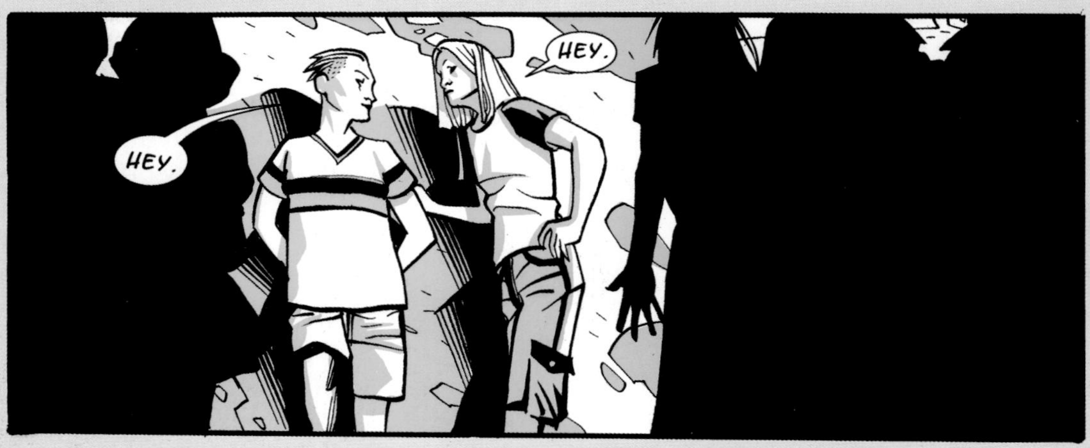
HEY.
HEY.

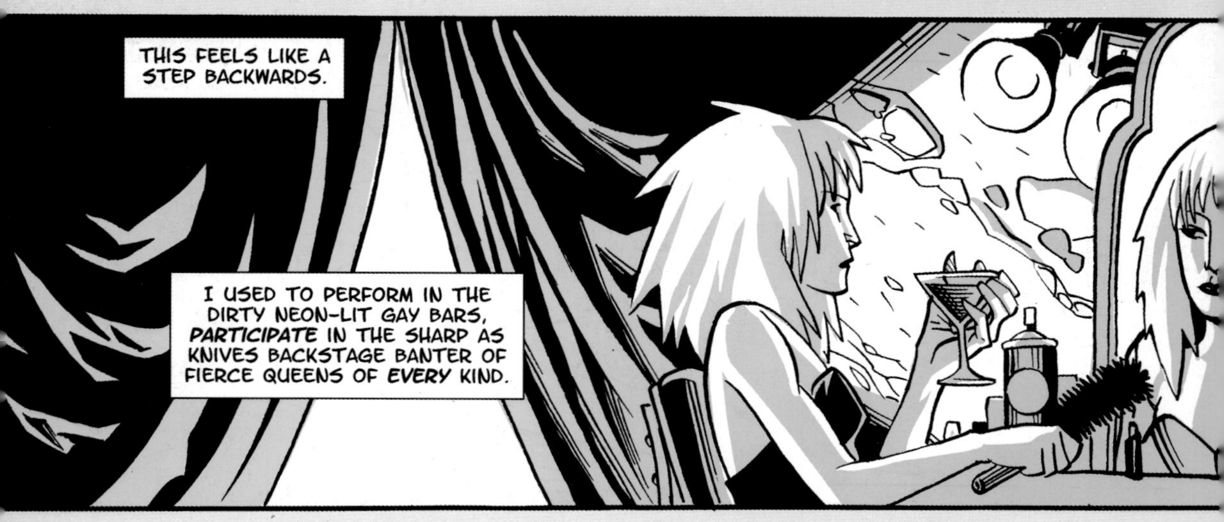
THIS FEELS LIKE A STEP BACKWARDS.
I USED TO PERFORM IN THE DIRTY NEON-LIT GAY BARS, PARTICIPATE IN THE SHARP AS KNIVES BACKSTAGE BANTER OF FIERCE QUEENS OF EVERY KIND.

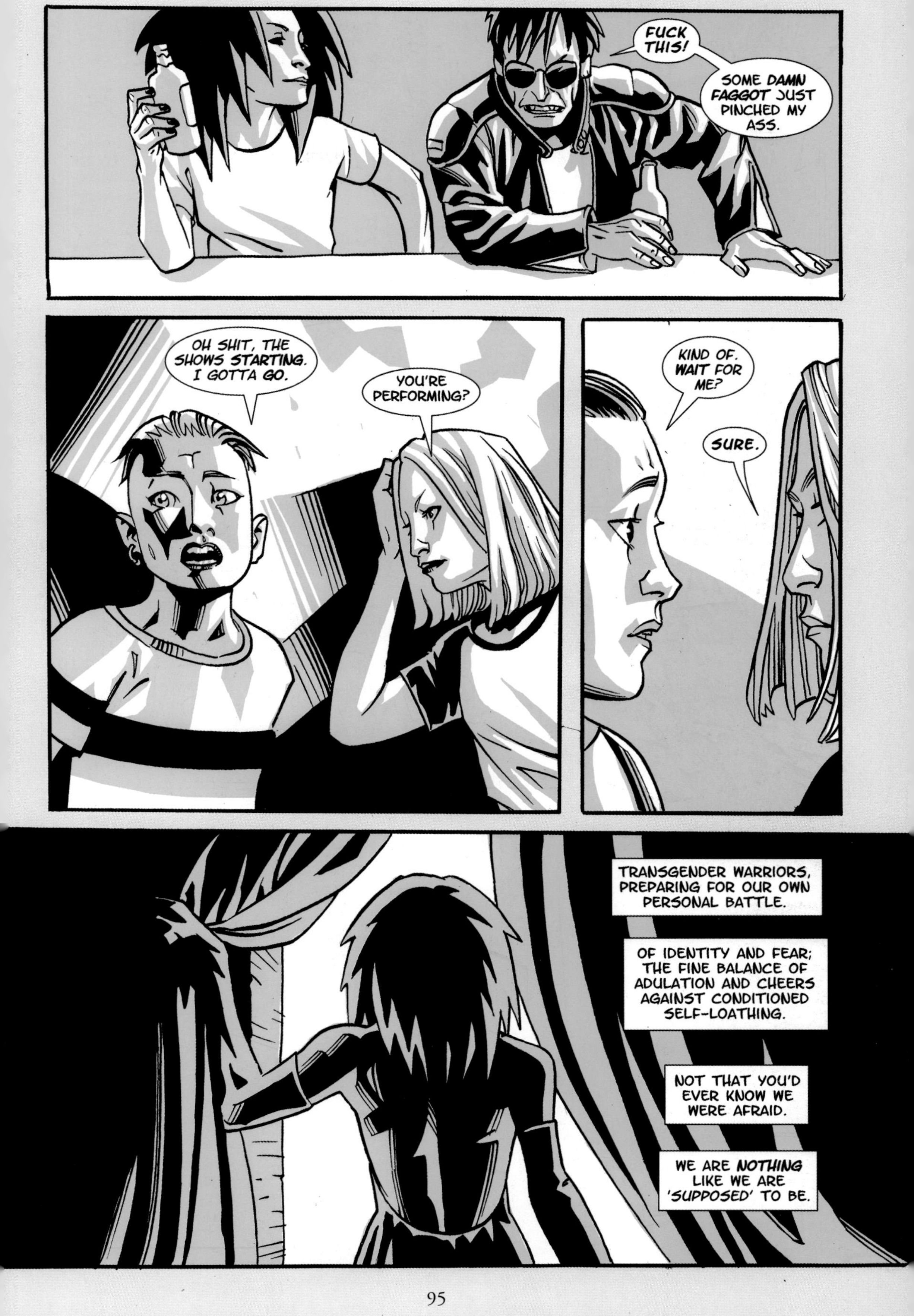
FUCK THIS!
SOME DAMN FAGGOT JUST PINCHED MY ASS.
OH SHIT, THE SHOWS STARTING. I GOTTA GO.
YOU'RE PERFORMING?
KIND OF. WAIT FOR ME?
SURE.
TRANSGENDER WARRIORS, PREPARING FOR OUR OWN PERSONAL BATTLE.
OF IDENTITY AND FEAR; THE FINE BALANCE OF ADULATION AND CHEERS AGAINST CONDITIONED SELF-LOATHING.
NOT THAT YOU'D EVER KNOW WE WERE AFRAID.
WE ARE NOTHING LIKE WE ARE 'SUPPOSED' TO BE.

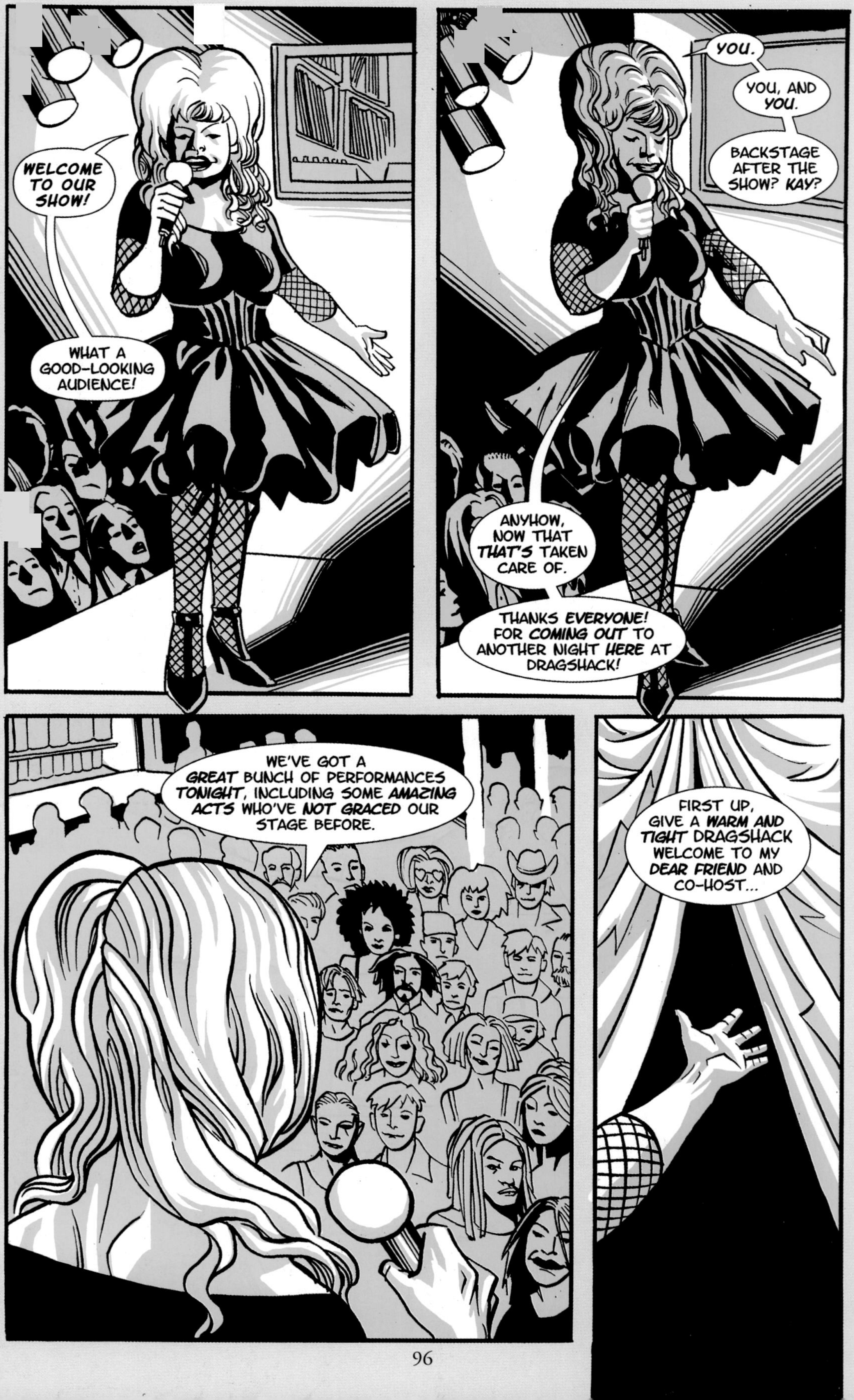
WELCOME TO OUR SHOW!
WHAT A GOOD-LOOKING AUDIENCE!
YOU.
YOU, AND YOU.
BACKSTAGE AFTER THE SHOW? KAY?
ANYHOW, NOW THAT THAT'S TAKEN CARE OF.
THANKS EVERYONE! FOR COMING OUT TO ANOTHER NIGHT HERE AT DRAGSHACK!
WE'VE GOT A GREAT BUNCH OF PERFORMANCES TONIGHT, INCLUDING SOME AMAZING ACTS WHO'VE NOT GRACED OUR STAGE BEFORE.
FIRST UP, GIVE A WARM AND TIGHT DRAGSHACK WELCOME TO MY DEAR FRIEND AND CO-HOST...

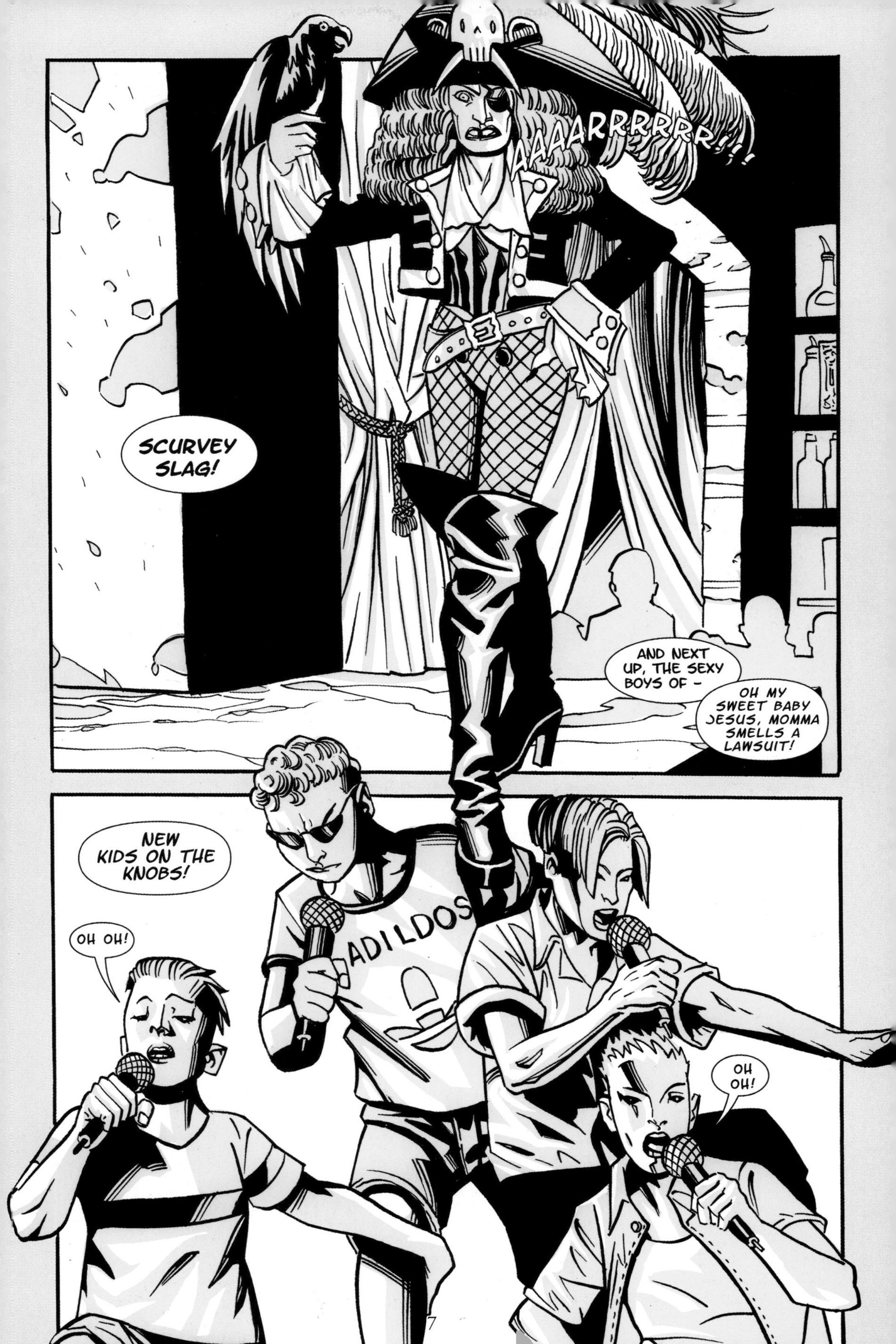
AAAARRRRRRR!!!
SCURVEY SLAG!
AND NEXT UP, THE SEXY BOYS OF –
OH MY SWEET BABY JESUS, MOMMA SMELLS A LAWSUIT!
NEW KIDS ON THE KNOBS!
ADILDOS
OH OH!
OH OH!

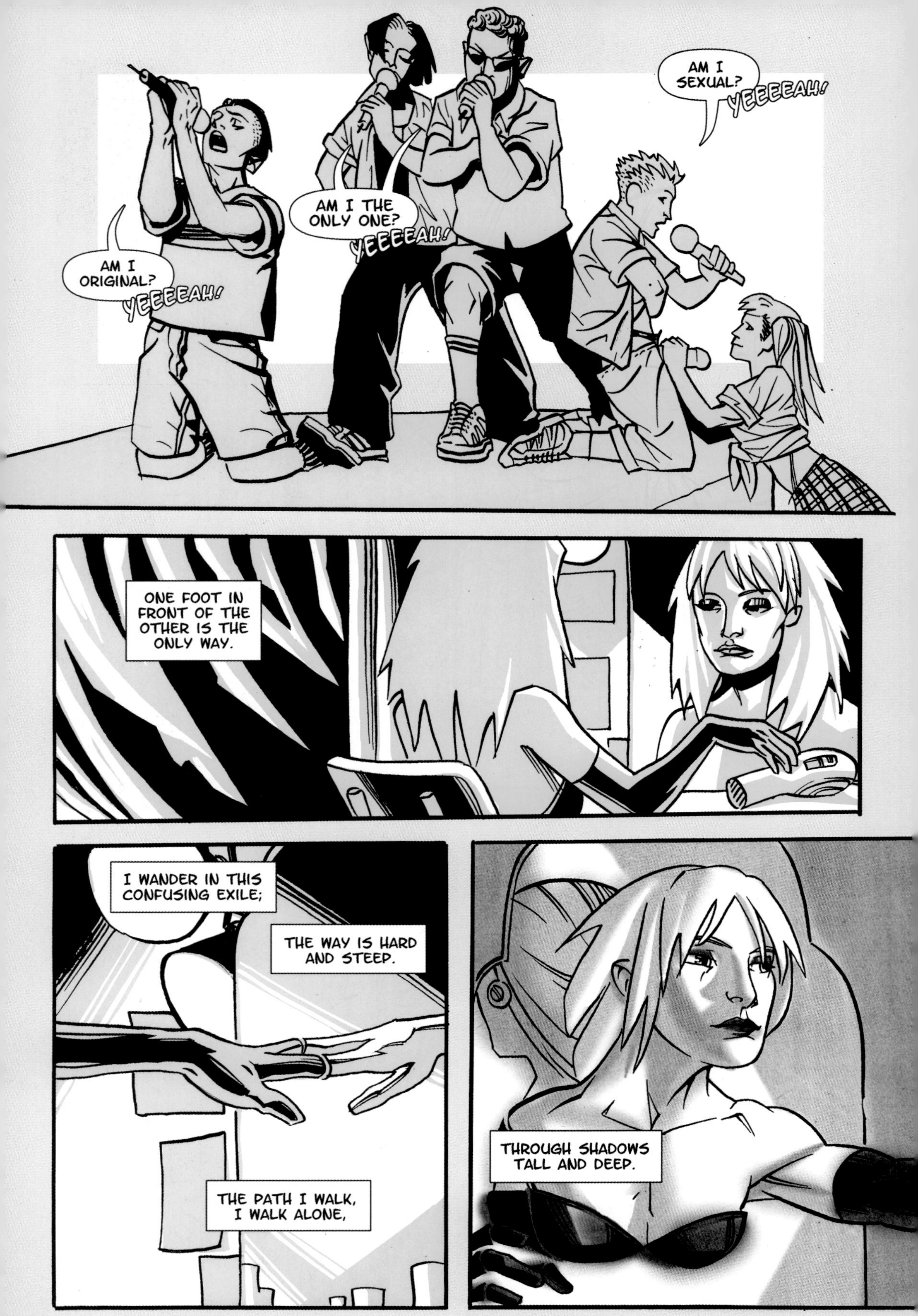
AM I ORIGINAL?
YEEEEAH!
AM I THE ONLY ONE?
YEEEEAH!
AM I SEXUAL?
YEEEEAH!
ONE FOOT IN FRONT OF THE OTHER IS THE ONLY WAY.
I WANDER IN THIS CONFUSING EXILE;
THE WAY IS HARD AND STEEP.
THE PATH I WALK, I WALK ALONE,
THROUGH SHADOWS TALL AND DEEP.

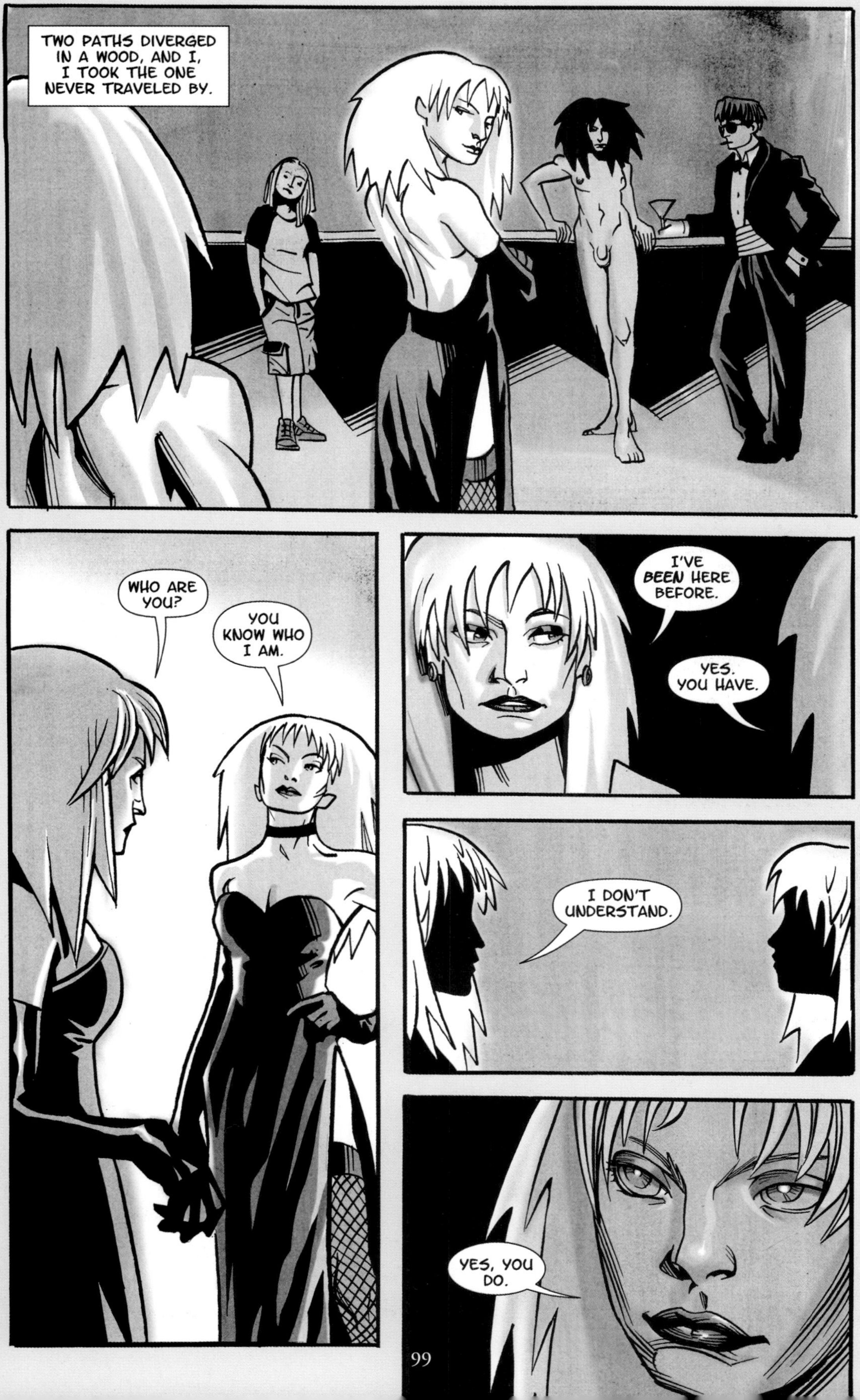
TWO PATHS DIVERGED IN A WOOD, AND I, I TOOK THE ONE NEVER TRAVELED BY.
WHO ARE YOU?
YOU KNOW WHO I AM.
I'VE *BEEN* HERE BEFORE.
YES. YOU HAVE.
I DON'T UNDERSTAND.
YES, YOU DO.

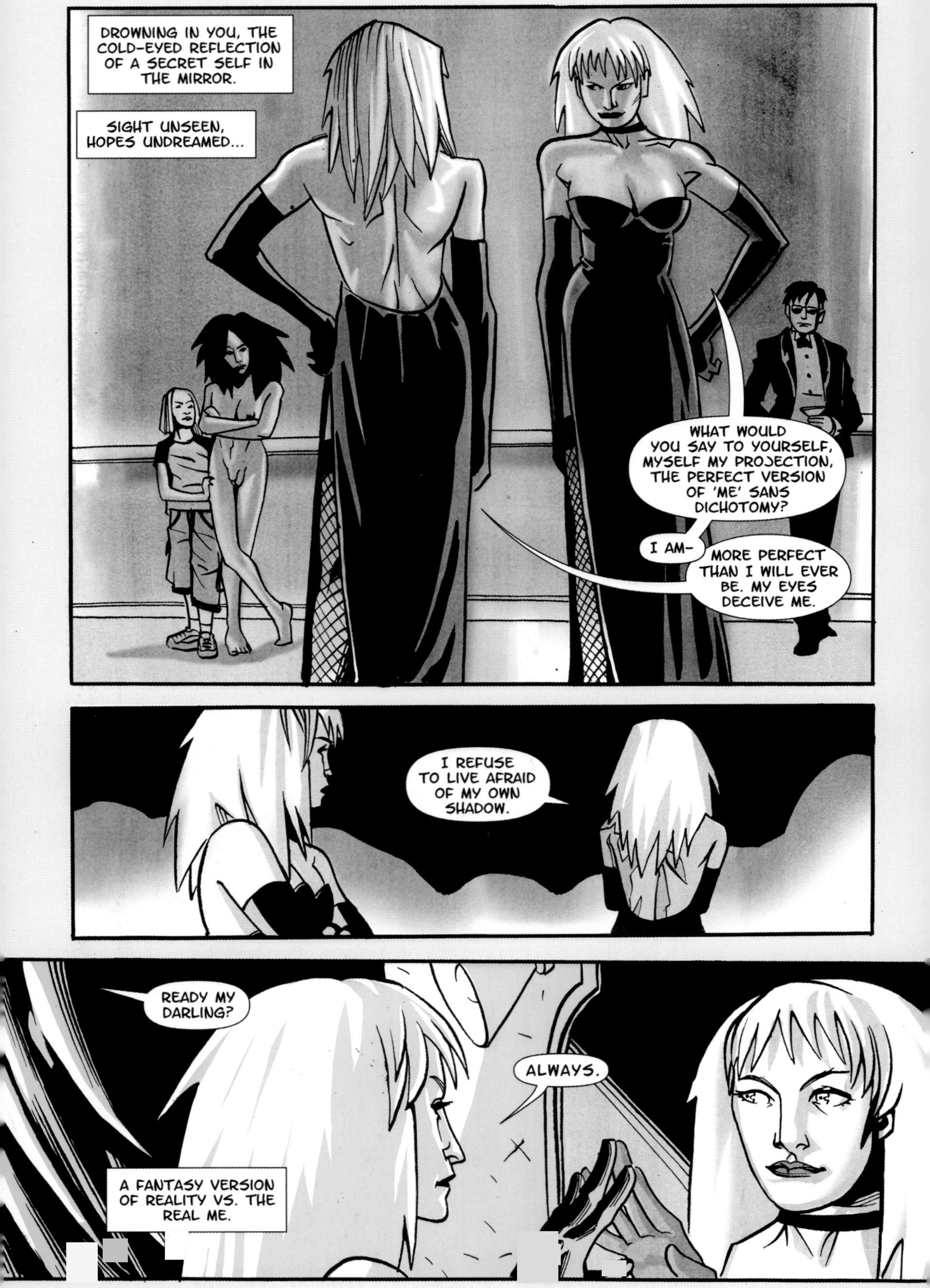
DROWNING IN YOU, THE COLD-EYED REFLECTION OF A SECRET SELF IN THE MIRROR.
SIGHT UNSEEN, HOPES UNDREAMED...
WHAT WOULD YOU SAY TO YOURSELF, MYSELF MY PROJECTION, THE PERFECT VERSION OF 'ME' SANS DICHOTOMY?
I AM-
MORE PERFECT THAN I WILL EVER BE. MY EYES DECEIVE ME.
I REFUSE TO LIVE AFRAID OF MY OWN SHADOW.
READY MY DARLING?
ALWAYS.
A FANTASY VERSION OF REALITY VS. THE REAL ME.

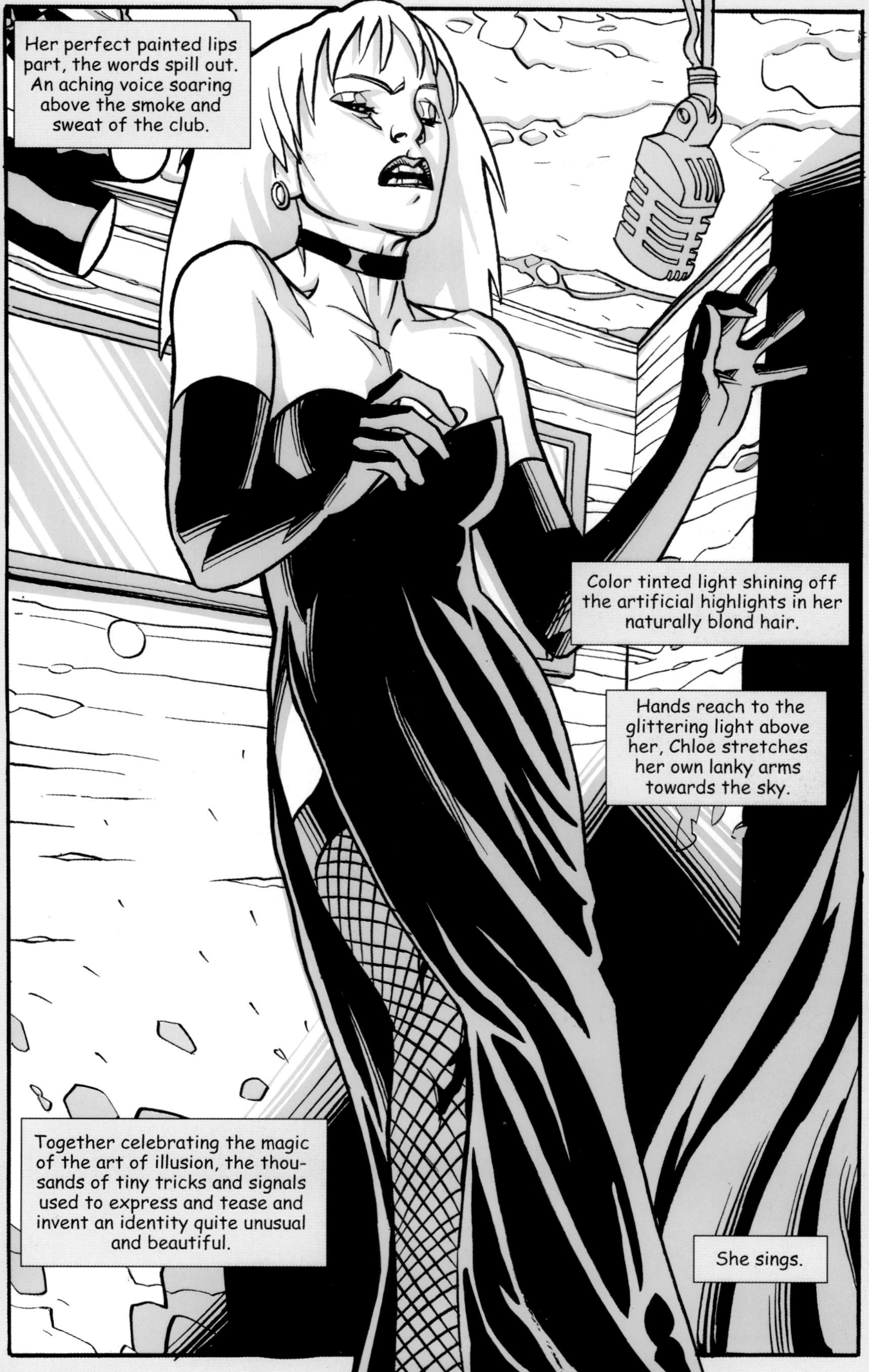

Her perfect painted lips part, the words spill out. An aching voice soaring above the smoke and sweat of the club.
Color tinted light shining off the artificial highlights in her naturally blond hair.
Hands reach to the glittering light above her, Chloe stretches her own lanky arms towards the sky.
Together celebrating the magic of the art of illusion, the thousands of tiny tricks and signals used to express and tease and invent an identity quite unusual and beautiful.
She sings.

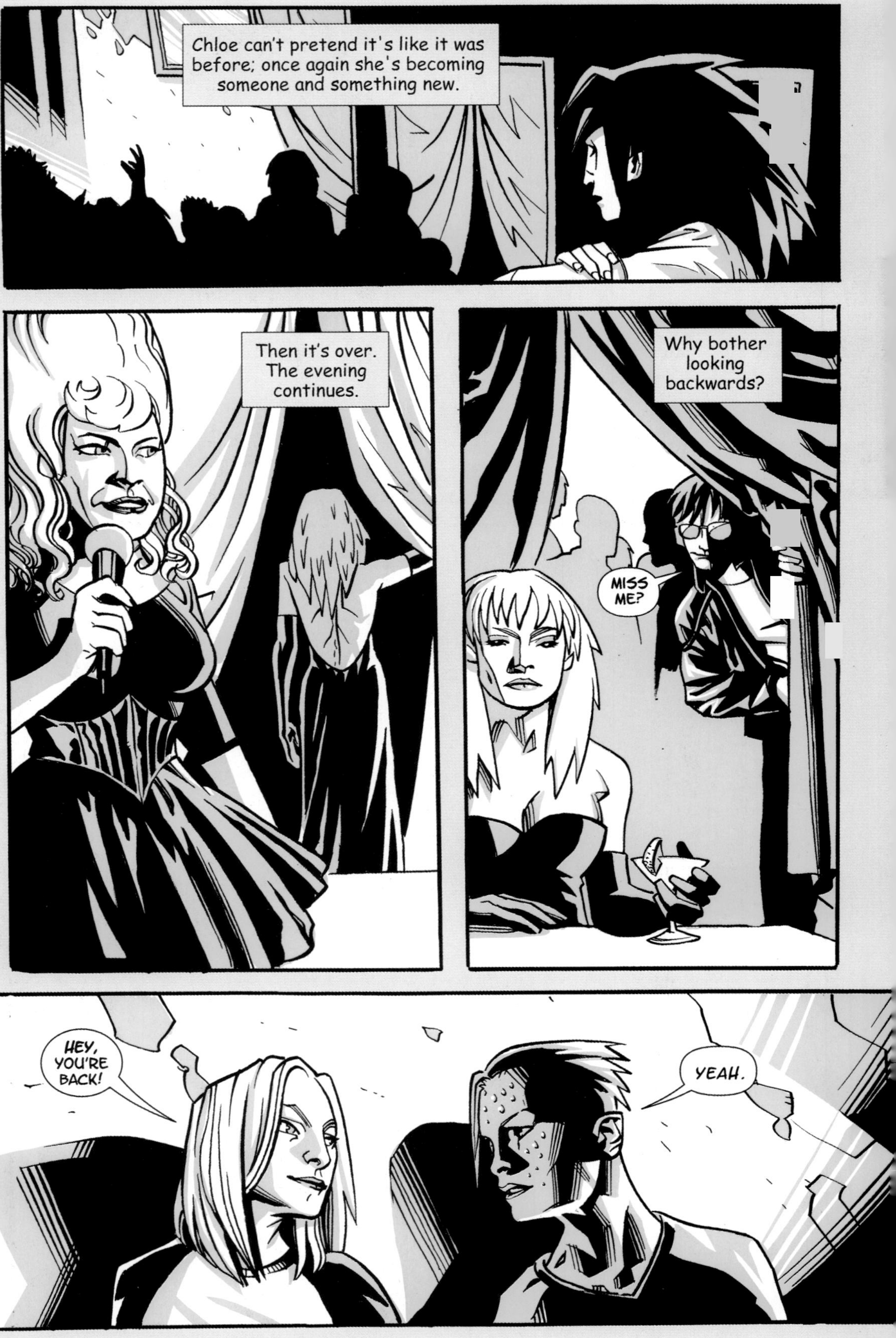
Chloe can't pretend it's like it was before; once again she's becoming someone and something new.
Then it's over. The evening continues.
Why bother looking backwards?
MISS ME?
HEY, YOU'RE BACK!
YEAH.

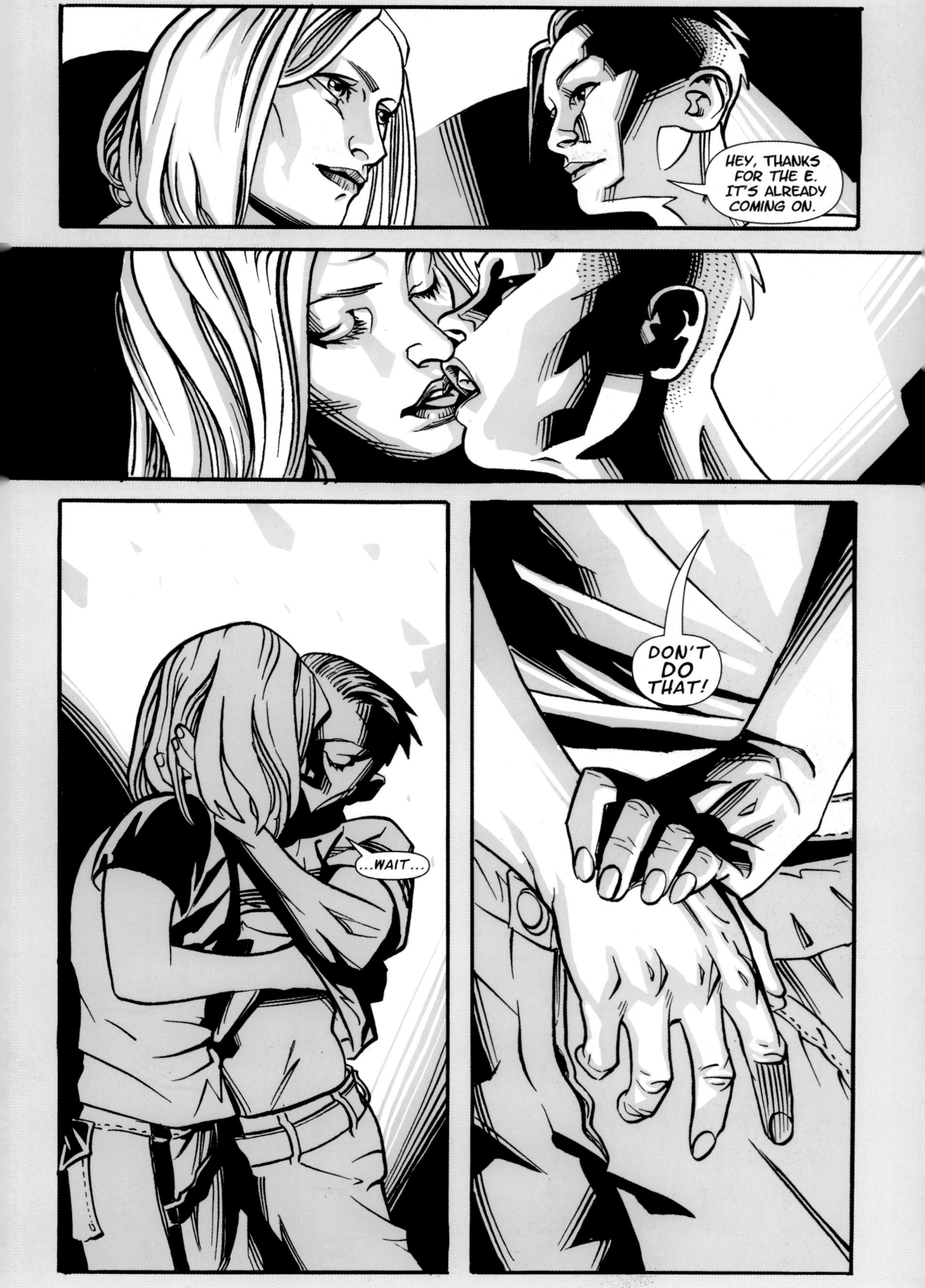
HEY, THANKS FOR THE E. IT'S ALREADY COMING ON.
...WAIT...
DON'T DO THAT!

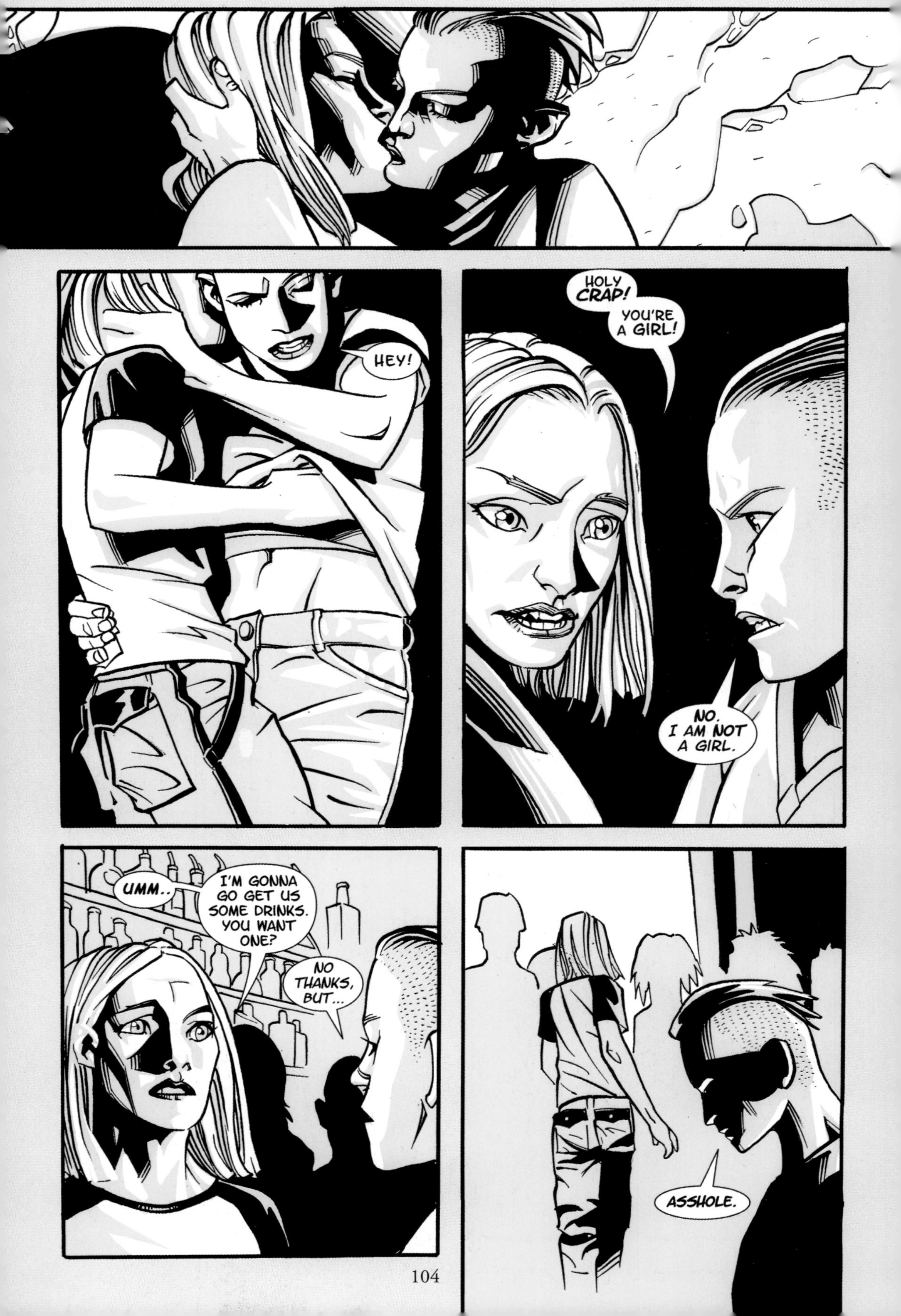
HEY!
HOLY CRAP!
YOU'RE A GIRL!
NO. I AM NOT A GIRL.
UMM..
I'M GONNA GO GET US SOME DRINKS. YOU WANT ONE?
NO THANKS, BUT...
ASSHOLE.

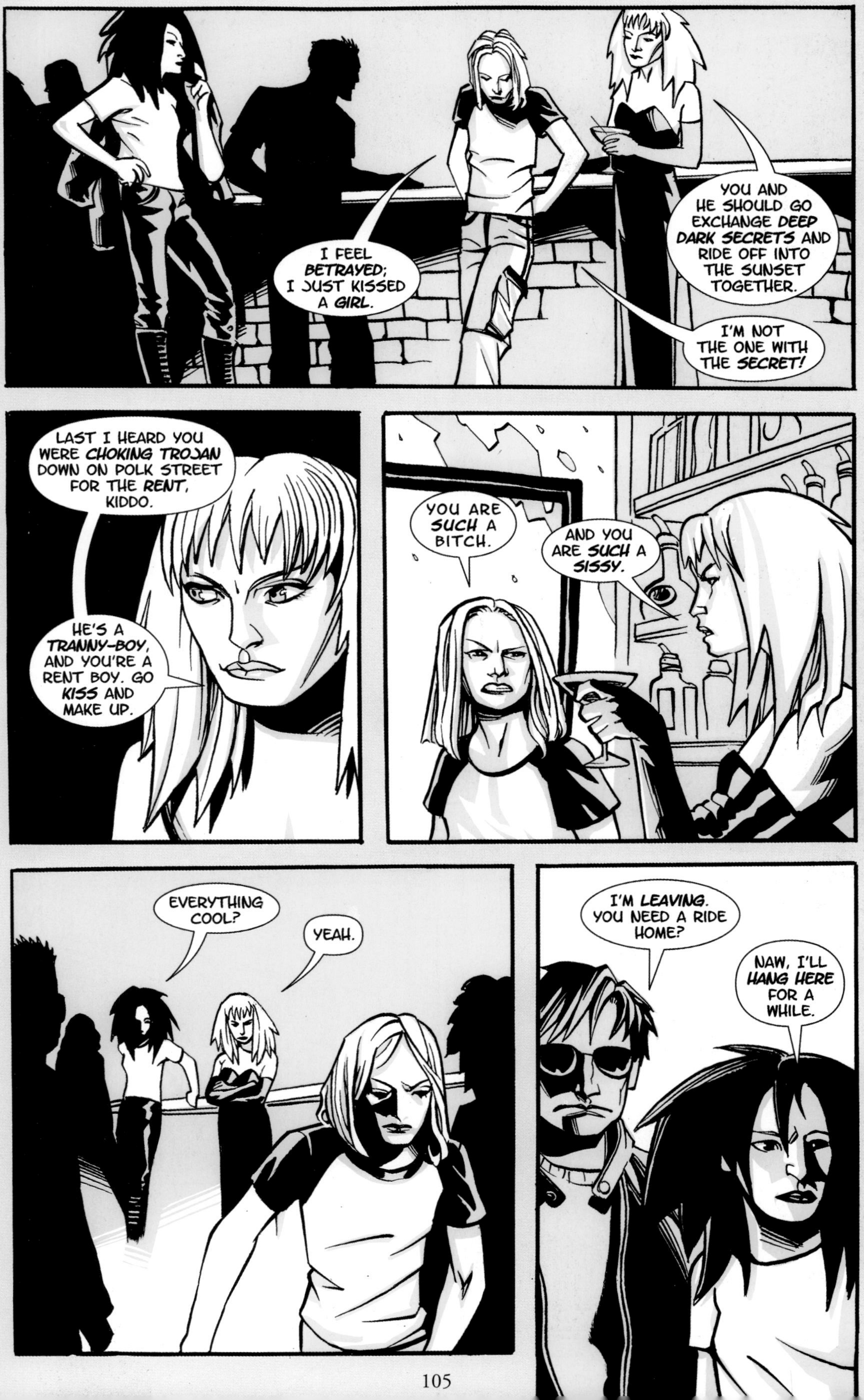

I FEEL BETRAYED; I JUST KISSED A GIRL.
YOU AND HE SHOULD GO EXCHANGE DEEP DARK SECRETS AND RIDE OFF INTO THE SUNSET TOGETHER.
I'M NOT THE ONE WITH THE SECRET!
LAST I HEARD YOU WERE CHOKING TROJAN DOWN ON POLK STREET FOR THE RENT, KIDDO.
HE'S A TRANNY-BOY, AND YOU'RE A RENT BOY. GO KISS AND MAKE UP.
YOU ARE SUCH A BITCH.
AND YOU ARE SUCH A SISSY.
EVERYTHING COOL?
YEAH.
I'M LEAVING. YOU NEED A RIDE HOME?
NAW, I'LL HANG HERE FOR A WHILE.

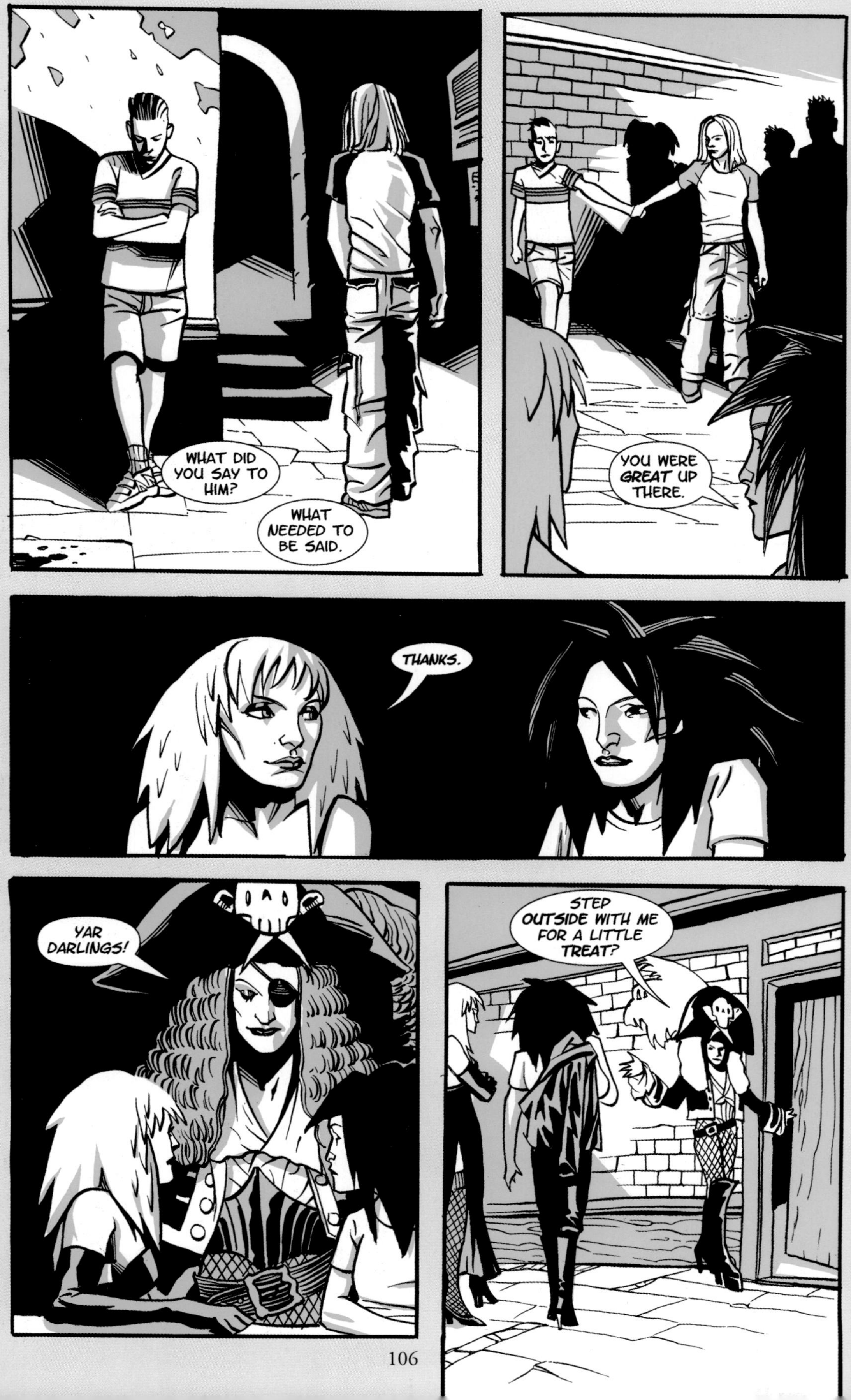
WHAT DID YOU SAY TO HIM?
WHAT NEEDED TO BE SAID.
YOU WERE GREAT UP THERE.
THANKS.
YAR DARLINGS!
STEP OUTSIDE WITH ME FOR A LITTLE TREAT?

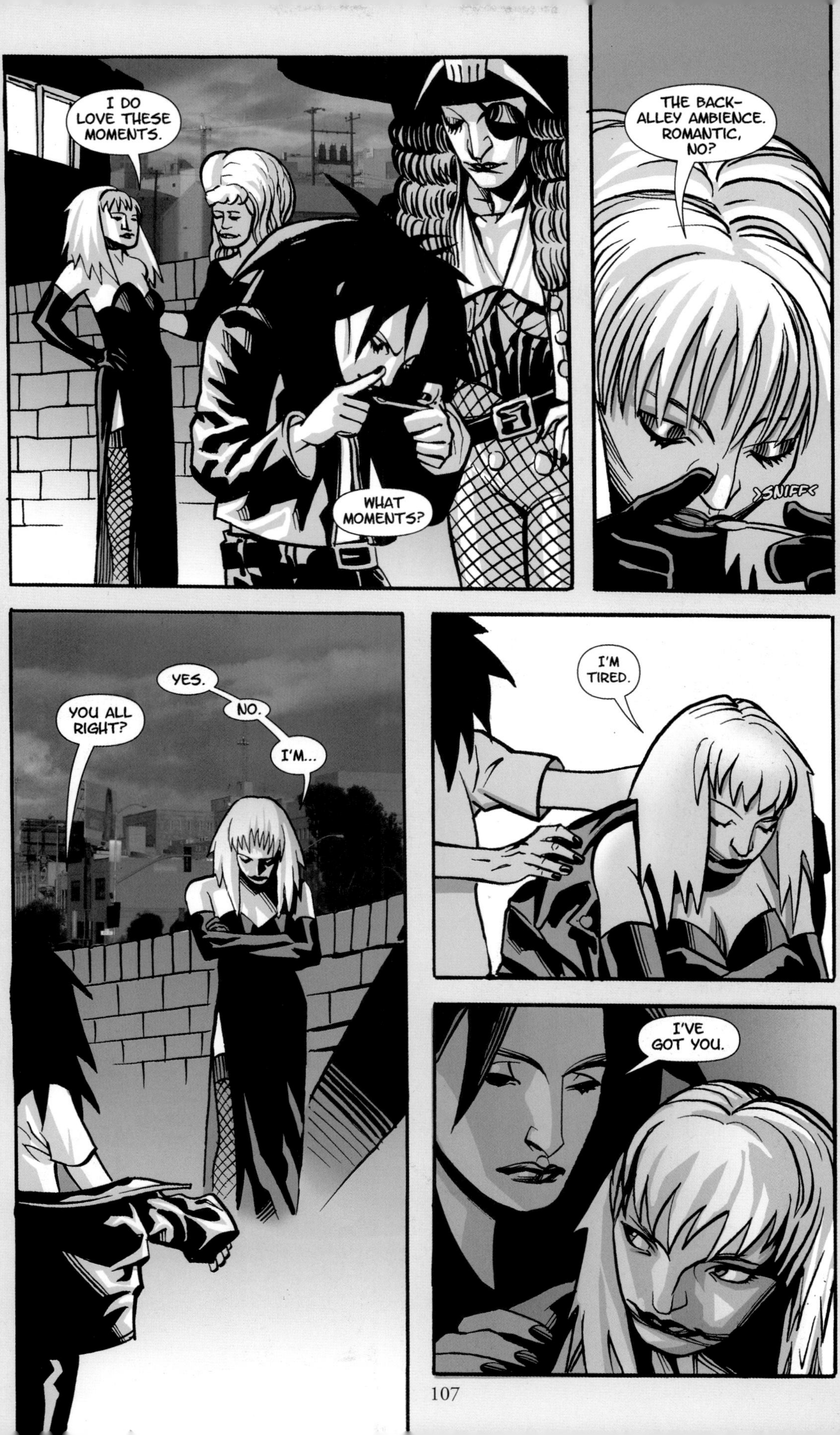
I DO LOVE THESE MOMENTS.
WHAT MOMENTS?
THE BACK-ALLEY AMBIENCE. ROMANTIC, NO?
SNIFF
YOU ALL RIGHT?
YES.
NO.
I'M...
I'M TIRED.
I'VE GOT YOU.

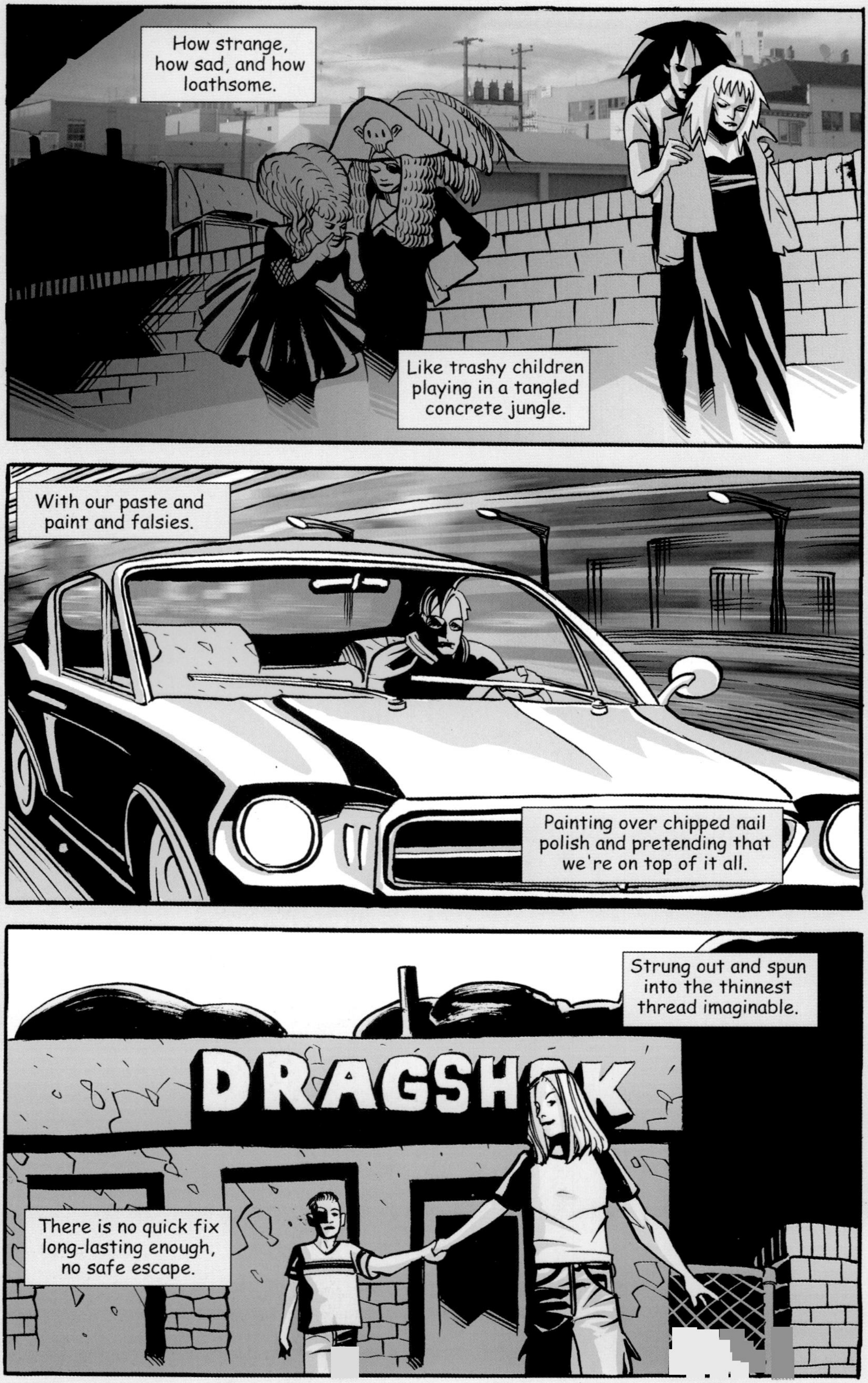
How strange, how sad, and how loathsome.
Like trashy children playing in a tangled concrete jungle.
With our paste and paint and falsies.
Painting over chipped nail polish and pretending that we're on top of it all.
Strung out and spun into the thinnest thread imaginable.
There is no quick fix long-lasting enough, no safe escape.

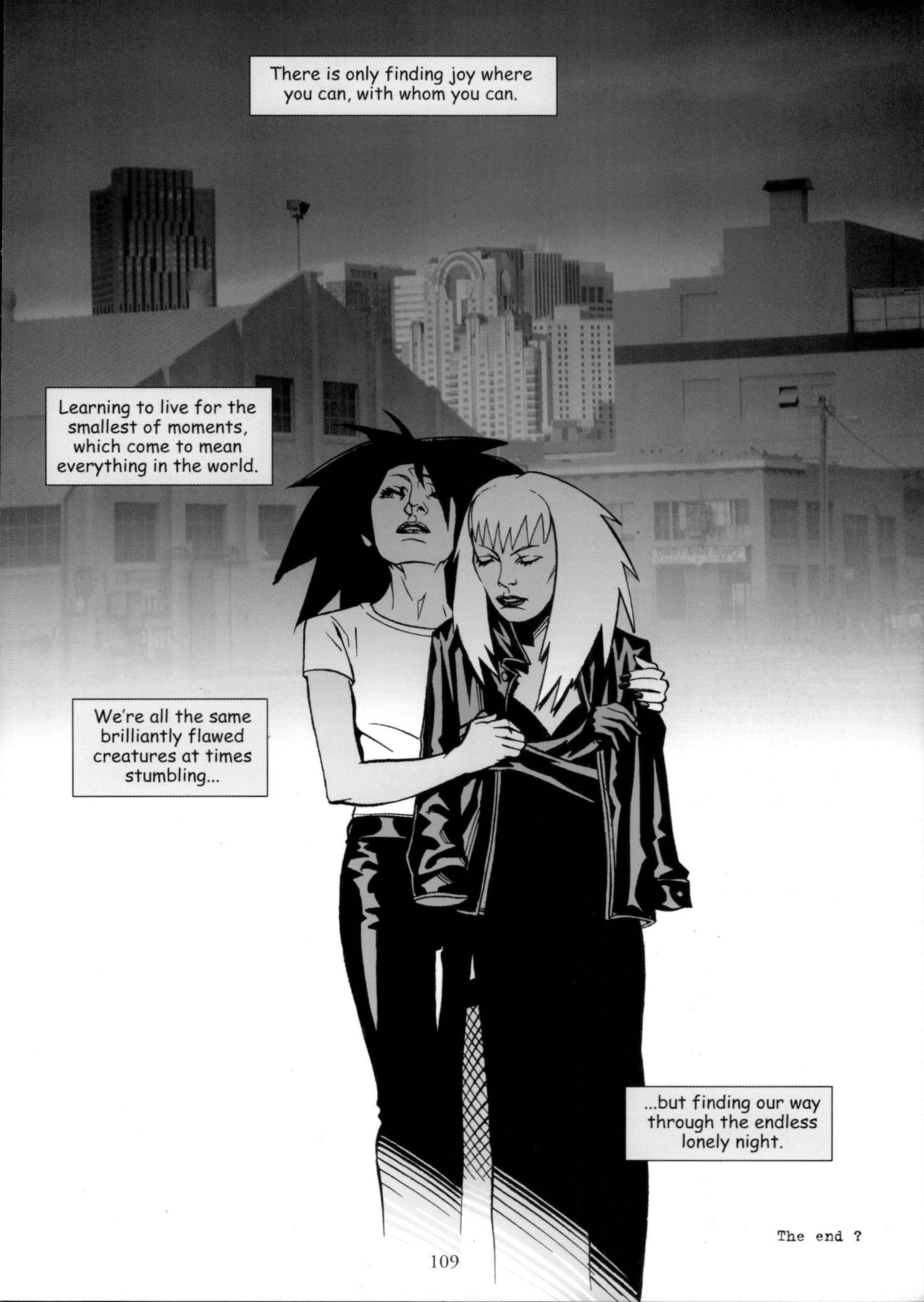
There is only finding joy where you can, with whom you can.
Learning to live for the smallest of moments, which come to mean everything in the world.
We're all the same brilliantly flawed creatures at times stumbling...
...but finding our way through the endless lonely night.
The end ?

Acknowledgements

Tristan would like to thank Terry and Howard Crane, for their endless support, patience, and acceptance.

Ted would like to thank Kelly Crumrin for day by day support, and Ron and Magic for helping to build the foundation.

Much thanks and appreciation to:

Amanda Strain, Eden Crane, eM Trucco, Vylet Hemlock, Brent Goodbar, Tracy St. Cyr, and Laurenn McCubbin.

Comrade Cid, Sherilyn and Katrina, Joe Palmer and PRISM, Ed Matthews and everyone at Popimage, Warren Ellis, Denise Sudell and the rest of the Sequential Tarts, Greg McElhatton, Andrew Wheeler and the rest of the crazy Ninthart peeps, Christopher Butcher at Previews Review, and Randy and Don at The Fourth Rail, and everyone else who supported us and this project through the years.

Special thanks to Terry Nantier and his team at NBM Publishing, Tony Shenton, the Bay Area comic book retailers ...

...and most especially Danielle Willis.

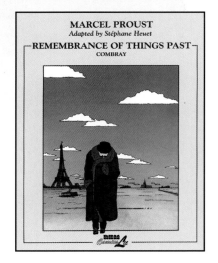

ComicsLit is an imprint
and trademark of

NANTIER · BEALL · MINOUSTCHINE
Publishing inc.
new york